California
DISASTERS
1812 - 1899

Firsthand accounts of fires, shipwrecks, floods, epidemics, earthquakes and other California tragedies

William B. Secrest, Jr.
&
William B. Secrest, Sr.

Word
Dancer
Press

Sanger, California

Printed in the United States of America
Published by Quill Driver Books/Word Dancer Press, Inc.
1254 Commerce Avenue
Sanger, California 93657
559-876-2170 • 1-800-497-4909 • FAX 559-876-2180
QuillDriverBooks.com

Quill Driver Books' titles may be purchased in quantity at special discounts for educational, fund-raising, business, or promotional use. Please contact Special Markets, Quill Driver Books/Word Dancer Press, Inc. at the above address or at 1-800-497-4909.

Quill Driver Books/Word Dancer Press, Inc. project cadre:
Doris Hall, John David Marion, Stephen Blake Mettee,

First Printing

To order another copy of this book, please call
1-800-497-4909

ISBN 1-884995-49-7

Library of Congress Cataloging-in-Publication Data

Secrest, William B., 1957-

California disasters, 1812-1899 : firsthand accounts of fires, shipwrecks, floods, epidemics, earthquakes and other California tragedies / by William B. Secrest, Jr. & William B. Secrest, Sr.

    p. cm.

    Includes index.

    ISBN 1-884995-49-7

1. Disasters--California--History--19th century. 2. Natural disasters--California--History--19th century. 3. California--History--19th century.

I. Secrest, William B., 1930- II. Title.

    F861.S35 2005

    979.4'04--dc22

2005026098

CALAMITY, n.

A more than commonly plain and unmistakable reminder that the affairs of this life are not of our own ordering. Calamities are of two kinds: misfortune to ourselves, and good fortune to others.

From
The Devil's Dictionary
by Ambrose Bierce

Table *of* Contents

Introduction

Disasters are the events which both history and popular culture are loath to forget. In a relatively short span of time—sometimes, only an instant—legions of people are injured or killed, and the mighty creations of civilization are reduced to rubble. What takes decades or even centuries to build is laid to waste, efficiently if not neatly, and the inherent delicacy of civilization and the human race is emphasized. We are compelled to contemplate how powerless we have been, and frequently remain, at the twin gargantuan hands of Nature and Fate.

For these reasons, disasters spark interest and hold our collective attention. We find ourselves enraptured and captivated by tragedy, especially when some time has elapsed and the human suffering and horror factors have ebbed. We devour the newspaper stories, pore over the smallest details with friends and family, and even tolerate the endless replays offered on television. Ask anyone about the Missouri Compromise and Manifest Destiny, and few definitions will be offered; tilt conversation toward the Chicago Fire, the Titanic or the Hindenburg, and the answers are likely to be dense with talk of cows, lanterns, icebergs and volatile gases.

The authors of this book confess to a long-standing fascination with disasters, for the reasons cited above, and especially since they reside in a state in which one of history's greatest calamities took place—the 1906 San Francisco earthquake and fire. While undeniably important, the magnitude of what happened in the City by the Bay has obscured a fundamental truth: Because California is situated at a continent's edge, where tectonic plates and other risk-bearing geographical features converge, and has experienced dramatic cycles of population influx and urban expansion, it offers—sadly enough—an ideal stage for the twin hands to conjure tragedy. And how those hands have busied themselves, for two centuries and more!

We begin with that great constant in California disasters, the earthquake. Few realize that the 1872 Owens Valley temblor was the strongest to ever hit the state, and the 1812 and 1857 quakes compiled a startling record of property damage for hundreds of square miles. Earthquakes are, arguably, the most terrifying of natural phenomena. One can often find refuge from advancing water or foul weather, but there is no place to go during an earthquake, and the feeling of helplessness is total. It is a feeling known only too well to millions of Californians, past and present.

If not quite as dramatic, fire is a subject seen even more pervasively in these pages than earthquakes. California experienced widespread destruction during the 1850s, primarily because of the many flimsy wooden buildings, shacks, and canvas tents in the gold rush towns. "The town is but one great tinderbox," wrote a '49er in San Francisco to his wife back home. Built hastily and on the cheap, it surprised no one that almost every major town in the early Golden State experienced a devastating blaze—or several, in the case of San Francisco, Sacramento and Marysville—and fires remained a serious danger throughout the nineteenth century.

Floods were another bane of early California, since few dams and weirs were in existence to check their advances. Large rains, sometimes combined with melting snowpacks, flushed huge volumes of water down streams and rivers in 1853, 1861-1862, 1871-1872, and 1890. None of these incidents were confined strictly to any area, and the entire state was within the path of destruction. People were drowned or stranded for days, vast herds of livestock were lost, crops were ruined, structures were swept away, and much property of every kind was destroyed.

Always a society on the move, Californians grimly accepted the risks of early ship and rail travel, and a great many passengers paid with their lives. Defective boilers blew up the steamboats *Sagamore* and *McClelland*, foul weather dashed the ships *Brother Jonathan* and *Elizabeth* to pieces, and failure to reckon properly with gravitational forces resulted in runaway trains at Santa Cruz and Tehachapi. Once again, in an era with less technological sophistication and government regulation, what were happenstances by definition were, in fact, more like inevitabilities.

Also in these pages are a few extraordinary disasters—nitroglycerin and mine explosions, epidemics, and even a balloon ascension gone wrong. A state always noted for its diversity of peoples and places, California is no exception where the realm of calamity is concerned. In fact, the roster (for the nineteenth century alone) is so dense that the main text covers only the events that, to us, are especially significant. To complete the record, an appendix treats numerous lesser disasters in summary form.

So let us take a trip back in time. Walk up the gangplank of a luxurious riverboat, commencing a trip from which you may never return. Imagine the ground shaking beneath your feet, or shiver on an isolated island while a flood rages around you in pitch darkness. And contemplate watching the town you live in, and everything you own, burning to the ground in a howling, fiery holocaust. More important, observe how the victims picked themselves up and plunged ahead, in the face of constant devastation, to build a state that took its place at the forefront of our great United States.

The Authors

Acknowledgments

Our first debt is to the editors and reporters of California's frontier newspapers, and the reminiscences and interviews of pioneers, without whom the all-important records of disasters past would not exist. Surprisingly, it appears that this account is the first of its book-length kind; our exhaustive bibliographical searches failed to uncover any other comprehensive histories of California disasters.

A few volumes treat California disasters in specialized fashion, and were of help to us. Noteworthy among them are Don B. Marshall's *California Shipwrecks*, James A. Gibbs, Jr's *Shipwrecks of the Pacific Coast* and *Disaster Log of Ships*, Bonnie J. Cardone and Patrick Smith's *Shipwrecks of Southern California*, and Sidney D. Townley and Maxwell W. Allen's valuable and helpful *Descriptive Catalog of Earthquakes of the Pacific Coast of the United States, 1769 to 1928*.

Ray Silvia and Melissa Scroggins, our colleagues at the Fresno County Library's California History and Genealogy Room, have been a constant source of technical assistance and moral support. We are likewise grateful to Gary Kurutz and John Gonzales and their staff, of the California State Library, for cheerfully tolerating our incessant requests for materials, copies, and spare change.

Longtime friend and historian John Boessenecker pointed out a valuable photograph, owned by William Jaeger, to us. Other persons and institutions who provided assistance were Lee Edwards of Bakersfield; Gary Rodgers of Cazadero; John Walden of the Kern County Library; the University of the Pacific's Holt-Atherton Special Collections; and the Trinity County Historical Society, Weaverville. Our thanks as usual to Steve Mettee and his always-helpful staff at Word Dancer Press.

1812
EARTHQUAKE

Where: Southern California Coast
Details: Casualties unknown

Santa
Barbara

The Spanish mission system and its pueblos, established in the late eighteenth century to colonize California and Christianize its native residents, were dealt a severe setback by a series of earthquakes that hit the southern region during this period. Serious damage was inflicted on the scattered settlements and crudely-constructed buildings at San Juan Capistrano, San Gabriel, San Fernando, San Buenaventura, Santa Barbara, Santa Ines and La Purisima. Reconstructing exactly what happened is difficult, since records consist mainly of priests' reports, eyewitness accounts recorded after the fact, and later reconstructions.

There had been some rumblings and tremors in October 1812, but early on the morning of December 21 a series of major shocks struck the California coast. At Mission San Juan Capistrano, the bells had just rung for the next mass when the church tower began to rock and the outside walls shook and fell outward. The unsupported dome over the chapel collapsed as the terrified Indians inside tried to flee. Falling rocks and support beams sent up a cloud of dust as the screaming natives were buried in the rubble. A total of thirty-nine bodies were recovered and buried. Several others were later discovered in the wreckage.

Simultaneously, other missions and presidios to the north were struck by the violent tremors. At Mission San Gabriel the main altar in the church was overturned, and four

THE SANTA BARBARA MISSION WAS
THE MOST MAGNIFICENT IN THE CHAIN. *Secrest Collection*

statues broken. The steeple was toppled and much damage was done to the sacristy walls and the friars' houses in the form of cracks. Mission San Fernando's walls were weakened to such an extent that thirty new beams were used to provide needed support.

Further to the northwest, three heavy shocks were reported at Mission San Buenaventura, weakening the tower and much of the facade, all of which had to be rebuilt. As the local priests and Indians fled to higher ground, they noticed that the sea had receded. This was a new terror—to see such a vast and powerful body of water suddenly retreat from the shore, and further observe a distant, tall wave later estimated to be between fifteen and thirty-five feet tall. This tsunami, or seismic sea wave, indicated that the earthquake had been generated offshore. When this huge wave crashed onto the shore at San Buenaventura, and some thirty miles north at Santa Barbara, it flooded inland at least a half-mile, and perhaps more.

MRS. ANGUSTIAS DE LE GUERRA ORD.
Secrest Collection

Mission Santa Barbara was equally hard-hit. Father Zephyrin Engelhardt, noted historian of California's missions, later wrote:

> During the month of December, 1812, several earthquake shocks were felt. These shocks were so severe that all the mission buildings were badly damaged; the church in particular had suffered so much that it was thought more expedient to take it down and erect a new one than to make repairs. A new stone church was accordingly commenced in 1815, but not completed until September, 1820.

Santa Ines was the next mission, up the coast and to the north. Here it was reported that two shocks, fifteen minutes apart, brought down a corner of the church, ruined the complex roofs, cracked its walls and destroyed a fourth of the new houses near the church.

Beyond Santa Ines and to the north was Mission La Purisima Concepion. Engelhardt chronicled the devastation there:

> The earth shook so violently that it was difficult to stand. A brief examination sowed that the church walls had been thrown out of plumb. Just before 11 o'clock there came another more violent shock which brought down the church and nearly all the mission buildings, besides about one hundred neophyte houses of adobe.

The earth opened in several places and emitted water and black sand. Several persons were wounded, but none killed. Subsequent floods completed the devastation so that very few buildings were worth repairing.

The seven missions mentioned were the most seriously damaged; others along the coast seem to have been spared. Jose Arguello, comandante of the presidio at Santa Barbara, gave a spare account of the disaster in a report he wrote that month:

Almost daily shocks this month. Several buildings ruined and damaged at presidio and mission. Earth opened in several places, with sulfur volcanoes.

Tremors continued to be felt during this period, particularly in January and February. A ball, suspended from a string at Mission Santa Barbara, was in almost continuous movement through April 1813. A dispirited Father Jose Francisco de Paula Senan summed up the situation in his biennial report from Mission San Buenaventura:

The already severe conditions have been rendered even more severe by the horrible temblors and earth-quakes that have been experienced in this province and which will constitute a special epoch in it because of the great resulting damages. The violence of these occurrences have been extraordinary.

As a result of the ruinous events we have to build anew the churches of Missions San Fernando and Santa Barbara. Mission San Gabriel suffered somewhat. At Missions Santa Inez and San Buenaventura quite some time will be required to repair the damage which I consider annoying to describe in detail. Concerning the last named mission I will say only that the tower partially fell and that the wall of the sanctuary was cracked from top to bottom. At Mission Purisima the bells rang out without the aid of a bell ringer and in a few minutes the

THE VILLAGE OF SANTA BARBARA AS IT APPEARED SOME YEARS AFTER THE EARTHQUAKE. THE MISSION IS ON HIGH GROUND TO THE FAR LEFT.
Secrest Collection

mission was reduced to rubble and ruin presenting the picture of a destroyed Jerusalem.

SAN JUAN CAPISTRANO, LARGEST AND MOST BEAUTIFUL OF THE MISSIONS, WAS NOT REBUILT AND IS SHOWN HERE IN 1876. *California State Library*

The missions and their subsidiary buildings were constructed of rough-hewn timbers, with adobe and rock walls bound with a primitive mortar. Roofs were of red tile made of native clay, while structures housing the Indian neophytes were adobe and roofed with thatch of some sort. Unfortunately, at this point in California (and for that matter, world) history, seismic safety procedures and earthquake-resistant building methods would not be known for decades. Had more substantial construction materials been used, the earthquake damage might been much less extensive.

In terms of human and property loss, the 1812-1813 earthquake season was the first major event of its kind in California's recorded history. The relative lightness of population and building density restricted its impact; the same earthquake today would result in billions of dollars in damage and untold casualties.

1833

EPIDEMIC

Where: Sacramento and San Joaquin Valleys
Details: Thousands die

In the autumn of 1833, two buckskin-clad American trappers rode up to Mission San Fernando, twenty miles north of Los Angeles. Jonathan Warner, a visitor, observed that one of the men was "feeble and emaciated by disease." The trapper helped his sick companion to a spot under a mission porch, making him comfortable on his blanket. By signs, the trapper indicated to several bystanders that he and his partner had come over the mountains from the Tulare (San Joaquin) Valley. He then asked if they could stay the night, but was told that would not be allowed. In late afternoon some food was brought and the two men enjoyed a good meal, with the sick trapper feasting on chicken soup and wine.

When one of the mission priests made an appearance later, he stood off at a distance and gestured in an excited manner that the two strangers could not stay. He became so excited in his arm waving that the trappers concluded it might be dangerous to stay. Saddling their mules, the two men mounted and headed south that evening. They realized that word of a disease epidemic in the Sacramento Valley had preceded them. Hundreds, if not thousands, of Indians had already died in part of a continuing cycle that had begun centuries before.

Early scholars believed that some 1.15 million inhabitants peopled North America in 1491. In 1966 Henry F. Dobyns, using extensive archeological and documentary evidence in the western hemisphere, scaled this figure upward—to between 90 and 112 million people. This changed drastically with the coming of the white man. Dobyns further estimated that, in the first 130 years of contact with Europeans, about 95 percent of the Americas' indigenous people died!

Smallpox arrived in Peru about 1525, sweeping south from Mexico and destroying more than half the population of the Inca empire. In succeeding years, typhus, diphtheria and measles further demolished populations lacking immunity, helpless against the deadly diseases brought by the Spanish. The Maya and other native races were similarly decimated in Mexico, while the same fate awaited the natives of North America.

The lower Columbia River, in what is now Oregon, provided the 1833 California epidemic's breeding ground. Its might be traceable to British ships that dropped anchor at the river's mouth in 1829-1830, or to trappers traveling west from swampy areas of Missouri. An exhaustive comparison of early accounts by biologist Sherburne Cook leave little doubt that the disease in question was malaria, introduced during trading with the Indians and spread south by trapping parties in the valleys of California. John Work's expedition, to give one example, was known to include members suffering from the intermittent symptoms of malaria, as carried by the anopheles mosquito. While most whites stricken by affliction recovered, the natives died in droves.

Jonathan Warner joined Ewing Young's trapping party in the fall of 1832. Leaving San Gabriel, the party crossed the Tehachapi Mountains and headed north through the San Joaquin and Sacramento valleys. They were looking for beaver, but found the country already trapped out by rival groups. Warner later recalled: "The number of Indians living along and in the vicinity of the banks of the rivers, was so much greater than I had ever seen living upon the same area of country, that it presented a constant source of surprise."

Warner's comment on the great number of Indians was verified by the journal of John Work, who was in the area at the same time. According to Work, Indian villages and smaller groups of huts lined the rivers and streams. Along a five-mile stretch of the Feather River, Work recorded in his journal four villages of forty to fifty houses each, with 250 to 300 Indians in each village, and a total of 15,000 Patwin and Nisenan

Indians living along that particular stretch of ground. This was just one area, and an indication of Warner's amazement that so many natives had been seen on the trip. "On no part of the continent over which I had then, or have since traveled," Warner later wrote, "was so numerous an Indian population, subsisting upon the natural product of this soil and water, as in the valleys of the San Joaquin and Sacramento."

JONATHAN WARNER, AS HE APPEARED IN LATER LIFE. *California State Library*

Young and his men proceeded north up the Sacramento Valley, which was also heavily populated with native inhabitants. The party then continued its beaver search in Oregon. In the late summer of 1833, Young's party headed south again, retracing their steps through interior California. The men were staggered by what they now saw. Warner noted:

On our return, late in the summer of 1833, we found the valleys depopulated. From the head of the Sacramento, to the great bend and slough of the San Joaquin, we did not see more than six or eight live Indians, while large numbers of their skulls and dead bodies were to be seen under almost every shade tree, near water where the uninhabited and deserted villages had been converted into graveyards. On the San Joaquin River, in the immediate neighborhood of the larger class of villages, which, the proceeding year, were the abodes of a large number of those Indians, we found not only many graves, but the vestiges of a funeral pyre.

At the mouth of the Kings River, we encountered the first and only village of the stricken race, that we had seen after entering the great valley. This village contained a large number of Indians, temporarily stopping at that place.

We were encamped near the village one night only, and during that time, the death angel , passing over the camping ground of these plague-stricken fugitives, waved his wand, summoning from the little remnant of a once numerous people, a score of victims to muster in the land of the Manitou, and the cries of the dying mingled with the wails of the bereaved, made the night hideous in that veritable "valley of death."

JIM BAKER WAS A TYPICAL APPEA TRAPPER OF THE ERA. *Secrest Colle(*

Resuming their journey south toward Los Angeles, Young's party was also attacked by what Warner described as a "violent type of remittent fever." Two young Indians with the trappers died, and Warner himself "came near dying from it." Young and his men made it safely over the Tehachapis to San Gabriel and Los Angeles. In the latter city, Warner eventually became a successful merchant, rancher and political figure.

Estimates of the mortality during this epidemic, based on information by Warner and various other groups and informants in

A CALIFORNIA INDIAN VILLAGE OF THE 1830s. *Secrest Collection*

the area at that time, are startling. Sherburne Cook, who assembled and examined all the available data, was convinced that fully three-quarters of all the Indians in the Sacramento and San Joaquin valleys were destroyed in that cruel summer of 1833. Perhaps more important, Cook's figures are always conservative. This indicates that only a pitiful remnant of the native Indian population was around fifteen years later, during the greatest gold rush in history, when miners ruthlessly overran their settlements and lands.

1847

The DONNER Party Tragedy

Where: Mountain pass in Sierra
Details: Nearly half of wagon train perishes

Sutter's Fort

Emigrants in the Mountains —It is probably not generally known to the people, that there is now in the California mountains in a most distressing situation, a party of emigrants from the United States, who were prevented from crossing the mountains by an early heavy fall of snow. The party consists of about sixty persons, men, women and children. They were almost entirely without provisions, when they reached the foot of the mountain, and but for the timely succor afforded them by Capt. J. A. Sutter one of the most humane and liberal men in California, they must have all perished in a few days.

This brief item in the *California Star* heralded one of the most tragic and horrifying incidents in the American west's history. Leaving Iowa in the spring of 1846, Patrick and Margaret Breen headed west for California with their seven children. They had three wagons and were accompanied by Pat Dolan, who had his own wagon. By the time the Breens and Dolan reached Fort Bridger in Wyoming, they were attached to the wagon train of the families of George and Jacob Donner, James Reed and others. There were eighty-seven people in some twenty-three wagons at this point, as they prepared for the final leg of their journey.

It was critical that wagon trains cross the Sierra Nevada Mountains before winter set in. Jim Reed had heard of a new, shorter route to California called the Hastings Cut-Off, promoted by Lansford Hastings, who had earlier ridden the route on horseback. Solo travel and wagon piloting were two different things, however.

ELITHA DONNER'S FACE SEEMS TO REFLECT THE HORRORS SHE HAD SEEN.
Secrest Collection

Hastings' poor estimation of distances and circumstances proved a fatal blow to the emigrants, as they spent far too much time cutting roads through the mountains and crossing barren deserts.

By the time they reached Truckee Meadows (now Reno) in late October, the travelers knew they were in trouble. Indians had stolen or maimed some of their

JAMES AND MARGARET REED AND THE BREENS WERE THE ONLY FAMILES TO REMAIN INTACT DURING THE TERRIBLE SIERRA ORDEAL. *California State Parks*

stock, they were low on provisions, and Jim Reed had been banished from the company after he killed another of the train in a dispute. With snow now threatening the caravan, the group pushed ahead to Truckee Lake. Along the way five men died from accident, starvation or disease. Reed and three others rode ahead, hoping to obtain supplies at Sutter's Fort in the Sacramento Valley and replenish the stranded party's supplies. Patrick Breen and Dolan tried to get over the last mountain pass, but when they failed to get through the heavy snows, they returned, killed their animals for food, and began building log shelters.

Reed and the three others who had pushed ahead made it through to Sutter's Fort, where six pack mules and supplies were quickly assembled. One of Reed's men, Charles Stanton, immediately headed back, with Sutter sending along two Indians

THE TRUCKEE LAKE CAMP WHERE THE GRAVES AND REED FAMILIES LIVED IN THE DOUBLE CABIN AT LEFT, WHILE THE BREEN CABIN AND KESEBERG'S SHELTER IS AT THE RIGHT. THE DONNERS WERE CAMPED SEVERAL MILES AWAY. *Secrest Collection*

to help tend the animals. Stanton made it back, although it was an incredibly difficult trip, the snow being nearly twenty feet deep in the higher elevations. With fierce snow storms harassing the trapped emigrants, Patrick Breen and his family, and other party members, ate ox hides and saved meat for the desperate times ahead.

Stanton, William Graves, the two Indians and six other men and five women left on December 15, utilizing crude snowshoes they had constructed. They became lost and staggered through the snow for some thirty days, during which Stanton became snowblind and froze to death.

YOUNG CHARLES STANTON HAD NO FAMILY AT THE MOUNTAIN CAMP, YET HE RISKED HIS LIFE AND DIED FOR HIS FRIENDS. *Secrest Collection*

Patrick Dolan was the next to die and was cannibalized, as were the two Indians, who were later reported murdered by William Eddy and William Foster. All five of the women made it to Johnson's Ranch (thirty miles from Sutter's Fort), but only seven of the men. Meanwhile, high in the mountains, the dead were buried in the snow, now piled much too deep to reach the frozen earth.

On March 1, Reed finally made it past the storms and deep snows, arriving with the second relief expedition of ten men. Daniel Rhoads, Britton Greenwood and other seasoned frontiersmen distributed the supplies they carried and then prepared to remove as many of the survivors as possible. Dan Rhoads later described the ordeal in a letter:

We walked on snowshoes over the snow; it was from 5 to 25 feet deep. At the end of the days travels we cached provisions so as to lighten our loads. We was 7 days going to their tents and cabins. They had been living on raw hides for 3 weeks. They was dieing every day. In some of the tents there was 3 and 4 on a pile of dead persons. We started [back] with 23 persons—all that was able to walk.

A third relief party rescued all but Lewis Keseberg, who had a painfully injured foot; Tamsen and George Donner were at their camp some miles away, but when her husband died, Tamsen went to stay with Keseberg and Mrs. Lavinia Murphy.

DANIEL RHOADS ACCOMPANIED JAMES REED'S SECOND RELIEF EXPEDITION. *California State Library*

The fourth and last rescue party left Johnson's Ranch on April 13 under the command of trapper and mountain man William Fallon. Fallon's party were scavengers, hoping to recover salvage and money left behind by party members as they rescued the last few survivors. Nonetheless, they were brave and resolute men, carrying packs of supplies on their backs over snow that was ten and twenty feet deep. They successfully guided the remaining survivors back to Johnson's Ranch and Sutter's Fort.

Fallon's journal of the expedition, published in the *California Star*, is the final ghastly chapter in the Donner tragedy:

BRITTON GREENWOOD. *Secrest Collection*

April 17th. Reached the cabins between 12 and 1 o'clock. Expected to find some of the sufferers alive, Mrs. Donner and Keseberg in particular. Entered the cabins and a horrible scene presented itself—human bodies terribly mutilated, legs, arms, and skulls scattered in every direction. One body, supposed to be Mrs. Eddy, lay near the entrance, the limbs severed off and a frightful gash in the skull. The flesh from the bones was nearly consumed and a painful stillness pervaded the place...Upon entering [a cabin we] discovered Keseberg lying down amidst the human bones and beside him a large pan full of fresh liver and lights [organs].

MARGARET BREEN'S FAMILY WAS FORTUNATE ENOUGH TO SURVIVE THE TERRIBLE ORDEAL IN THE MOUNTAINS. *California State Parks*

The Donner party, all told, included about ninety members. Forty-seven had survived, while nearly half, forty-three, had died. The ordeal brought out both the highest and lowest of man's instincts, while it traumatized others for years to come. Only those who have endured similar trials are fit to pass judgment on what happened within that cruel mountain encampment.

1850

CHOLERA EPIDEMIC

Where: San Francisco/Sacramento
Details: At least 700 deaths

Sacramento
San Francisco

With people streaming in from all over the world to join in the California gold rush, at a time when public health and sanitary conditions were frequently substandard, it now seems amazing that only one major plague ravaged the Golden State during those tumultuous days. While its duration was reasonably brief (about three months), the death toll of the 1850 cholera epidemic was nevertheless horrible—no fewer than 600 and perhaps in excess of 1,000. At its height, more than forty people a day were succumbing to the disease.

The cholera's advance has sometimes been attributed to the steamer *Carolina*'s arrival in San Francisco's harbor on October 7. During its voyage from Panama, fourteen passengers on board were lost to the disease, and it was from that time that the cases reported began to increase. However, an account published in the *San Francisco Alta California* of October 9, 1865 noted: "About the first of

ONE OF THE THEORIES CONCERNING THE SPREAD OF CHOLERA WAS THAT PASSENGERS OFTEN TOOK PASSAGE ON SMALLER RIVERBOATS TO SAVE MONEY. THE SMALLER CRAFT, HOWEVER, WERE CRAMPED, OFTEN SERVED BAD FOOD AND USED VARIOUS COMMON UTENSILS SUCH AS WATER CONTAINERS. *California State Library*

October, one or two deaths from cholera were reported in San Francisco. At the same time the newspapers reported the disease at Carson Valley, hundreds of miles in the interior, where it was said to have broken out among the overland immigrants."

Transportation conditions of the time no doubt accounted for some of the disease's rapid spread. An article in the June 8, 1890 *San Francisco Morning Call* laid much of the blame on small, cramped schooners, sloops and sailboats used by those wishing to beat the higher travel rates of the steamboats. If the ticket prices were low, the sanitary conditions were likely poor— and the presumed use of common eating and drinking utensils provided an excellent host for the cholera bacteria, which is borne via water.

AD IN AN 1850 SAN FRANCISCO NEWSPAPER.
Secrest Collection

The *Call* account further states: "One schooner left Sacramento with forty-two passengers for San Francisco. On the third day she arrived with only three of the number alive. The others had been seized with cholera on the passage and died. A printer named Bugbee was one of the survivors and was the only one of his companions on the schooner who was able to walk ashore on arrival."

San Francisco's mortality figures from the epidemic spread from the earliest part of October to just before Christmas. The tents, boarding houses and hotels of the city were packed with victims, and given the poor condition of the streets ("thickly covered with black rotten mud," as the *Annals of San Francisco* put it), the fact deaths were restricted to 250 or thereabouts was almost miraculous. Many prominent citizens were claimed by cholera, including the city's treasurer, George W. Endicott, jeweler W. A. Woodruff, and businessman Sam Maynard.

On October 27, the *Alta*'s "Sacramento Intelligence" column noted: "Five or six cases only have been reported since our last issue. This indicates no increase, and encourages the hope that with the thorough precautionary measures now on foot, the malady may not assume an epidemic character." This proved to be a too-optimistic prediction. In a year when Sacramento was hit by both severe flood and fire, the cholera epidemic became the worst disaster of all, claiming casualties which will never be ascertained accurately. Local newspapers attributed no fewer than 325 deaths to the disease, with the actual total likely being even higher.

By the end of October and the beginning of November, Sacramento reached its mortality peak. A temporary hospital for the indigent was set up on L Street, and the wails of the sick, dying and bereaved were audible throughout the city. John Morse's brief history of the early city said: "As soon as the daily mortality became so great as to keep men constantly employed in carrying away the dead, the citizens began to leave town in every direction and in such numbers as to soon diminish the population to probably not more than one-fifth of its ordinary standard." According to the round figures available for the time, this meant that approximately 8,000 people had fled from the cholera's onslaught. Contemporary reports indicate that practically all business and recreation in the city ground to a stop.

Hardin Bigelow, the mayor of Sacramento, fell victim to cholera —while visiting San Francisco—and was taken back for burial on November 28, when the plague was at last on the wane at his home base. A total of ninety physicians were practicing in Sacramento during the outbreak and, as noted in Dr. E. S. Fenner's account of this episode, all stood their ground to minister to the victims and did not participate in the pell-mell exodus from the city. He also paused to note that female mortality was much less than male, claiming only seventeen lives in total, "and the majority of these were from the abandoned class. This fact goes far to corroborate the oftrepeatedobservation, that the better classes of communities are not so liable to the disease."

Cholera also made inroads within other California towns and cities during this time—perhaps not to the extent seen in San Francisco and Sacramento, yet apparently appreciable. The December 26 *Alta* commented that "whole families have been swept away" in Santa Barbara. It was further reported that the disease hit Marysville and San Jose, particularly affecting the Mexican and Indian populations at the latter city.

During the plague's course, the newspapers spent considerable column space complaining about the constant accumulation of filth and rubbish in California's urban areas, and pleaded for the abatement of this ongoing menace as a way to combat disease transmission. As the science of public health was in its infancy at this time, and reports are largely anecdotal, it is difficult to tell whether the cholera's toll produced cleaner streets and conditions, and less susceptibility to disease. Whatever the reason, it is interesting to note that cholera-stricken steamer passengers who arrived in San Francisco in 1853 and 1854 (and who were hospitalized in town) failed to set off a similar pandemic, and it would be decades before the Golden State experienced a urban disease outbreak of similar magnitude.

1850

San Francisco

EXPLOSION of the *SAGAMORE*

Where: San Francisco
Details: Nearly 50 people killed, many injured

The California gold rush inaugurated the era of steamboat travel in California waters, with boats competing with stage and wagon transportation. Some large steam vessels were able to travel from the East to the West Coast by water, while smaller craft were dismantled and brought to California in pieces on boats, then reassembled on arrival. By the spring of 1850 there were some seven steamboats operating out of San Francisco and Sacramento, carrying miners and supplies from Stockton to the lower Feather and Yuba rivers.

By its very nature and location as a port, San Francisco became a ship repair and building center. Materials, craftsmanship and safety standards were dubious in the early Gold Rush days, however, and the results were sometimes tragic. The *Fawn*, a riverboat of obscure origins, was built in 1848. While operating out of San Francisco Bay in August 1850, the *Fawn's* boiler exploded, causing the first tragedy of its kind inside of California.

PORTSMOUTH SQUARE AS IT APPEARED DURING THE ADMISSION DAY FESTIVITIES IN OCTOBER 1850.
Secrest Collection

Slightly before the *Fawn*'s demise, the steamboat *Sagamore* was built or assembled in San Francisco by early 1850 and was serving the Bay Area by June. It operated for a number of months without any problems of note.

On the late afternoon of October 29, one of the *Sagamore*'s passengers was a fascinating character named James Kirker. Born in Ireland in 1793, young Kirker came to America in 1810, worked as a grocer, and at various times was a privateer in the War of 1812, a Southwest trader, a scout and guide during the Mexican War, and an Apache scalp hunter. In 1850, he had settlerd down and was running cattle in Contra Costa County.

Jim Kirker lived a few miles south of what was then called New York of the Pacific (now Pittsburg). Located some fifteen miles above the Carquinez Straits, this was the river route to Stockton. Kirker had traveled to the bay city on the *Sagamore*, perhaps to attend celebrations being held on the occasion of California's admission to statehood. Late on the afternoon of October 29, Kirker boarded the same steamer for the trip home.

For STOCKTON, touching at Benicia—The new and fast sailing steamer SAGAMORE, Capt. Geo. D. Griflin, will leave Central wharf, THIS DAY, (Saturday,) at 4 o'clock P. M. for the above places. For freight or passage, apply to the Captain on board, or to
aug17   G. M. BURNHAM, Central wharf.

DAILY ALTA CALIFORNIA, AUGUST 19, 1850.
Secrest Collection

The old mountain man was late boarding the *Sagamore* and sought out the captain to secure his ticket. Deck hands were getting ready to cast off amid the clanging engines and whistle-blowing. Then it happened, as reported in the October 31, 1850 San Francisco *Daily Alta California*:

> At five o'clock, just as the steamer *Sagamore* was casting off from Central wharf, with a large number of passengers, bound for Stockton, her boiler burst with a terrible explosion. Masses of timber and human bodies were scattered in every direction. Many bodies were blown into the water, from which they were recovered by the numerous boats which thronged about the scene of the disaster. The boat was a complete wreck, and from among the fragments were taken the dead and the dying, mutilated in a manner shocking to behold.

The number of persons on board at the time of the accident cannot be accurately ascertained as the passenger list has not been found. We have heard it variously estimated at from seventy-five to a hundred. Many bodies were so much mutilated that it was found impossible to identify them. Limbs and fragments were gathered up in baskets— a shocking sight.

Kirker's account of the disaster was published in the same issue of the newspaper, and is most interesting:

I had just got on board and was going aft to pay my passage, when the explosion took place and I was thrown some ten or fifteen feet in the air and lit on the bodies of two (dead) persons. When I recovered my presence of mind, and the steam had cleared away, I saw as many as twenty-five persons on deck, who were apparently not hurt, and a great many who were either killed or very badly wounded. I saw two hanging on the side of the wreck, badly wounded and crying for help. I caught hold and pulled them in. By this time several boats had got alongside and were busy picking up those who were thrown into the water. I should think there were as many as 130 persons on the upper deck when the explosion took place. I have seen some service as well as being in some tight places, but this being blown sky high by a little hot water is a little more than I have been accustomed to, and in future I shoulder old "Kentucky" and take Walker's line; driving tandem, (i.e. one foot afore the other) in preference to traveling on these blow-up concerns.

Miraculously, Kirker received no injuries. Captain Cole, the ship's master, was also blown high in the air and into the water, but was not seriously injured, either. Initially, thirteen of the dead were identified, while some seven others were too mutilated to establish just who they were. There was a long list of injured, some of whom eventually died from the blast's effects. Since there was no passenger list, there were undoubtedly even more dead.

Oddly, and for unclear reasons (if any), a number of bystanders refused to

AN OLD WOODCUT ILLUSTRATES THE EXPLOSION OF A STEAMBOAT AT THE WHARF. *Secrest Collection*

aid in removing the injured. One of the reluctant individuals was turned over to the police, and the chief engineer of the fire company directed the Sansome Hook and Ladder Company to render any necessary aid, which they did. To compound the tragedy, a hospital tending to the injured caught fire during the night, and some of the *Sagamore* victims were burned in the conflagration.

At the inquest it was decided that the explosion was the result of carelessness on the part of the engineer. After all, the boiler was a new one and had just recently been inspected. G. N. Johnson, another passenger, had testified that he had passed the engine room just a moment before the explosion, "but saw no engineer." The engineer, who was severely scalded, could not defend himself.

JAMES KIRKER HAD MANY WILD ADVENTURES DURING HIS WESTERN CAREER, BUT BEING BLOWN UP ON A STEAMBOAT WAS AN AWESOME EXPERIENCE, EVEN FOR HIM. *Missouri Historical Society*

Whatever their causes, the sudden and ugly demises of the *Fawn* and *Sagamore* initiated a half-century of deadly steamboat disasters in California.

1849 - 51

SAN FRANCISCO FIRES

Where: San Francisco
Details: Up to $17,000,000 in losses

San Francisco

In early San Francisco, few worried about the threat of fire. Everyone was thinking of gold— either the gold dug out of the ground, or the gold made by supplying the Argonauts' needs. And in 1848 and '49, there were few buildings in town worth much, in any case. Although there were several water pumpers in town, there was no water supply. No fire codes, either. There were plenty of experienced firemen—men from New York, New Jersey, Chicago and so on. All of which led to a false sense of security on the part of the citizens. Their wake-up call came at 5:45 A.M. on the morning of December 24, 1849.

The fire started in Dennison's Exchange on Portsmouth Square, a large, three-storied frame building utilized as a saloon and gambling hall. The flames spread quickly to the wooden structures on the eastern side of the plaza, and up Washington Street. With no formal fire department, there was little time to do anything but flee with valuables in hand. Some fifty buildings were destroyed at a loss of $1,000,000. When some Australian thieves quickly began pilfering the

DENNISON'S EXCHANGE. *From* Annals of San Francisco

ruins, it was surmised the conflagration had been started for that purpose. An early resident, one John Henry Brown, explained what actually happened:

> It was an unwritten axiom in gold rush San Francisco that a black man could order a drink in a white saloon, but after the one drink he was expected to leave. In December, 1849, Dennison's Exchange was

being operated by one Thomas Bartell, a recently arrived Southerner. When a young black man ordered a drink from the scowling Bartell, the bartender attacked him, beating him severely. Leaving the saloon, the black man threatened vengeance and was seen in the vicinity of the saloon several times just before the fire.

Two days after the fire, a chastened town council appropriated $800 to purchase axes, ropes, hooks and ladders and a wagon. These were to be given to the freshly organized "Independent Unpaid Axe

SAN FRANCISCO BAY IN THE EARLY 1850S WAS FILLED WITH SHIPS FROM AROUND THE WORLD, MANY OF WHICH HAD BEEN DESERTED BY CAPTAINS AND CREW WHO WERE IN THE GOLD FIELDS. MANY OF THESE SHIPS WERE USED TO STORE PROPERTY DURING THE GREAT FIRES. *California State Library*

Company." Two months later, resolutions to organize a general fire department were enacted, with a Chief Engineer to supervise the men and equipment of all the fire companies in the city. His salary was to be $6,000 yearly, a princely sum in those days. Meanwhile, the burnt-out section was rebuilt within a few weeks.

A little over four months later, on May 4, 1850, the city's second great fire flared into existence, discovered smoldering at 4 A.M. Again, it took place on the eastern side of Portsmouth Square, this time in the United States Exchange. Great crowds flocked to the scene, both to watch and to help contain the fire or save property. Some refused to help unless they were paid. The fledgling city police force was on hand to help keep order and prevent looting. Several buildings were torn down or blown up to stop the fire from spreading, but this often caused even more damage. A young Swiss eyewitness to the scene noted the explosions caused when the Americans "throw kegs

NOTICE.

A NOTICE, POSTED AFTER THE DECEMBER 1849 FIRE, CALLING FOR A MEETING OF THE TOWN COUNCIL TO DISCUSS RELIEF OF THE MANY VICTIMS OF THE DISASTER. *Secrest Collection*

of powder into the middle of a conflagration to raze the houses and isolate the fire. Indeed, the buildings collapse, but all too frequently fiery debris tumbles to the other side of the street and sets on fire the houses opposite which catch on fire like matchsticks."

It was noon before the fires were halted. Three blocks of the most valuable structures in the city had been destroyed, at a cost of some $4,000,000. Again, incendiaries were blamed, the Australian ticket-of-leave men—paroled convicts. Some were arrested, but none were convicted of any offenses. Once again, the clearing and rebuilding commenced before the glowing embers had even cooled.

There were still no city fire codes or an organized fire department when yet a third large fire occurred just a month later, on June 14, 1850. Most accounts place the blame on the faulty chimney of a small bakery shop behind the Merchants Hotel, located between Sacramento and Clay streets. Once again, it was in the general area of the city's main plaza, Portsmouth Square. With the aid of a strong wind, the blocks between Clay, California and Kearny streets were sheathed in flames

A CITY BURNS! AN EARLY LITHOGRAPH DEPICTS THE GREAT FIRE OF MAY 4, 1851. *Calfornia State Libary*

within an hour. There was another huge loss of property, with estimates running up to five million dollars.

It was at this time also that fire engine companies began to burst forth like flowers in spring. Between June and October, no fewer than seven were created, all staffed with experienced firemen from the East Coast. The new fire companies, coupled with the construction of brick buildings thought to be fire-proof, now gave an additional false sense of security to San Franciscans.

AUGUSTUS ELLIS, A VOLUNTEER FIREMAN OF CALIFORNIA ENGINE CO. NO. 4 IN THE EARLY 1850s. *Courtesy the New York Historical Society, New York City*

For the following eight months the citizens of the bay city were relatively free of the fire fiend. Then it struck again on the night of May 3, 1851, as reported in the following day's San Francisco *Evening Picayune*:

About eleven o'clock last night, the cry of "Fire" startled everyone like an earthquake. The fire had just commenced in a paint shop on the west side of Portsmouth Square, adjoining the Bryant House, formerly called, but more recently the American. It was but a slight blaze when first seen, but in five minutes the whole upper story was full of flame. We have never seen flames spread so rapidly. Before the engines could get upon the ground and commence playing, the American on one side, and a store occupied by Messrs. Rhodes as a furnishing establishment, were in flames.

The buildings in the vicinity being all of wood and extremely combustible, the fire spread up Clay street, back towards Sacramento, and down Clay towards Kearny, with frightful rapidity. It soon had full command, and the Fire Department could only work upon the borders, and endeavor to check its progress by anticipating it. In this they succeeded on the north side before it reached Dupont street, but in every other direction in which it could spread, it took its own course. There was little chance to save much of the movables—for ere they were aware of their danger in most cases, the flames were wrapping them in destruction.

Three men at the building of Wells & Co. were burned to death. One man on Washington street fell dead from over exertion. Three men were burned to death in the Union, one of them the bookkeeper by the name of Willard.

And the brick buildings that were to be the city's salvation—
Theodore Barry and Benjamin Patten, two early city saloonkeepers,
recalled the disappointment of that experiment:

> We remember, as well as if it were but yesterday, being in front of
> Jo. Bidleman's fine, three-story brick, fire-proof store, on the east side
> of Montgomery street when the fire of May 4, 1851, reached it.
> Everyone said "Oh, the fire will stop there! It can't get through those
> walls and shutters!" But when the dreadful heat had turned its all-
> devouring breath upon the firm, thick walls, and bolted, massive
> shutters he saw, along the iron window-shutter's edge, a line of thin,
> smoky fringe, like an angora edging for a lady's robe. For a moment
> it slowly curled about the window-casing; then, with a sudden puff,
> the delicately waving border quickly changed to a thick frame of wool-
> like smoke. The doubled sheets of bolted iron burst their fastenings,
> belching long-tongued flames that soon consumed the costly structure.
> Our faith in "fire-proof" was shaken.

The fire burned for some ten hours, the glow said to have been
seen one hundred miles at sea and down the coast as far as Monterey.
Some 1,500 to 2,000 houses were destroyed, with damage estimated at
$12,000,000. Many people died, and some suffocated in the "fireproof"
brick buildings. The population was so transient, and the holocaust so

SAN FRANCISCO AFTER THE
GREAT FIRE OF MAY 4, 1851.
From Annals of San Francisco

complete, that the true number of deaths was never established. The destruction seeming so overwhelming that many seemed to think it was the end of the world—certainly, the end of San Francisco. But, once again, construction of new buildings began immediately by these indomitable people. Piping water into the city was at last seriously discussed and more fire companies were created.

Another fire in June succeeded in destroying most of the old wood and adobe landmarks of the city. "During the progress of the flames," reported the Stockton *San Joaquin Republican*," the city was attempted to be fired in six places by a gang of villains. Many of the incendiaries and thieves have been arrested." Early reports indicated losses up to $3,000,000.

Only the future devastating destruction of 1906 could compete with these last several fires as the residents of San Francisco again resumed the rebuilding of their legendary and beautiful city.

1851-87

FIRES in MARYSVILLE

Where: Marysville
Details: At least $1,500,000 in damage

Marysville

cisco

During the Gold Rush era and in the ensuing years, few California cities were as hard hit by fire as Marysville. Thompson and West's *History of Yuba County* states that the county seat managed to avoid major conflagrations for the first two years of its existence, but this record was first broken on August 31, 1851, and repeatedly for almost three decades following.

For sheer destructive force and property loss, the first fire was the worst of them all. It was said to have started about 12:30 A.M., when a sleepy Chinese laundry proprietor left a burning candle near some clothing, and the flames spread to the fabric while he dozed. His business was one of the first to go, with many others following in fast succession.

In the space of an hour and a half, three entire blocks of Marysville's downtown district were burned out, along with substantial portions of the city's central plaza and levee. Wet blankets were hung out windows to help check the fire, and succeeded in keeping the large U.S. Hotel on D Street from succumbing to the blaze. It was thought that this large structure's salvation kept the city's entire eastern portion from going up in smoke. Similar efforts along E Street checked damage in the opposite direction. That damage was widespread was hardly surprising, as the firefighters were an ad hoc and completely volunteer force.

Not all, however, seem to have been intent on smothering the rapidly-moving flames or help in any way. The *Marysville Herald* was quick to complain:

> Most of the citizens worked nobly during the fire, but we noticed some instances where persons in the shape of men stood looking on apathetically, with their hands in their pockets, refusing to lend a helping hand.

This inaction, combined with the general overwhelming of the townsfolk, propelled total losses to the then-staggering sum of $500,000. The Farish and Adams auction house was said to suffer the most property destruction, to the tune of $30,000, and a similar operation conducted by John J. Jacobs lost $12,000. In all, about a quarter of the city was gone.

While rebuilding began as soon as the embers had cooled, misfortune was quick to strike Marysville again—all of ten days after the first fire. Thompson and West related the particulars:

> At one o'clock Wednesday morning, September 10, 1851, flames were seen issuing from the rear of the wholesale liquor store of Mitchell and Nunes, on the south side of First Street, west of D Street. In half an hour twenty-five buildings situated between D and First streets, Maiden Lane and the river, were in ruins. Water carts were used to convey water to the scene of the conflict, and this was thrown upon the burning buildings by the excited citizens. The estimated loss was eighty thousand dollars. Steps were immediately taken to form a fire department, which resulted in the organization of Mutual Hook and Ladder Co., No. 1, on the eighteenth of September.

The firefighters' organization was overdue and sorely needed. No sooner was the burned district repaired than it was revisited by fire, on November 7, 1852. This time, the area bounded by First, Second, C, and Maiden Lane was leveled; three hotels, three livery

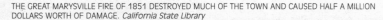

THE GREAT MARYSVILLE FIRE OF 1851 DESTROYED MUCH OF THE TOWN AND CAUSED HALF A MILLION DOLLARS WORTH OF DAMAGE. *California State Library*

businesses, and a number of smaller establishments were destroyed, with the losses piling up to approximately $75,000.

Worse yet were the blazes of 1854. The first of these, on May 25, was reputedly the work of an arsonist, and struck familiar territory: First, Second, D and High streets, along with Maiden Lane. Once again, the flames took an extraordinarily short time to furrow a wide swath of destruction. In two and a half hours, the post office, city hall, theatre and 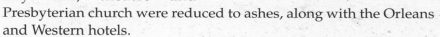 Presbyterian church were reduced to ashes, along with the Orleans and Western hotels.

When flames returned on the following July 27, they seemed determined to confound the citizenry even further. As in the earliest fire, the source was a Chinese business (of a less respectable kind: a brothel). This time, five blocks—likewise situated in the heart of the business district—were razed in the fleeting span of fifty minutes, with 200 houses destroyed and losses mounting to $250,000. "Flames spread so rapidly that but very few were able to save their household effects and in many instances articles of furniture were consumed on the spots where they had been carried to safety," reported the *Daily Alta California*.

Compounded disaster hit during August 1856, when alarms again sounded throughout the riverbank and the entire firefighting force—three hand engines and a hook and ladder company—raced to battle the flames. It was thought most expedient to mount the engines on a ferry boat, but before the equipment could do its job, the ferry sank. A contingent of volunteers struggled to keep the losses down, which nevertheless amounted to $145,000.

Smaller blazes erupted in 1864 and 1871, with Marysville's final severe fires of the nineteenth century taking place on September 7, 1879, and September 19, 1887. The first hit a number of buildings along High Street, and consumed the stores of E. C. Ross and N. D. Popert. The second was concentrated along C, D and Fourth streets, and caused the greatest amount of destruction at the Union Lumber Company and the municipal water works. Loss of the latter company's wooden tanks , holding fluid at the time, helped quench the flames—at the expense of the works' storage capacity. For days after the fire, mains had to be supplied by direct pumping from local wells. Reported damages exceeded $150,000, more than three times that of the 1879 blaze.

All told, Marysville's losses to conflagration over a thirty-six year span topped $1.5 million in under-inflated dollars, with no fewer than five significant swaths of destruction cut through the downtown area on different occasions. Save for Georgetown (see later chapter), few California cities have endured such a sustained, relentless trial by fire.

1852
GREAT FIRE in SONORA

Where: Sonora
Details: $700,000 in damage

Sonora
cisco ❋

From its beginning in 1850, Sonora was the county seat of Tuolumne County, located in the heart of the California Gold Rush country. Mexicans from the state of Sonora had established the village—hence the name—but by 1852 , the town was also peopled by Americans and a generous sprinkling of Europeans. J. D. Borthwick, an early arrival in town, wrote: "It consisted of a single street, extending for upwards of a mile along a sort of hollow between gently sloping hills. Most of the Houses were of wood, a few were of canvas, and one or two were solid buildings of sun-dried bricks." No doubt this lack of substantial construction provided ample tinder for a severe fire that hit on June 19, 1852.

It was after midnight when the dreaded cry of "fire!" was heard on the streets of Sonora. It had started in the Hotel de France,

SONORA WAS WELL ON ITS WAY TO BECOMING THE QUEEN CITY OF THE SOUTHERN MINES WHEN DISASTER STRUCK IN JUNE 1852. *California State Library*

FIREMEN AND THEIR APPARATUS IN NEARBY COLUMBIA. THE FIRE COMPANIES WERE ALSO PRESTIGIOUS SOCIAL ORGANIZATIONS, RACING OTHER COMPANIES TO BE FIRST AT FIRES AND COMPETING TO SEE WHAT COMPANY HELD THE MOST LAVISH DANCES AND PARTIES. *Secrest Collection*

operated by a Madame Landreau. Strangely enough, she and her family had lost everything in the great San Francisco fire of the previous year. In a letter to her husband Madame Landreau described her Sonora ordeal, in which she also lost all she owned:

> It was nearly two in the morning when two of the men servants observed a light in the hall. They saw from whence it came, rushed into the unhappy man's room; the flames burst out furiously! I was fast asleep, but my faithful servants did not forget me. They ran to my apartment, and I was saved. I rushed to my children's room; they were gone. I sought for them amidst the flames. Great God what was my agony! Several voices were then heard crying, "Save yourself; come to your children!" I then escaped all but naked and found our two children in the same condition. Eight lodgers on the same floor jumped from the windows and fell on the balcony. They were not hurt, but nothing could be more appalling than the remains of the young man who brought so much misery on us all. I saved nothing. We are now in a hut with some of our unfortunate country people. They are all kindness, but alas, this misfortune is overwhelming.

Francois Molliere, a French boarder and the "unhappy man"referred to in the letter, had been cautioned by Madame Landreau several times against reading in bed with a candle. "He perished in the flames," reported the Sonora correspondent of the *San Francisco Herald*, "and this morning his bones were gathered from the ruins and decently interred." That candle had snuffed out not only his life, but that of the whole town. Borthwick, who had been rooming nearby, rushed downstairs and helped carry as much property outside as he could before the fire arrived:

> The house was about a hundred yards from where the fire broke out, but from the first alarm till it was in flames scarcely ten minutes elapsed. The fire spread with equal rapidity in the other direction.
>
> On the hills, between which lay the town, were crowds of the unfortunate inhabitants, many of whom were but half dressed, and had barely escaped with their lives. One man told me he had been obliged to run for it, and had not even time to take his gold watch from under his pillow.
>
> The whole hillside was lighted up as brightly as a well-lighted room, and the surrounding landscape was distinctly seen by the blaze of the burning town.

In the midst of this horrendous disaster, a new threat surfaced. Thugs and unprincipled miners now began staking new claims among the ruins. "Men who had just seen the greater part of their property destroyed," commented Borthwick, "were not likely to relinquish very readily what little still remained to them; and now, armed with pistols, guns and knives, their eyes bloodshot and their faces scorched and blackened, they were tearing up the stakes as fast as the miners drove them in."

A published catalog of destroyed property listed all the principal buildings in town. Captain Alonzo Green sustained a loss of some

THIS OLD LITHOGRAPH OF THE SACRAMENTO FIRE OF 1852 DRAMATICALLY SHOWS THE FURY OF FIRE IN THE LARGELY WOODEN STRUCTURES OF A CALIFORNIA TOWN. *California State Library*

$40,000; Theall, Perkins & Co. were out some $35,000, and another merchant $30,000. First estimates of losses were $2,000,000, but later figures scaled this down to some $700,000. Whatever the proper figure, it was a great loss.

"The city," groaned a correspondent of the Sacramento *Daily Union*, "from the Philadelphia restaurant to the Barnum House, a distance of full three-fourths of a mile, has been almost entirely swept away. On Main, or Washington street, not a single building remains."

The next day, a large public meeting appointed committees to begin restoring order and planning the rebuilding of the city. Better fire and police protection was made a priority, and serious threats were directed at anyone attempting to locate on another's property. The claim jumpers quickly vanished.

Sonora began rebuilding before the embers had even cooled, but despite the new measures, the town was once again destroyed by fire the following year. A combination of poor construction, few regulations and little advance planning made the 1850s a fire-plagued decade, not only in Tuolumne County, but throughout all California.

GREAT FIRE IN SONORA.

Mr. Harry J. Raphael, who left Sonora at about 4 o'clock this morning—arriving here at noon, informs us of a dreadful catastrophe which has happened at Sonora. It is expected that all the business portion of the mountain city is in ashes. At one o'clock this morning, it was discovered that the French Hotel was on fire, and in a short time the greater part of Main street was enveloped in a sheet of flame. At 4 o'clock, when our informant left, over two thirds of the town had been destroyed, and the fire was still raging with unabated fury. We regret to say that no provision had been made for an event of this character by the authorities or by the people: there was no water, no engine, no hooks or ladders; all was confusion, and as might have been expected, but few goods were saved. Many persons but narrowly escaped with their lives. This sad event will be severely felt by the enterprising citizens of our sister city. Mr. Raphael is agent for Todd's Express.

FIRST NEWS OF THE SONORA FIRE ARRIVED VIA THIS NOTICE IN THE STOCKTON *SAN JOAQUIN REPUBLICAN* JUNE 19, 1852. *Secr[e] Collection*

1852

SACRAMENTO'S GREAT FIRE

Where: Sacramento
Details: Four dead, $10,000,000 in damage

As a town built in a Gold Rush hurry, with extensive canvas and wood construction, severe fire was no stranger to early-day Sacramento. On April 4, 1850, its first major blaze hit Front Street, prompting formation of the city's first fire department. Only seven months later, on November 9, another conflagration caused four hotels and a number of smaller buildings to go up in smoke. However, as significant as these incendiary events were, they all paled next to the catastrophe of November 2-3, 1852. In the space of seven hours, seven-eighths of the city was rendered into smoldering ruins, and losses totaled $10 million—a staggering sum for those days.

The fire broke out at the Madam Lanos dry goods store, near the corner of J and Fourth streets, at half past eleven on the night of the 2nd. Heavy winds managed to push the flames up and down the block, and even across the street to the Crescent City Hotel, in

the space of only five minutes. Thompson and West's *History of Sacramento County* explained why the fire cut such a quick and deadly swath through town: "The wind, which at the commencement of the fire blew very strong and, as the flames gathered headway, increased to a hurricane, carried burning boards several feet in length through the air, and lighted the roofs of buildings often one or more blocks in advance of the main conflagration. This fact, of course, rendered abortive all attempts to check or control the fire."

It took only a few minutes for the fire to head south, to the vicinity of K and Fourth streets, where it attacked a number of brick stores and the Phoenix Hotel. The heavy winds then whipped the flames east and south, destroying the city's Catholic, Baptist and Methodist churches. The sole survivor among the city's houses of worship was the Congregational Church on Sixth Street.

VOL. IV.—NO. 504.   **SACRAMEN**

SACRAMENTO DAILY UNION.

THURSDAY MORNING, NOVEMBER 4.

Ourselves.

We present the *Union* this morning in rather reduced size. For a few days we shall issu · on a cap sheet, but as soon as we can get things in order, we shall resume our original dimensions. We are compelled to adopt this course, having saved but a single cap press. Persons having business with us will apply at the counting room of Mr. J. B. Starr, on Front street.

AWFUL CONFLAGRATION!
Sacramento in Ruins—Loss of Life—Immense Destruction of Property!!

That terrible destroyer which has heretofore laid in ashes every other important town in this State, has at last visited our own fair city of the plains, and in a few brief hours swept almost every vestige of it from existence. Amid the excitement and confusion which prevails, it is impossible for us to give our readers abroad more than a brief summary of the painfully thrilling events of the last thirty hours.

At ten minutes past 11 o'clock, on Tuesday night, the appalling cry of fire was sounded, and almost instantly

ALTHOUGH BURNED OUT OF BUSINESS, THE UNION MANAGED TO GET OUT A SMALL SHEET, A PORTION OF WHICH IS SHOWN HERE. *Secrest Collection*

At this point, the fire whipped to the northwest, destroying the large brick Overton Building, and many allegedly fireproof buildings in the same vicinity. Hard efforts by citizens and firemen kept the flames from spreading any farther east than Ninth Street. At first the fight was conducted by hook and ladder, but all involved became overwhelmed quickly, and explosives were brought in as the major firefighting tool.

It seems there were at least four fatalities, and half a dozen firemen were injured in their frenetic race to smother the flames. All seventy patients at the county hospital at I and Seventh streets had to be evacuated to other quarters. While the enterprise was largely successful, the bones of one patient, and a "fleshy mass" thought to be another, were later found in the building's charred ruins. With so many buildings unsafe or gone, ships along the waterfront were hastily commandeered for emergency use: the *Camanche* became the city's new, floating hospital, and a number of other vessels (the

Confidence, *Antelope* and *Senator*) became emergency shelters. Women and children were the primary residents, as all the men were conscripted into firefighting efforts.

The *State Journal* newspaper was burned out of its printing shop and the Sacramento *Daily Union* was all but destroyed, the owners being able to salvage two small printing presses, type cases, and enough paper to print reduced-format "cap size" editions for several days. When the November 5 issue appeared, a remarkable story was related:

"Mrs. M. A. Acherson furnishes us with the following thrilling incident of the fire. When the flames broke out in the Crescent City Hotel, she was borne along by the tumult into the street, where she heard her little daughter, a child six years old, calling 'mother! mother!' Her feelings under such circumstances can well be imagined. The flames were bursting out of the upper windows of the building. Its eastern side was rapidly yielding to their influence and no hope commended itself to the mother's agonizing heart for her child's safety. At this moment Mr. William P. McGrath, at the peril of his own life, made his way through the rushing fire and smoke, and by an almost superhuman effort reached the little child which he bore to its mother's arms in safety."

While there was no real reason to rejoice in the fire's wake, Sacramentans could take comfort in the fact that the disaster, nevertheless, could have hit much harder. The brick vaults of Adams & Company, along with several other express and financial institutions, withstood the heat and kept their contents free from harm. Paradoxically, the winds did their part to keep losses in check. Dry goods and other articles had been moved out near the riverbank for safekeeping, and when these were threatened by floating embers, gusts whipped up to smother and blow away the threat. It was still a scene of heartbreak and despair, as the *San Francisco Herald* noted: "The levee presents a singular spectacle of promiscuously piled merchandise, household effects, and melancholy looking people, crouched among their goods or searching for lost articles of property."

By any measurement, Sacramento had taken a near-mortal blow. The 1852 fire remains secure in its status as one of California's great urban disasters, and no flames have since hit the city with such comprehensiveness or ferocity. The area bounded between J, L, and Ninth streets and the river was all but completely consumed, and many adjacent blocks were hard-hit as well. Like San Francisco in the wake of the 1906 earthquake and fire, the city had to be rebuilt almost from scratch. Remarkably, it took the citizens only a matter of hours to rise and begin meeting that challenge.

On the Sunday following the fire, the *Union* counted upward of sixty buildings being rehabilitated or under construction. It offered this summary of the city's prevailing mood: "The bustle of preparation and of re-building renders our city a spectacle of industry seldom witnessed. The ruins of those splendid brick blocks which so ornamented our city, at frequent intervals on J and K streets, are rapidly being removed. In a few days the bricks will again be occupying a position in some newly devised edifice. Our citizens have too much energy to permit them long to lie idle."

1853

EXPLOSION of the *JENNY LIND*

Where: South San Francisco Bay
Details: Thirty-one killed, many injured

T he *Jenny Lind* was a small sternwheeler of 61 tons and 145 feet in length, built in 1850. In 1853 she was making routine runs between San Francisco and Alviso at the southern end of the bay, providing a ferry-type service along with a number of other steamships. It was a functional boat that possessed no pretensions of elegance; travelers of the day found decrepitude and squalor to be its most noticeable characteristics.

On the morning of April 11, 1853, the *Jenny Lind* took on about 125 passengers at the Alviso wharf. It was just before noon, and the boat was getting up steam while passengers boarded for the thirty-mile journey north to San Francisco. As it headed north up the bay, the boat was gathering steam, and a pleasant but ordinary trip was anticipated. Nearly half the passengers were in the dining room for lunch as the steamer *Express* passed to the south. About ten minutes later a "violent tremor" resembling the concussion of a cannon shook the boat, followed immediately by a tremendous explosion. A plate on the boiler had blown off, and a scalding torrent of steam and water blew out and enveloped the dining room cabin. The San Francisco *Herald* described this terrible scene:

RIVERBOAT SCHEDULE IN SACRAMENTO DIRECTORY.
Secrest Collection

> The terror, the agony of the scene as described by eye witnesses, baffles all description, and surpasses almost the power of conception. Men, women and children assembled together within a contracted space, unconcious of danger and preparing for a pleasant meal, were suddenly writhing amid volumes of the terrible vapor, stricken with

death in its most dreadful form, or surviving awhile only to endure the most exquisite torture to which the human frame is susceptible.

Those in the forward part of the boat, with the exception of a fireman, who was standing in front of the furnace door, escaped; the latter, a powerful, fine looking man, was struck in the head by the flying open of the furnace door, so that the skull was laid open and the brain exposed; persons came to is assistance, but he motioned them away saying, "No, I'm a dead man, go help others," and soon after breathed his last. But in the after part of the boat but few escaped unhurt; many standing near the guards, were wither blown overboard or leaped into the water in their sudden alarm; of these, but one was picked up, the balance, as many as twelve, we are told, meeting a watery grave.

FOR SAN JOSE AND ALVISO, The fast running and favorite steamer JENNY LIND, Captain Charles Thorn, will leave Long Wharf every MONDAY, WEDNESDAY, and FRIDAY, at 9 o'clock A. M.. for the above: returning. leave Alviso at 8½ o'clock every TUESDAY. THURSDAY. and SATURDAY. connecting with Hall & Crandall's line of stages to San Jose.
For freight or passage. apply on board.   ju27

SCHEDULE FOR THE JENNY LIND ON HER BAY ROUTE. *SAN FRANCISCO HERALD,* AUGUST 13, 1852. *Secrest Collection*

Those within the cabin and on top nearly all died. Survivors, rushing into the cabin to aid the injured, found a hideous scene. Terribly burned and wounded victims were writhing in agony on the floor in six inches of scalding water. Hurtling chunks of wood and metal had cut down people like a deadly scythe. Some screaming people were terribly scalded and when attempts were made to take off their clothes, their skin peeled off with the garments.

EXPLOSION
OF THE
STEAMER JENNY LIND.
AWFUL DESTRUCTION OF LIFE!
HEART-RENDING PARTICULARS
FIFTEEN KILLED.
THIRTY-SIX WOUNDED.
Many Supposed to be Drowned.

Until lately it has not been our fate to chronicle many serious steamboat disasters occurring upon the Pacific or upon our inland waters. but now the intelli-

NEWSPAPER HEADLINE IN *SAN FRANCISCO HERALD,* APRIL 12, 1853. *Secrest Collection*

San Francisco businessman James Tobin was standing, talking to a friend outside the cabin, when the explosion occurred. Tobin had frequently traveled on the Mississippi River and, when the first tremor came he flattened himself on the deck and covered himself with the heavy cape he was wearing. His friend was killed, but Tobin suffered only a minor burn due to his quick thinking. After his narrow escape, Tobin stayed up all night caring for the injured. As soon as this situation was recognized, anchor was dropped and a passenger jumped into the water and swam for shore to secure aid. About the time, a schooner and several small boats arrived from a nearby ranch. The

CONTEMPORARY LITHOGRAPH OF THE DISASTER THAT BEFELL THE *JENNY LIND* IN 1853. *Huntington Library*

nearby steamer *Union*, noting the *Jenny Lind*'s flag upside down in a distress signal, pulled alongside her and took off all the injured and uninjured passengers.

Word of the tragedy was sent to San Francisco, where Mayor Charles Brenham quickly made preparations to aid the stricken passengers. Before he could charter a relief boat, however, the owner of the *Jenny Lind* chartered the steamer *Kate Kearny* and began stocking it with medical supplies, while a half dozen physicians boarded the steamer for the trip. The *Kearny* left just after nine o'clock, but after an hour's trip met the *Union* with some thirty-six wounded and ten dead aboard.

The *Kearny* pulled alongside and the supplies, physicians, several reporters and others went aboard. The *Alta California* reporter was horror-stricken at the scene before him:

> The scene on board beggars all description. Here a fond wife, herself sinking in the arms of death, looking at the last struggles of an affectionate and long tried husband, surrounded by the dead

bodies of their four innocent offspring, but a few hours before buoyant with life, health, happiness and hope. In another spot was the dying mother, endeavoring with her raw and scalded arms to embrace the only child of her bosom, a cold, stiff corpse, untimely hurried to eternity by a violent and dreadful death. There laid a strong man, convulsively wrestling with Death, whilst the hoarse rattle in his throat and the galvanic quivering of his eyes, gave token of rapid dissolution. In another spot were the torn and mangled remains of a once beautiful woman, wearing even in her horrible death a sweet smile of peace and tranquility. Arranged side by side were the dead, dying and the sufferers of excruciating agony. Medical attendance was on hand, and everything done that human skill and ingenuity could do; but the circumstance will leave an indelible impression on the minds of all who saw it.

When the *Union* reached San Francisco, the injured passengers were given rooms in various hotels and rooming houses. Seventeen bodies were examined by the coroner's jury, but it was assumed others had died and drowned. The deaths of the injured brought the known count to thirty-one. Nineteen others were wounded or mortally injured. With only a partial passenger list to go by, the exact number of dead was unknown and unknowable.

FOR SAN JOSE MISSION.—The fine steamer UNION, J. A. Trefry master, will leave her berth in the basin, between Pacific and Broadway wharves, for Union City, on Wednesdays and Saturdays, connecting with the stage for San Jose Mission.
Returning, will leave Union City on Mondays and Thursdays.
For freight or passage apply on board, or to
HORNER & CO.,
ap1   Broadway wharf.

THE *UNION* BROUGHT THE DEAD AND ALIVE PASSENGERS OF THE *JENNY LIND* TO SAN FRANCISCO. A SCHEDULE IN THE *ALTA CALIFORNIA*, APRIL 10, 1853. *Secrest Collection*

The stricken steamer was towed to the Brooks shipyard, where many came to view the wreckage. Actually, although the boiler and cabin were destroyed, the rest of the *Jenny Lind* seemed undamaged. It was an inglorious end to one of the lowlier commuter boats plying the bay. One traveler, Frank Marryat, later commented on "the intolerable filth of the *Jenny Lind*," noting also that "she has since 'blown up,' which is about the only thing that could have purified her."

1853

FLOODS in the VALLEYS

Where: Much of California
Details: Much hardship and loss of stock

Lacking today's extensive network of dams, levees and canals, floods were a constant threat in early California, especially during the seasons of bad weather and high runoff. Few areas of the state were spared when the rivers and lakes jumped their banks, and the consequent difficulties in transportation and disruptions in everyday life affected almost everyone. All this came true in the first flood season of note, during 1850, but the latter months of 1852 brought on an even more extensive siege of deluges.

Just how badly the rains and impassable roads had paralyzed the young state was indicated by Weaverville merchant Franklin Buck, who wrote the following in his journal for December 18, 1852:

> There is a right smart chance of a famine. No mule trains can get through and we are reduced to beef and some of us are fortunate enough to have a few potatoes. There is no flour nor meal nor beans. I was fortunate enough to buy of a man on the river just before the snow set in, 2200 lbs of potatoes. We saved a few to eat and I sold the rest in one day for 37½ cents per pound (made $250 easy). This is awful business for the miners but owing to the rise in everything, we have made more than in all the previous summer.

A report from El Dorado County, published in the Sacramento *Daily Union* on January 3, 1853, offered additional details of this increasingly desperate situatiom:

> For a week past the rain has fallen almost incessantly. Since the middle of November [1852], with but few intervals, it has rained or snowed. The ground is thoroughly soaked, and the gulches, ravines, creeks and rivers full to overflowing. The river at this place, on Wednesday night last, rose to an alarming height, but without doing any serious injury. Fears were entertained for the safety of the bridge, but it firmly resisted the rise, and stands almost uninjured. It was much higher than last spring, and a few inches higher than in '49.

The roads between this place and Sacramento are almost impassable, and in consequence provisions are exorbitantly high. At present the stock on hand is extremely light, and holders are not disposed to part with it so long as the weather continues so unsettled.

Thus far the weather has been infinitely worse than it was in '49. More snow and rain have fallen already than during the entire winter of '49.

Sacramento was already flooded, with continual efforts necessary to keep the city's river levee from crumbling. To make matters worse, the City Common Council was currently deciding how to finance a city indebtedness of some $575,000. Losses from the previous year's disastrous fire (see earlier chapter) had compounded the financial woes of a city where boats were now necessary to navigate streets in the downtown area. The *Union* commented on the situation in its January 1, 1853 issue:

The Flood—The waters above gathered new strength towards the evening of Friday and came down upon us in augmented volumes. Between noon and twilight they arose considerably, and at dark had attained two inches above the highest mark of the flood of two weeks ago and consequently, higher than at any period since the Americans have occupied the country .

At present writing (9 p.m.) the waters continue to flow in, though with no alarming rapidity. Everything now depends upon

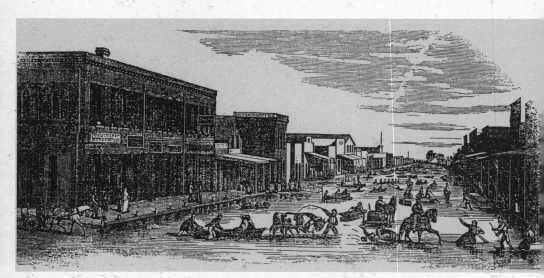

J STREET IN SACRAMENTO ON JANUARY 1, 1853. *California State Library*

the levee immediately encircling the city, which is considered sufficiently strong to allay apprehensions. Should a breach unfortunately occur either along the wharf, or on I street, a great destruction of property must undoubtedly ensue, as the water on the outside of the levee stands some four feet higher than on the inside.

10 o'clock—Small boats are being rowed about on J Street, as low down as Front.

Reports from other parts of the state were much the same. In Shasta, to the north, incessant rains were reported, as well as heavy snowfall. The town of Tehama was inundated, while ranchers scrambled to save their livestock. One large stock raiser reported losing eighty-one cattle in a slough, while the balance of a herd of five hundred were not expected to escape the rising water. Provisions were low everywhere in the mountains, with the *Shasta Courier* reporting: "The road between Tehama and Shasta is strewn with the wrecks of wagons and teams stuck fast in the mud."

According to the *Marysville Herald*, many of the mining camps on the upper Feather River were out of supplies, and local miners were unable to get out of the area due to the high snowpack. Drifts at one location was reported as being twelve feet deep, while at Frenchman's and Buck's Ranch the snow was reported as "bottomless." Two Hawaiians perished trying to get out, and some ninety men from various camps also left, but were later reported as stopping at various places along the road, gathering their strength before moving on. Five men were drowned while trying to cross the Yuba River in early January. On January 10, the *Herald* further commented:

The loss in drowning of stock has been immense, and the damage to perishable property almost incalculable. The greatest pecuniary loss, however, will result from the almost entire suspension of business of every kind for so long a time—country communication having been almost entirely cut off during the past month.

In early January, only two stage lines were reported operating between Stockton and the mines, but by the 7th the *Stockton Journal* stated all lines had been shut down until recently:

By Mr. Todd, who arrived from Sonora last evening, in the first stage that has run on that route for eight or ten days, we learn that the markets of the mountain towns are all entirely barren of provisions, the last flour having been used in Sonora the day he left. There is at present, however, a large lot on the road, which, in all probability has reached its destination ere this, and the folks in those diggings are again feasting on hot cakes and biscuit.

The *Journal* also carried other, more serious news:

The flood in the region about the headwaters of the San Joaquin has risen to an unprecedented height. On the Four Creeks the whole country is under water, Woodville being ten feet below the surface, and all the settlers have been driven to the highlands. The stock, in a great many instances, is drowned.

All the bottoms on the San Joaquin are one vast sheet of water, and at Graysonville, when our informant left, a large herd of cattle were on the opposite side of the stream, standing in water up to their sides, with no prospect of being extricated. In the country for twenty miles back was a great lake, through which it would be impossible to cross them. The owners offered to charter the boat to transport beef to this market, but it was so heavily laden, and in such haste, that the offer was refused. The cattle were inevitably bound to perish, as there existed no possibility of saving them.

At the mouth of the Merced [river] the owners of the ferry had taken up their residence in the boats, and, in many places on the river, rancheros had adopted the same precaution against all possible contingencies.

This is dreadful news from the Four Creeks, as that settlement had but sprung up this last year, and was in highly prosperous

PACKING PROVISIONS INTO ISOLATED MINING CAMPS OVER SNOW-COVERED MOUNTAINS WAS EXHAUSTIVE WORK, EXPENSIVE AND DANGEROUS. THIS GREATLY INFLATED THE PRICE OF GOODS, ALSO. *Secrest Collection*

circumstances, all busily engaged in planting their crops, building and otherwise improving the homes they had adopted.

The flooding and incessant rainstorms had made the streets of many California towns a dangerous quagmire. Just how bad the situation became was illustrated by a tale that unfolded in Sacramento on January 10, 1853. On that day, two men were seen walking together down the Sixth Street sidewalk when the streets were a slippery, muddy nightmare to traverse. They turned into I Street to continue their journey, but stopped at an alley entrance where the sidewalk ended. One of the pair thought it best to take a roundabout route to the next section of sidewalk, while his companion thought he saw a board partially sunk in the mud that would serve as a means to cross. Both took their separate routes, but only one showed up on the next section of sidewalk. Looking around and calling to his friend, the lone pedestrian now found himself in for a shock, as reported in the next day's Sacramento *Union*:

ISOLATED MINING CAMPS, SUCH AS WEAVERVILLE, WERE OFTEN CUT OFF FROM THE OUTSIDE WORLD IN BAD WINTER WEATHER. *Secrest Collection*

He retraced his footsteps to the mouth of the alley and found the glazed hat of his friend lying mouth downwards, but no man. He stooped down, reached in, and lifting the hat, saw numerous bubbles arise, which contained a monosyllable utterance resembling "elp!" The alarm was immediately given when a crowd repaired to the spot. A negro man, arriving in advance of all others, tore a board from the fence adjoining, and casting it across the mouth of the alley aforesaid, jumped on it and forcing his arms elbow deep into the soft mud, immediately under the bubbles, grasped hold of something which felt like hair. Pulling on this with all his strength, an object arose slowly to the surface, but which was not distinguished to possess any definite form. Many declared it to be an old mat that had been submerged by the action of the water. Others thought it might be the unraveled end of a very thick cable, while some contended that it was a *man!*Someone thought

RATS AND DEEP MUD IN CITY STREETS ADDED TO CALIFORNIA'S 1853 FLOOD PROBLEMS. *From* Annals of San Francisco

to throw a bucket of water on the discovery and the exposed head and shoulders became quite clear. The black man and several others now pulled and tugged and exposed more of the victim. When another bucket of water was sloshed on the man, a woman screamed and two nearby Chinese were said to have fainted. While everyone was talking and asking questions, an Irishman exclaimed, "And a dead men, too, howly Virgin be gracious." Some movement appeared where the man's eyes and mouth would be as his voice bellowed, "Damnation! Are you ever going to pull me out?"

This brought the crowd to their senses. Jacks were then procured, propped on boards under the man's arms and he was soon extricated. As the dejected figure finally stood on the sidewalk, the crowd began arguing as to the best means of fully resuscitating him.

"Give him some Chile Colorado," suggested a Mexican in the crowd.

A bartender said some whiskey would be more beneficial.

A passing teamster was more practical when he heard what had happened. "Water," he proposed, "was what he used to clean his mules and they got into that kind of scrape every day."

The advice was heeded, and everyone went on his way as the victim went home to bathe and change clothes.

1853

SINKING of the *WINFIELD SCOTT*

Where: Middle Anacapa Island, near Ventura
Details: Ship lost, no casualties

Santa Barbara

❄

A handsome sidewheel steamer built in New York during 1850, the *Winfield Scott* was named after the general of Mexican War fame and carried his likeness on her straight stem. First entrusted with runs between her home port and New Orleans, a subsequent sale to the New York and San Francisco Steamship Company caused her to switch oceans. By 1852 she was servicing the lucrative gold rush route between California and Panama, and continued to do so after her mid-1853 acquisition by the Pacific Steamship Mail Company.

Under the supervision of Captain Simon Frazer Blunt, an Annapolis graduate and allegedly capable seaman, the *Scott* spent a trouble-free six months under its new ownership. Unfortunately, a combination of foul weather and impatience on the skipper's part cut her career short, putting the five hundred or so crew and

AN OLD ENGRAVING SHOWING THE WINFIELD SCOTT LEAVING PORT.
Secrest Collection

passengers in harm's way, causing a large loss of property and the near-destruction of the mail on board. The last-mentioned was a particularly sensitive subject, since it was the primary means of communication between the gold miners and their families and friends in the East.

San Francisco printer Edward Bosqui, a *Scott* passenger, headed back to his ancestral home in Montreal, later wrote of troublesome signs afoot during the voyage's first day:

> At about nine o'clock in the evening the first officer of the ship crossed the threshold of the captain's cabin, where a group of army officers were telling war adventures, and diverted the attention of the party, of which I was a member, by very abruptly addressing Captain Blunt with the words: "Captain, the weather is dirty and squally. Shall we keep her out?" The captain answered, "No; let her rip!" None of us paid much attention to the incident, and soon afterwards separated for the night.

Though later praised in newspaper accounts for his coolness under fire, this carelessness on Blunt's part (and poor visibility due to fog) caused the *Scott* to run headlong into treacherous shallow waters off of Middle Anacapa Island, located southwest of Ventura. Bounced to and fro in the rough seas, the ship sustained considerable damage, as the December 7 *Alta California* noted:

EDWARD BOSQUI, A PASSEN● THE WINFIELD SCOTT, LATER OF HIS EXPERIENCE DURING FATEFUL TRIP *From his book* Memoirs of Edward Bosqui

> She struck bow on, staving two holes in her bow, and then, in backing off, her stern struck, knocking away her rudder. There was a good deal of alarm manifested among the passengers, most of whom had turned in; and even after she had struck, the fog was so dense that they could see nothing before them. After the loss of her rudder, the boat drifted off a distance of three hundred yards, and went ashore bow on, striking upon a bluff. She had already commenced filling, and soon after striking for the last time sunk up to her guards.

Passengers were by now scrambling to get ahold of life preservers and pile into the five lifeboats. A frightened group of men tried to jam themselves into one of the small craft, ahead of the women and children, and Blunt had to ward them off with his pistol. Despite the edgy situation, the evacuation to Middle Anacapa proceeded on an efficient basis, and all those aboard had been transported to land by the time daybreak hit.

SAN FRANCISCO DAILY ALTA CALIFORNIA, DECEMBER 7, 1853

The general confusion and disorder encouraged both passengers and outsiders to take advantage of the situation. Captain Martin Kimberly, a resident of nearby Santa Cruz Island, spotted the goings-on and, along with a sailor friend, decided to make a fast reconnaissance of the *Scott*. "They found it filled with the choicest sort of food and wines, and a great many other things," reported Kimberly's widow, Jane. "They made several trips in an open boat, appropriating what they wanted. My husband told me that one of the things he took off for his home was a large mirror."

Another passenger, Asa Call, wrote in his diary that some of the stranded were sneaking back to the wreck and making off with various goods: "Robbery and plunder has been the order of the day since the wreck. But today we appointed a committee of investigation and have had everything searched. A good deal of property has come to light, and two thieves have been flogged. I have recovered a pair of revolvers, a Bowie knife, and some clothing, but I am a good deal out of pocket yet. But probably my other things never came ashore."

Amazingly, given the hordes of people aboard the *Scott*, no more than two men (one of them a butcher named Underwood) were lost in the commotion. Their numbers presented an immediate food problem, mitigated by the appearance of George Nidever, a onetime fur trader and Santa Barbara resident. He sailed past Middle Anacapa soon after the lifeboats landed, and lent his lines and hooks for fishing. Before long, crews were fishing in shifts to feed the beached multitudes.

Crew and passengers had to wait only a matter of hours for relief. On December 4, the steamer *California* chanced upon the scene and began to cart away the stranded and the ship's cargo. Eventually, three other ships (the *Republic*, *Southerner* and *Goliah*) joined in these efforts, and in less than a week, all the passengers were headed to their intended destination. The precious mail was taken back to San Francisco, where it was hung over bonfires, dried carefully, slipped into new envelopes, stamped and sent on its way. One account claimed that only a single, wax-laden letter was lost during the execution of this process.

Aside from Underwood and the unidentified man, the other major victims in this tragedy were its captain and the ship itself. A footnote to Bosqui's memoir states that Captain Blunt died of a "broken heart" in mid-1854. Was it broken, perhaps, by shame over his recklessness? As for the *Scott*, she was pillaged for decades by treasure hunters until the Channel Islands National Monument was created, and park rangers began regular area patrols of the site. Often obscured by kelp and other sea debris, she remains where she landed, her rotting hulk sometimes protruding at low water but usually visible to divers only.

1854

EXPLOSION of the *SECRETARY*

Where: San Pablo Bay
Details: More than forty deaths

It promised to be an ordinary passage for the steamer *Secretary*. Heading north on San Francisco Bay on the morning of April 15, 1854, the crew and passengers were steaming toward a mid-afternoon destination of Petaluma, an easy ride along the inland waterways of northern California. Yet, as the *Secretary* neared the entrance of San Pablo Bay, those aboard the vessel felt its engines groan and shake as another steamer, the *Nevada*, came within sight. The latter, a swifter and more powerful craft, had little difficulty surging forward and then pulling alongside its competitor. Apparently, a race had started. Meanwhile, as the *Secretary* chugged and strained to stay in the running—and just when its rival got about sixty yards ahead—fate intervened to render the competition irrelevant.

With the *Nevada* a mere 100 yards away, the *Secretary* exploded, raining its contents over the suddenly-turgid waters. The *San Francisco Herald* of the following day offered this account of the desperate scene:

> In a moment the water was covered with the broken fragments of the boat, to which the wounded were seen to cling. It is thought the entire machinery was blown out, and what remained of the hull was quickly covered by water—the bow of the boat and the hurricane deck remained afloat; and upon the latter, several persons who had not

THE STEAMBOAT *SECRETARY* EXPLODED WHILE RACING WITH THE OPPOSITION STEAMER *NEVADA* ON THE WAY TO PETALUMA IN SONOMA COUNTY. IT WAS ANOTHER FOOLISH ACCIDENT THAT NEVER SHOULD HAVE HAPPENED. *Secrest Collection*

been blown off, remained, whilst others who had been thrown in the water, were drawn up by those already there. Of course all was consternation and confusion around, and had it not been for the presence of some experienced mariners, the destruction of life would have been greater. The cries of the women and children who escaped death, are said to have been most heart-rending.

No fewer than fifteen souls aboard the *Secretary*, or what remained of them, sank into the bay immediately and were never found. The crew was hard-hit, losing the engineer, Ansel Bessie, along with two deckhands and the ship's cook. Among the others who disappeared were John Ebbets, discoverer of the Sierra Nevada pass which has been known by his surname ever since, and Martin Gormley, a sloop captain and onetime private in the New York Volunteers which served in California during the conquest years.

The *Nevada*'s captain, J. H. Cornell, was quick to back up his boat and start searching for survivors. It picked up a total of thirty-eight treading water and clinging to the wreckage, but only one body, that of Mrs. Cecelia Clark. A few were soaked but otherwise unhurt; most of the survivors unsurprisingly had burns, bruises or broken limbs, including the captain, E. W. Travis. Worst-off of the survivors was Isaac Pailthorp, a badly burned Welshman, who was taken back to San Francisco for medical attention but died soon afterward.

No time was wasted in holding an inquest over Mrs. Clark's body, and a tale began to emerge which any modern plaintiff's attorney would envy. One of the slightly injured passengers, S. M. Terrill of Bodega Bay, reported that Engineer Bessie had complained of all the water leaking out of the *Secretary*'s boiler before the trip started—and to compound the worry, he had learned that Captain Travis intended to race his ailing ship against the *Nevada*, which regularly traversed the same route. According to Terrill's testimony:

> Before we started, I asked Captain Travis if the *Nevada* could beat us. He replied that she could in the bay, but that the *Secretary* would give her h—l in the creek. The captain said he would put us into Petaluma two or three hours ahead of the *Nevada*, and that the *Secretary* being a side wheel boat and the *Nevada* a stern wheel he would make better time in going through the creek.

Even more incendiary was the inquest statement of John Smith, another of the survivors:

> Went aboard the steamer about half-past ten o'clock to go to Petaluma. …I went into the engine room and *saw an oar lashed over the lever of the safety valve.* [Thus, the ship was running beyond full throttle capacity.] Heard somebody say to the fireman: "Shove her up. D—n it, shove her up." The blade of the oar was on the safety valve. I saw the engineer lift up the handle of the oar once. The Captain appeared excited during the trip. Heard the passengers say the boats were racing.

The accounts of Terrill and Smith were corroborated in part by that of another passenger, Mrs. Sarah V. N. Rodgers, who overheard Captain Travis tell Engineer Bessie "not to force the boat," indicating that he knew the *Secretary* was in less than perfect shape for a race. She further mentioned having been on the steamer the day before the explosion, during a trip to Contra Costa, and overhearing the engineer saying he wished to conserve his wood supply for the following day—presumably, for racing purposes.

A search of the San Francisco newspapers for several weeks following indicates that no legal actions grew out of the *Secretary* tragedy. With such clear-cut negligence on the part of the main crew

SAN FRANCISCO DAILY HERALD, APRIL 16, 1854

PASSENGERS LOVED THE SPEED AND CONVENIENCE OF THE RIVERBOATS, BUT A GOOD RACE REALLY LIVENED UP A TRIP.
California State Library

members, it seems surprising that the vessel's owners, George Gordon and Steen, were never held accountable for their employees' actions. Interestingly, none of the contemporary accounts quote a word from Captain Travis; did he go amnesiac or mute to protect his superiors? There was also the problem that Engineer Bessie, the other key witness, was lost and presumed dead. The owners were also careful to issue a highly apologetic public statement, going so far as to admit that the safety valve had been held wide open, and citing evidence that accidental combustion (rather than boiler strain) had caused the explosion. It would seem these factors, considered together, conspired to squelch any court sequels to the *Secretary*'s demise.

Fans of curses and jinxes will be interested to know that the *Secretary*, built late in the previous year out of scavenged parts, was equipped with the very engines that drove another ill-fated San Francisco ship—the *Sagamore*—whose demise is recorded in an earlier chapter.

1854

WRECK of the *YANKEE BLADE*

Where: Southern California coast
Details: More than thirty lost in shipwreck

Santa Barbara

"I n what manner the unfortunate accident, which led to the loss of the steamship *Yankee Blade* occurred, it is impossible for me to say." This was the first public utterance of the unfortunate steamer's captain, Henry Randall. It was not the worst shipwreck off California's coast, nor the first, but it was a unique disaster in many ways.

With the steadily increasing trade brought on by the gold rush, and the loss of ships by aging and in various disasters, steamships were constantly being built or purchased from Eastern capitalists anxious to turn a profit. When shipping magnate Commodore Cornelius Vanderbilt joined with Edward Mills to form the Vanderbilt Independent Line on the Pacific coast, Mills already had a new steamer under construction in New York. It was to be a magnificent and luxurious ship called the *Yankee Blade*, captained by Randall. A steamer with two huge sidewheels, the ship was also rigged for sail and was launched in November 1853. Originally scheduled to run between New York and the Isthmus, after one trip it was sailed around the Horn and put in service between San Francisco and Panama.

The new steamer was put into service amid a rate war, several ship disasters, and a fierce rivalry among feuding ship owners. From the beginning, the *Yankee Blade* itself seemed haunted with an aura of violence and death. While off the coast of

THE *YANKEE BLADE* AS DEPICTED IN AN OLD PRINT. *Secrest Collection*

Brazil, during its maiden voyage to San Francisco, a murder was committed on the new ship. A man smuggling a prostitute to California stabbed the woman while in a jealous fit, then tried to kill himself.

The *Blade* arrived in San Francisco on May 4, 1854 and prepared for service on the coast. Its maiden voyage to Panama and back encountered further problems. A married actress named Susan Denim was aboard, and when she was caught keeping company with a philanderer named Edward Bingham, her husband and other passengers attempted to throw Bingham overboard. The captain and others stopped the fracas, but after reaching port, Bingham was shot and badly crippled by an unknown assailant.

ADVERTISMENT IN THE *ALTA CALIFORNIA* FOR THE FIR
RUN OF THE *YANKEE BLADE* BETWEEN SAN FRANCIS
AND PANAMA. Daily Alta California, *May 20, 1854*

Later, when the ship had returned to San Francisco on July 1, 1854, two of its passengers engaged in a fight after drinking at a saloon called the Shamrock; one was knocked into the bay and drowned.

On the second trip to Panama, Captain Randall attempted to set a new time record and ran out of coal. The crew and some passengers went ashore on Coiba Island and cut enough wood to finish the run. Returning to San Francisco with 473 passengers, the *Blade* reported six of the group had died at sea of cholera. Remaining in port while it was cleaned and disinfected, the ship was scheduled to depart on September 30, 1854, on its third trip since arriving in California.

While some $355,650 worth of treasure was being loaded aboard the *Blade* for shipment to eastern banks, passengers were steadily arriving. Besides Captain Randall and 121 crew members, 812 passengers were listed for the voyage. As was the custom, fares collected after boarding were usually not immediately recorded. Steerage lists were also incomplete and the number of passengers, including stowaways, might have been as high as 1,200. Adding to this confusion was the presence of a notorious San Francisco thug named Jim Turner, stowed away in the *Blade's* bowels with several of his pals. Indicted earlier and facing six months in jail, he had decided to skip town for awhile.

The final bit of the tableau to come together was an ad in the *Daily Alta California* on September 29, 1854, announcing that a $5,000 wager had been made on whether the *Yankee Blade* or the *Sonora* arrived first in Panama. On the day of departure, the two ships, along with several others, left their respective wharves and sailed through a foggy Golden Gate and into the open sea.

Captain Randall took an early lead in the race and maintained it through heavy intermittent fog. When they passed Monterey about midnight the fog had lifted, but by morning they were again in the fog off Point Buchon, just west of San Luis Obispo. The sea was very rough and the weather cloudy and overcast.

A passenger on the steamer *Goliah*, accompanying the *Blade* and other ships, reported what happened two days later, as they approached Point Arguello through a dense fog:

> Just at this moment breakers appeared right ahead through the fog. The engine was immediately reversed, and while we were backing out of what might have been a bad scrape for us, we saw nearly off our starboard beam, looming through the fog, a large steamer. In an instant we saw that it was the *Yankee Blade*, with her bows run clear upon the rocks and her stern sunk in deep water to the wheel houses.
>
> Her bows and forward deck contained a dense mass of human beings who had climbed to the only place of safety left above water. We lowered our boats, and having manned and sent them off to the wreck, came to anchor at about a half mile distant. They brought back each a load of the passengers of the *Yankee Blade*, and from them we learned that she had run upon the rocks while under full headway, on the day previous.

HORACE BELL, A PASSENGER ON THE GOLIAH, GAVE A DRAMATIC ACCOUNT OF THE RESCUE. *Secrest Collection*

The stories told now by the survivors of the wreck were horrible tales of humanity running amuck. Captain Randall had immediately checked the damage and ascertained the *Blade* would not sink for some time as it was sturdily perched on a large reef. Next he took four of his men in a small boat and found a safe beach to land. Randall then returned to the *Blade*, only to find boatloads of women and children heading for shore against his orders. He took some into his boat and shouted landing instructions, but he was inaudible over the heavy surf. The passengers were swamped in the rough water and drowned. Going back to shore, Randall unloaded his charges safely, but then faced a new problem, as he later reported to the San Francisco *Daily Alta California*:

HEADLINES FROM THE SAN FRANCISCO *DAILY HERALD*, OCTOBER 10, 1854. *Secrest Collection*

> Those whom I had got to help row, jumped out and went away refusing to go off to the wreck with me again. Left with but one man, I rowed back to the wreck and ashore again four times, taking a load from the ship each time, and the last time was informed that all the women and children were off the ship.

Aboard the wreck, Turner and his gang were joined by unscrupulous members of the ship's crew. While the captain and crew frantically tried to save passengers, Turner and his drunken thugs were robbing luggage and stealing anything of value they could find. Many pass-

THE WRECKED *YANKEE BLADE* SITS ON THE REEF WHILE PASSENGERS CLUSTER ABOUT THE BOW TO STAY OUT OF THE WATER. SKETCHED BY A PASSENGER. *California State Library*

engers were beaten and robbed, and several murders were reportedly committed in the course of robberies. Lifebelts were collected and sold for exorbitant prices by both the thugs and crew members.

On shore, another horror story unfolded. Half-drowned passengers were dragged from the surf while bodies washed up on the beach. A woman heaved a man on her shoulder and carried him up a bluff to a campfire. A woman, still clutching her baby in her arms, was found in the surf and buried. When her frantic husband learned of her fate, he came ashore. Digging up the bodies, he kissed each, then re-buried them.

The *Goliah* dropped off many of the survivors in San Diego, while those on shore drifted to Santa Barbara and Los Angeles. All were eventually returned to San Francisco to pick up their lives. Some of the passengers, unaware of the captain's whereabouts during much of the ordeal, complained loudly to the press about Randall's presumed cowardice in leaving the ship. Most, however, hailed him as one of the tragedy's heroes.

Thirty lives were reported lost, but the incomplete passenger lists made an accurate count impossible. Much of the sunken treasure was recovered, some of it through the efforts of Captain Randall. Several of Turner's thugs were picked up later, but most of them either escaped or were reported drowned.

Despite his heroism, Randall still had to live with blame for the wreck. Returning to New York, he served as president of a bank, and—interestingly— invented various methods to promote safety at sea. Whether it was navigational error, fog, or the pressure of the race that caused the wreck, only Captain Randall could say, and it seems he never shared his knowledge of the incident with anyone.

1855

EXPLOSION of the *PEARL*

Where: Sacramento River
Details: More than twenty killed, many injured

While the sad tale of the *Secretary* (see earlier chapter) should have ended the dangerous and dubious racing of steam-powered vessels in early California, it seems that panache was valued over safety in those days, and the incident was more or less repeated the following year. On the morning of January 27, 1855, the passenger steamers *Pearl* and *Enterprise*, not long out of Marysville, were locked in a southbound competition on the Sacramento River. As both ships neared the state capital, the *Pearl* was lagging noticeably behind, but a fast throttle push got it ahead—for a few seconds. Then history repeated itself.

Under the title of "Notes by one of the Blown Up," the *San Francisco Herald*'s January 29 issue published a survivor's firsthand account of what happened, identifying him only as "Alabamian":

AN 1851 ENGRAVING OF MARYSVILLE. *Secrest Collection*

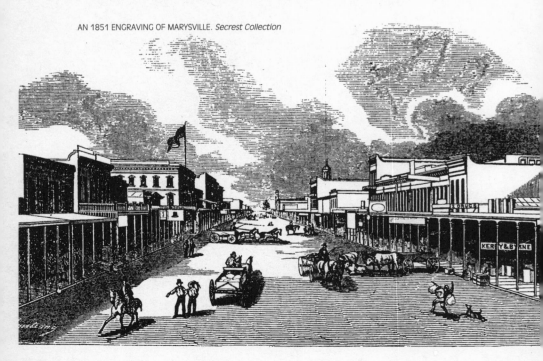

I was standing on the starboard side of the boiler deck , being above and little to one side of the boiler, which was not more than three feet from me; this deck was crowded with passengers who were getting their baggage preparatory to landing. I heard a tremendous and deafening crash, and next found myself in the water, about the middle of the river, I rose to the surface perfectly conscience [sic] of what had happened, and saw the steamer at a considerable distance; numbers were struggling around me; with one exception they appeared to be either badly wounded or had lost all presence of mind; the fragments around were so very small as to afford no assistance to the more desperate of the strugglers. Boats were hurrying to us from all directions, but the floating mass of ruins, while affording little or no buoyancy to help the drowning ones, prevented the boats reaching them in time to save. I saw but one picked up alive on my side of the boat, being hurt but little myself it required no struggling to keep afloat, but it was awful to behold the drowning struggles of those around me when I could not assist; though feeling perfectly safe myself I was convinced that if others grasped me it would be a desperate case. Of the forty or fifty who were with me on the boiler deck, not one in ten could have escaped, they were all blown up, as also those who were below on the main deck. I think there were more human beings on board than is given in any estimate that has yet appeared. There must have been 100 to 125 white persons on board, beside the number of Chinese, who were in the hold. It may not be amiss to note that an hour before the explosion my attention was attracted by a peculiarity in the working of the engines. If we had landed in safty [sic] I would not have thought of it again, not being a practical engineer. I do not feel warranted in laying any great stress on it now, even though I was blown up, or, more properly, blown out, for I am certain I did not go up far. As far as I can judge, my escape (almost unhurt) was by far the most providential of any.

"Alabamian" was right to discount his knowledge of the explosion's origin. Henry Keefer, a messenger for the Adams & Co. express firm and another passenger on board, noted that he saw no residual steam, smoke or fire immediately after the *Pearl*'s disintegration, strongly

STEAMBOAT RACING WAS VERY POPULAR, NOT JUST AS A SPORT BUT AS A MEANS OF SHOWING WHAT BOAT WOULD GET YOU TO YOUR DESTINATION FIRST.
California State Library

suggesting that her boiler had been strained to the breaking point, with its overheated contents vaporizing instantaneously. The coroner's jury convened after the tragedy ultimately decided that this was the blast's cause.

Since the tragedy took place within sight of the Sacramento levee, many witnessed the explosion and its grisly aftermath. Grotesque wounding and scalding predominated, and dismembered bodies and parts littered the riverbanks. The *San Joaquin Republican* of January 31 recited two of the more eyebrow-raising stories which issued forth:

When the body of Mr. [T. V.] Mount was found his watch was in his hand, he evidently having been noting the time the explosion occurred. The top of the watch case had been blown off.

On Sunday a boot was found containing a right foot and a portion of the leg. The body to which it belonged was found yesterday, but we believe has not been recognized. It is remarkable that although the leg was amputated so low down, the boot was wholly uninjured.

Those spared had tales no less amazing to report. The January 28 San Francisco *Alta California* said: "The pilot was blown some distance from the boat, and was picked up alive, with his leg only injured; his escape with life is miraculous, as the wheel that he held was blown all to fragments. A fine dog, that was on the Pearl, saved the life of a man by dragging him out of the water after he had sunk, twice." Less fortunate was Captain E. T. Davis, who was killed instantly, and whose body was later dragged out of the water.

Newspaper reports vary, but it seems that the *Pearl* had approximately 100 people aboard during its last river run. Of this number, more than half (fifty-three) were either killed outright or died later of injuries, with at least twenty-seven injured and ten escaping unscathed. A number of the dead were buried in Sacramento's city cemetery on the following Monday (January 29), amid a funeral procession of 2,500 or more, with a great many Chinese mourning the lost among their own.

As with the *Secretary*, the most puzzling part of the *Pearl*'s demise was the failure of the authorities to hold anyone responsible for what was likely a preventable disaster. At the inquest, the *Enterprise*'s captain testified that Andrew Wadleigh, the *Pearl*'s engineer, had been hired because he was a "hotter" man, willing to run the ship faster, and even lacking the technical expertise to do his job correctly. Worse yet, witnesses on the levee saw Wadleigh leap in the water and swim for shore seconds before the explosion. Though a subpoena was issued for him, he disappeared in the post-disaster confusion. It was a situation tailor-made for a latter-day plaintiff's attorney but, as with so many other grave and tragic incidents, it was fast forgotten in the hubbub of Gold Rush California.

1856

EXPLOSION of the *BELLE*

Where: Sacramento River
Details: More than thirty dead, wounded and missing

A dense fog hung over Sacramento on the early morning of February 5, 1856. The steamer *Belle*, docked on the city's waterfront, was scheduled to begin a trip upriver to Red Bluff at 7 A.M., but Captain Charles H. Houston looked outside and thought better of casting off at the assigned time. With fifty-odd passengers and crew members aboard, along with much valuable express cargo, the captain was determined to make the *Belle*'s passage safe. After waiting almost a half hour, he decided the thick mists had cleared enough, and told Chief Engineer W. J. Eirick to start firing the boiler.

As the *Belle* pulled away from the waterfront, subsequently passed the mouth of the American River and chugged further north on the Sacramento, Eirick was keeping a watchful eye on the ship's boiler. With the fog present, he started running at sixty pounds' pressure, and began a slow, careful buildup to eighty-six pounds, thus establishing a steady cruising speed. He asked Fireman William Green how he thought the boiler was running, and the answer was "easy." Seeing nothing amiss, Eirick stepped out to "key up a crank pin," by his own account—and at that moment, for reasons wholly unanticipated and ultimately unknown, the *Belle*'s boiler exploded.

The blast happened as the *Belle* came parallel to the Russian Ford, eleven miles north of Sacramento. Debris, bodies and corpses were blown high and pitched into the river and the surrounding country, with the remaining bulk of the ship sinking within seconds. The San Francisco *Daily Alta*

HEADLINE IN THE SAN FRANCISCO *DAILY ALTA CALIFORNIA*, FEBRUARY 6, 1856.

California of February 7 stated: "The only upper works of the Belle left standing and sound were the flag or steering staff, and the wheel. All else, save the aft-bottom, was completely mashed." Nevertheless, the wreck of the *Belle* was said to be more intact than that of the ill-fated river steamship *Pearl*, which had exploded a year before, and whose demise is related in an earlier chapter.

One of the more remarkable stories emanating from the tragedy was related in the following day's *Sacramento Daily Union*:

> William A. Mix [of Shasta], a passenger, while reading, was requested to move by a waiter who was sweeping, and passed into the cabin. While conversing with another passenger, the explosion occurred, killing the latter, himself escaping unhurt. [A more graphic account in the *Marysville Herald* mentioned that Mix was drenched with the man's brains.]
>
> Mr. Mix was thrown upon his face on a sofa in the cabin. He immediately jumped out the the window upon the deck, and saw 15 or 20 persons floating in the stream, all or most of whom he thinks he could have saved had there been a small boat at the stern. As soon as he recovered from the shock of the accident, and perceived those struggling in thewater, he commenced throwing overboard boxes, bales and everything movable that would float, for their assistance.
>
> A canary bird belonging to Mr. Mix was in a cage placed on a table in the cabin, at the time of the explosion. Although the table

THE SACRAMENTO LEVEE AND DOCKS IN 1856 AS THEY APPEARED AT THE TIME OF THE *BELLE* DISASTER. BOILER EXPLOSIONS WERE A NECESSARY RISK OF RIVER TRAVEL IN NINETEENTH-CENTURY AMERICA. *California State Library*

was almost entirely demolished by being cleared by portions of the boiler, the bird and cage escaped uninjured, with the exception of the latter being slightly bent. The bird is now singing as sweetly as ever, the accident having merely disturbed its plumage.

There was irony aplenty as the *Belle*'s toll was taken; much like Mix and his canary, some were left unscathed, including Engineer Eirick (despite his close proximity to the blast). James Hyland, a ship's steward, had his hat sheared neatly in half by a flying projectile, but was otherwise unhurt. A number of others were, of course, considerably unluckier. Captain Houston's badly disfigured body was plucked out of the Sacramento, and all that remained of Fireman Green was his lower half, floating in the *Belle*'s hold—rendered identifiable only by the presence of papers in his pocket.

Mercifully, relief was quick in coming to the scene of destruction. A local farmer, who heard the explosion, rushed toward the Sacramento and managed to pull five victims out of the water. Other residents hastily set up a tent near the riverbank, which served as a combination temporary hospital and morgue. It was a mere forty minutes or so before another steamship traveling downriver (the *General Reddington*) arrived, followed by the *Cleopatra* in its wake. Both were joined later by the *Gem*, whose crew spotted unexpected floating wreckage three miles south of the Russian Ford, and hastened to reach the disaster site. All three helped in the ensuing search, salvage and evacuation efforts.

The California Steam Navigation Company quickly sent a company of fifty men to remove freight from in and around the *Belle*, and to look for missing passengers. While they scored no notable success in accounting for the lost, the cargoes of the Wines and Pacific express companies aboard were, surprisingly, recovered intact. Many other odd dry goods carried on the ship were, of course, either destroyed or ruined.

Back in Sacramento, the coroner wasted no time in holding an inquest to determine the explosion's cause. In spite of an iron works proprietor, a boiler maker and a blacksmith testifying, no one could arrive at an adequate explanation for the *Belle*'s demise. The blacksmith, Jesse Morrill, contended that the *Belle*'s boiler should have easily taken ninety-five pounds of pressure, and should have gone to 120 pounds without any difficulty.

JOHN BIDWELL, PROMINENT CALIFORNIA RANCHER, MINER, POLITICIAN AND PRESIDENTIAL CANDIDATE, WAS SERIOUSLY INJURED IN THE EXPLOSION OF THE *BELLE*, BUT RECOVERED. *Secrest Collection*

If there was a passenger list for the *Belle*, it perished with the blast, so the exact toll of dead and injured will never be known. Comparisons between the newspaper accounts suggest that at least ten perished, eighteen were injured to varying extents, and four passengers were never found, making for a total casualty count of at least thirty-two.

An intriguing footnote to the *Belle*'s demise is that famed California pioneer John Bidwell happened to be on board that morning, was somehow hurled onto water or land, and was removed to Sacramento for treatment of a skull fracture. Despite Bidwell's being the only notable person on board, the *Union* obtained nothing more from him than his estimate of the number killed and wounded—and the standard biographies of him make no reference to the incident!

Towns and Waterways
of Nineteenth-Century
California

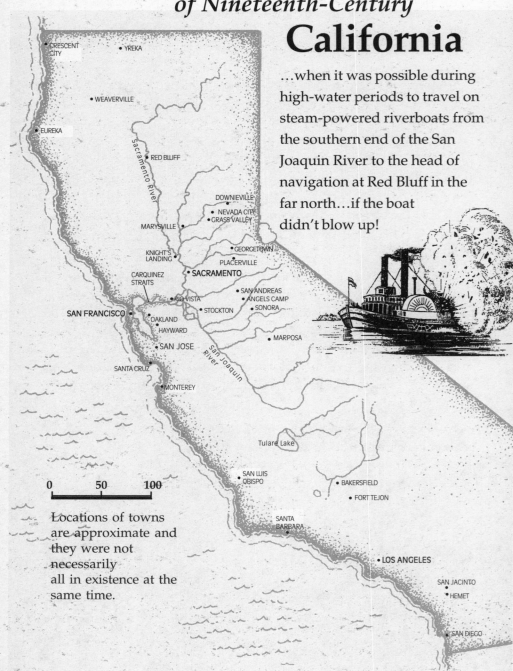

…when it was possible during high-water periods to travel on steam-powered riverboats from the southern end of the San Joaquin River to the head of navigation at Red Bluff in the far north…if the boat didn't blow up!

CRESCENT CITY

YREKA

WEAVERVILLE

EUREKA

Sacramento River

RED BLUFF

DOWNIEVILLE

NEVADA CITY
GRASS VALLEY

MARYSVILLE

KNIGHT'S LANDING

GEORGETOWN

PLACERVILLE

SACRAMENTO

CARQUINEZ STRAITS

SAN FRANCISCO

RIO VISTA

SAN ANDREAS
ANGELS CAMP
STOCKTON
SONORA

OAKLAND
HAYWARD

SAN JOSE

San Joaquin River

MARPOSA

SANTA CRUZ

MONTEREY

Tulare Lake

0   50   100

SAN LUIS OBISPO

BAKERSFIELD

FORT TEJON

SANTA BARBARA

Locations of towns are approximate and they were not necessarily all in existence at the same time.

LOS ANGELES

SAN JACINTO
HEMET

SAN DIEGO

70

GREAT NEVADA CITY FIRES

Where: Nevada City
Details: Ten deaths, over $2,500,000 in damages

Perhaps the most spectacular urban fire of California's gold rush era took place in the mining town of Nevada, early on the morning of March 11, 1851. ("City" was later appended to its name so as to avoid confusion with the state.) Begun by a trio of arsonists, who stealthily departed in the wake of the blaze's confusion, an early account painted an unusually vivid description of the flames and their progress:

> The buildings were extremely dry, of light construction, and burned with vast rapidity—the conflagration being accelerated by quantities of powder stored everywhere in the houses—which exploded momentarily at various points, as the heat overtook it, casting flaming timbers, brands and missiles of all descriptions into the air. Nevada was built in the midst of a pine forest, and many tall pines were left standing in the heart of the city, while the houses closely hemmed them in. These trees, extremely pitchy, caught the flames as they writhed round their stems, and shot them hundreds of feet into the air, where they danced and quivered like malicious spirits over the scene of a burning world.

Eventually, buildings had to be pulled down ahead of the flames to check their advance. A total of 125 buildings were lost to this fire, and half the town was left in ruins. The total losses amounted to a half-million dollars, a staggering-enough sum for the 1850s; but even this high figure was eclipsed five years later, when an all-encompassing inferno destroyed Nevada and anywhere from $1.5 to $3 million in property went up in smoke.

The 1856 fire started in the late afternoon of July 19, at an indeterminate location on Pine Street. It took only a brief half-hour to consume the town and its adjoining areas, in all 800 buildings and more than 150 acres, burning all the way to the banks of Deer Creek. Lost was the newly-built Nevada County Courthouse and its contents; twenty-two of twenty-eight allegedly fireproof brick business establishments; four churches; and ten souls, perhaps even more. Among those who perished were William B. Pearson, one of the *Nevada Democrat*'s proprietors; Peter Hendrickson and G. A. Young, prominent merchants; attorney S. W. Fletcher; and banker A. J. Hager.

An eyewitness account in the July 21 *San Francisco Bulletin* depicted the scene's extreme desolation and pathos:

> I have just come from Nevada (that was). I have this afternoon seen it enveloped in flames, and *nothing* of what it was, at 3 o'clock today, remains but ashes—ruins. There is not a place of business left standing. The people are without a single provision store, butcher shop, clothing store, or any place to supply the necessities of life. As to dwelling houses, not one stands in the town. A few in the suburbs remain, but not enough within the area of a square mile to give lodging to a tenth part of those who are houseless tonight....

> I had left Georgetown, a few days ago, a charred spot on the face of the earth. I thought nothing could be more complete than the destruction there seen. But Nevada—the proudest city of the

NEVADA CITY IN A VIEW THOUGHT TO HAVE BEEN MADE IN 1856. *Secrest Collection*

> mountains—has, within the last four hours, met with an entire obliteration. I have seen *all* the great fires of San Francisco, but nothing that carried with it such annihilation.

> I saw one poor fellow making his escape from a house—the fire burning on both sides of the street with intense heat, and he running between the fires, his clothes in a blaze, and crying "Save

me! Save me! For God's sake, save me!" I afterwards learned, that some noble fellow had thrown a wet blanket over him, and smothered the fire about his person, and it was believed his life would be saved.

Amazingly, the Nevada citizens had failed to form a fire department in the wake of the 1851 disaster. This egregious mistake no doubt accounted for much of this blaze's destructive force, and it obligated some attention to mitigating measures. By August a system of round-the-clock fire patrols had been inaugurated—though not a full-fledged fire department—and it seemed to be effective, at least for the first two years of its existence. Then, on May 23, 1858, a Chinese laundry located near the corner of Broad and Commercial streets went up in flames, and soon many nearby buildings were afire. The creative use of buckets and blankets soaked in water kept the damages down to a quarter-million dollars this time, and a couple of other fires in 1860 at last convinced the townsfolk that creation of a hook and ladder company was necessary.

The last major early-day Nevada conflagration took place on November 8, 1863, at a time when the city should have been at the ready—and was not, due to inexplicable low pressure in the water lines, the reason for which was never determined. Beginning at noon and stretching until five o'clock, the central portion of the area reduced to ashes in 1856 was overrun by flames once again, with approximately 250 buildings destroyed. The county courthouse was unlucky this time, too, and burned down; also lost were all the town's hotels and restaurants, all but one church, and a high proportion of the homes.

Nor was the lack of efficient hoses the only problem to complicate this disaster. Bean's *Directory of Nevada County* later remarked: "Let it pass into history that the Chief Engineer at that time, when his services were needed, was engaged in saving the duds of his strumpet."

The foregoing account says nothing of a number of smaller blazes that also plagued Nevada during its first few decades of existence. It vies with Georgetown and Marysville for the unfortunate title of California city worst-hit by fires during the nineteenth century.

1857
EARTHQUAKE at FORT TEJON

Where: Southern California
Details: Second largest quake in California history

In early January, 1857, ranched John Barker and a neighbor were searching for some stray horses on the eastern shore of Tulare Lake, a large runoff basin for the many rivers and creeks of central California. Knowing their horses would not drink from this particular area of the lake, the two ranchers rode to a nearby waterhole to look for tracks. Years later, Barker recalled that memorable day:

> I dismounted and led my horse by the bridle and walked to the edge of the water. Just as I reached it, the ground seemed to be violently swayed from east to west. The water splashed up to my knees; the trees whipped about, and limbs fell on and all around me. I was affected by a fearful nausea, my horse snorted and in terror struggled violently to get away from me, but I hung to him, having as great a fear as he had himself. The lake commenced to roar like the ocean in a storm, and, staggering and bewildered, I vaulted into the saddle and my terrified horse started, as eager as I was to get out of the vicinity. I found my friend, who had not dismounted, almost in a state of collapse. He eagerly inquired, while our horses were on the run and the lake was roaring behind us, "What is this?" I replied, "An earthquake! Put the steel to your horse and let us get out of this!" and we ran at the top of our speed for about five miles.

> We returned the next day and found that the lake had run up on the land for about three miles. Fish were stranded in every direction and could have been gathered by the wagon-load. The air was alive with buzzards and vultures eager for the feast, but the earth had acquired its normal condition.

Barker's recollection was validated by other intelligence, as reported in the January 13, 1857 San Francisco *Herald*:

> In every portion of the state from which we have heard, up to the present, the earthquake of the 9th inst. was very seriously felt.

TULARE LAKE WAS A VAST RUN-OFF FOR THE STREAMS AND RIVERS FLOODING DOWN FROM THE SIERRA BEFORE THE LAKE DISAPPEARED WITH THE ADVENT OF DAMS. *Secrest Collection.*

It is by no means improbable that it extended to the extreme North. We clip the following additional particulars from our upcountry exchanges—

A gentleman from Mokelumne Hill informs the *Sacramento American* that it was severely felt in that region, and seemed to shake the hills for miles around. Reports were numerous of the caving in of several tunnels and burial of a number of men, but he could not obtain the particulars.

By all we could learn, says the *Stockton Republican*, the commotion was very visible, lasting some minute or two. We have heard two or three gentlemen describe the sensation as being so violent as to cause a kind of sea-sickness. In our establishment, the shock was quite apparent. The lamps, which are suspended from the ceiling, swung to and fro for the distance of more than a foot. One of them was thrown against the walls so violently that its jingling was heard in every part of the office .

JOHN BARKER.
Secrest Collection

Barker could hardly have exaggerated the extent of the tremor. Others reported the Kern River, to the south, flooding its banks as it actually reversed course and ran upstream. The quake, generally regarded as one of the most powerful in U.S. history, was felt throughout a large swath of California. Surface ruptures ran all along this tract. Artesian wells in the Santa Clara Valley suddenly went dry, while other wells appeared suddenly near San Fernando and Santa Barbara. Both the Los Angeles and the Mokelumne rivers, some 350 miles apart, flung water from their beds, leaving dry spots in some areas. As far north as San Francisco, much notice was given to the frightening phenomena, as proven by the January 10, 1857 *Herald*:

At five o'clock, yesterday morning, and again at fifteen minutes after eight o'clock, the earth was shaken to its centre by the throes which seem to have become a part of the peculiarities of our state. In February last a severe shock was felt, and then all those who experienced the sensation of the "firm earth" moving beneath their feet were frightened to a degree that led many to believe the wildest and most absurd predictions: —that some weather-wise gentleman of Castillian descent had, one hundred years ago, carefully noted the geographical position of the Bay of San Francisco, and had concluded there would be a great city grow up on its shores—that it would be five times destroyed by fire, and finally swallowed up by an earthquake.

In San Francisco, the shock was measured in a particularly unique manner, according to the city's *California Chronicle*:

A gentleman informs the *Town Talk* that he determined the direction of the shocks and the extent of the vibrations, from the results of the same on the material of his breakfast table, while engaged at his matinal meal, previous to the last shock. A plate of beefsteak, swimming in gravy to its very edge, was the instrument. After the motion ceased, it was found that the gravy has been ejected from the dish on two sides for about two inches each way, in a line east and west by the compass.

Sacramento, even farther north, was no stranger to the jolts, as reported in the January 10 *Sacramento Daily Union*:

It was but a few seconds duration, but sufficient in force to cause chandeliers to vibrate about a foot from the center, to create a rattling among the crokery and other wares of our dealers, to rock several of the hulks (boats) at the levee and impart to many a sense of motion produced by some general unseen cause. The clocks in the banking houses of Drexel, Sather & Church and D. O. Mills & Co., and in the Magnolia and other places, were stopped and many persons being unable to appreciate the cause of their sensations at the moment, imagined that they were attacked with vertigo.

The January 14, 1857 *San Jose Tribune* reported effects that seemed to indicate the city's closer proximity to the epicenter:

The effect of the motion in San Jose was such as to produce in almost everyone to whom we have spoken on the subject a severe nausea, in several instances even to vomiting, and a similar effect is said to have been produced on certain hotels and boarding houses, which threw out the contents of their breakfast saloons with emetical precipitancy. At Hillman's Temperance House, when the earthquake motion was laid on the table, the motion to adjourn to the street was immediately put and unanimously carried. And we have been informed of another instance, where several strangers who were just finishing their breakfast at one of the city restaurants, were so alarmed by the unwanted movements of the knives and forks, that they not only gathered up their hats and rushed out of the room, but altogether forgot to return and settle their bills.

Santa Barbara was even closer to the area of the quake, but was separated from the San Andreas Fault (which caused it) by the Coast Range of mountains. Still, the January 15, 1857 *Santa Barbara Gazette* reported this activity:

A RUINED ADOBE STANDS NEXT TO A RESTORED STRUCTURE AT OLD FORT TEJON. *Secrest Collection*

> In this city, the morning of the eventful day was ushered in by the same genial sun; the air was tranquil, and no unusual atmospheric phenomena indicated that any danger was at hand. At about half past 8, or at 22 minutes past 8 o'clock, according to those who assert that they had the "correct time," the severest shock commenced, and which continued from 40 to 60 seconds. It was universally noticed throughout the city, and was so violent in its vibrations that all of the inhabitants fled from their dwellings, the majority of whom, on bended knees, and hearts throbbing with terror, made fervent supplications that the imminent and impeding danger might be providentially averted.
>
> This "shock" commenced with a gentle vibration of the earth, which gradually increased, accompanied with an undulating motion, until it attained its culminating intensity, and then as gradually decreased, until it ceased its action altogether. It passed without causing material damage to the city.

A preponderance of one-story structures in town undoubtedly reduced serious damage. Still, inhabitants remained apprehensive for the next few days, as they wondered if aftershocks would evolve into an even greater disturbance.

When an express rider from Fort Tejon arrived in Stockton on January 15, he brought additional news of the quake's effects in the vicinity of his post. There was a light, barely perceptible shock about six o'clock that morning, with a heavier one following at 8:30. This second jolt lasted from three to five minutes, accompanied by a sound resembling the rumbling of a train of railroad cars. Nearly all the adobe buildings in the area were damaged to some extent as chimneys tumbled down, plaster cracked and walls fell. Several adobe buildings at the fort were under construction and were all but destroyed. Miraculously, no one at the post was injured, although there were some close calls. A man in the kitchen of one of the adobes rushed outside just as the walls caved in, and a Dr. Tenbrock was thrown to the ground violently.

At the government sawmill located some twenty miles distant, a mule team was thrown to the ground, oak trees were uprooted, and large branches fell to the ground. At Reed's nearby ranch, a Mexican woman was killed by the caving-in of an adobe house. A Reverend Bateman, who rode through the surrounding country, reported that there were great fissures in the earth, indicating a very violent upheaval. He was informed by a vaquero that the mountain road to Los Angeles was nearly impassable due to rockslides. "From the accounts detailed by Mr. Cannady," commented the *Stockton Daily Argus*, "we are confident that the shock was more severely felt at Fort Tejon, than at any other point in the state."

Although it could not be measured in any way, most scientists of today agree that the quake was very large based on eyewitness accounts. It is generally agreed also that the quake was perhaps as large, or larger, than the San Francisco quake of 1906. It was only due to the sparse population, and lack of high population densities throughout California, that much greater damage and loss of life did not occur.

1858

Disastrous DOWNIEVILLE Fires

Where: Sierra County
Details: $650,000 in damages

Downieville

cisco

Northernmost of the major Gold Rush outposts, and sharing the danger of major combustion with its brethren, it is hardly surprising that Downieville was largely destroyed by fire twice. The first of the blazes erupted on the evening of February 19, 1852, at approximately 11 P.M. It continued to burn throughout the morning hours, leaving the town in ruins by the following afternoon.

The fire's origin was traced to the vicinity of north Main Street, where it proceeded to engulf the Magnolia saloon and Yuba House of Gardner and Janney, the Morris and Pullman theater, and a number of other businesses. From there it traveled south, wiping out the post office and no fewer than four other hotels situated on Main, and then made its path down Craycroft Street to swallow up a number of stores, bakeries and professional offices. Estimates vary as to the total loss, but it was no less than $150,000 and probably a great deal higher.

There was a bit of luck amid the devastation. Most of the town's warehouses were outside its proper limits, and these were spared. Another quirk of good fortune was reported in the February 24 San Francisco *Alta California*:

The fire having occurred in the immediate vicinity of S.W. Langton's express office, that gentleman was unable to save anything but what was deposited in his

THE MINING CAMP OF DOWNIEVILLE AS IT LOOKED IN 1851.
Courtesy Downieville Museum

vault, which, notwithstanding the intense heat surrounding it, owing to a large quantity of liquors and other combustible matters, proved perfectly fireproof. Mr. L.'s loss has been immense, but the security of his excellent vault must prove a great blessing to himself as well as to many of his friends and depositors....With his usual energy he has already bought a building and his business will go along as usual.

When they rebuilt, the citizens took care to widen Downieville's streets to forty feet and purchased a hook and ladder rig, but these measures proved no match for the disaster which hit on New Year's Day of 1858. The flames first broke out at the St. Charles Hotel

A LITHOGRAPH FROM A SKETCH MADE BY MRS. M. N. HORTON IN 1852 SHOWS THE MINING CAMP OF DOWNIEVILLE AS IT LOOKED AT THE TIME OF THE FIRST FIRE. *California State Library*

around 6 P.M., and in the space of an hour and a half had blackened much of Bridge and Commercial streets, along with the lower part of Main Street. Destroyed were a recently-built Congregational church, Fraternity Hall (shared by both the Masons and Odd Fellows), and the offices of the *Sierra Citizen* and *Sierra Democrat*, the town's two newspapers (the *Citizen* occupying the upper floor of Fraternity Hall). Another complete loss was the bridge leading out of the business section to Jersey Flat. It was said that while the fire raged, the air was almost solid with burning embers and other debris. Saved, thanks to much hard and frantic work, were the Sierra

County Courthouse, along with several other important buildings. The January 5 issue of the *San Joaquin Republican* described the scene:

The Methodist Church was saved by tearing down two of the buildings nearest it, and by the almost superhuman efforts of those engaged; by which means, the valuable private buildings situated on the upper end of Commercial Street were saved. The Catholic Church was on fire several times and was saved with difficulty, as also the dwelling house of S. A. [sic] Langton, which was within a few yards of one hundred kegs of powder when it exploded. The powder was the property of Eastman & Co. The explosion was heard distinctly fifteen miles.

Amazingly, a broken arm seems to have been the only human casualty caused by this fire, whose losses were later tallied at almost $500,000. Although relief donations collected by the surrounding towns amounted to a paltry $1,604.25, Downieville was soon back on its feet, via insurance and self-help, and has yet to experience devastation of similar magnitude.

1858

The *LUCAS* Disaster

Where: Farallon Islands
Details: Ship and 10 to 20 passengers lost

San
Francisco

On the early morning of November 8, 1858, the ship *Lucas* was a little more than twenty days out of Victoria, British Columbia, and was headed toward port in San Francisco. Having met with a succession of gale-force winds while proceeding down the coast, and coping more immediately with extremely thick fog and rough seas, the captain and crew were using the utmost caution in guiding their vessel to the end of its voyage. Captain Daggett had a special interest in employing his best judgment, as he happened to be a half-owner of the boat.

Sadly, the crew's best efforts were no match for the tempest. Some time after 1 A.M., it was noticed that the *Lucas* was going headlong into a row of breakers. The order went out fast to "put down the helm" and turn the ship away from the hazards. It came too late, and the vessel smashed hard against a cluster of rocks. It was eventually noticed that the ship had sailed straight into a treacherous spot between the main Farallon Island and a lesser outcropping, known as Seal Rock, three hundred yards to its southeast. The islands, known to generations of mariners, are situated some twenty miles west of San Francisco; hence, the *Lucas* was only a matter of minutes away from docking when it rammed into its final resting place.

An account in the November 12 *San Francisco Alta California* described what happened after the initial impact:

> The ship, after a few thumps, swung round broadside on, and rolled heavily over against the rocks with every breaker. Amidst all the confusion, the Captain tried to get a kedge anchor out, but without avail. As there were six boats and two canoes on the ship, five of the boats were soon launched and filled with passengers.... During this time, as the ship rolled over, many of the passengers jumped for the shore, and scrambled up to the top of the island out of the reach of the surf. A number of them jumped on the rocks,

and not getting a foot or hand hold, fell back into the surf and were dashed against the shore, or crushed between the ship and the rocks. The cries for help were heard in every direction, but in the wild confusion, each one was endeavoring to save himself.

Considering the fact that all this took place in the morning's wee hours, when it was foggy and pitch black, with momentary bursts of light supplied by a lighthouse on the main Farallon, it was a miracle that anyone saw his way onto the island's crags—or managed to set the extra craft into the Pacific's turbulent waters.

THE FARALLON ISLANDS WERE EASILY SEEN AND AVOIDED IN GOOD WEATHER, BUT IN ROUGH SEAS AND AT NIGHT THEY COULD BE A DANGEROUS IMPEDIMENT TO A SHIP APPROACHING SAN FRANCISCO. *Secrest Collection*

The *Alta* continued:

About an hour and a half after the ship struck, most of the passengers had got on the Island, or on to boats. At this time a heavy sea struck the vessel and she slid off, and went down, sinking up to the topsail yards. Most of the passengers, who were still on board, clambered into the rigging, though some of them are said to have gone down. Captain Daggett and the second mate were taken off the mizzen rigging by means of a rope, which was thrown from the shore.

Later on Wednesday morning, a group of Italian fishermen sighted the *Lucas* wreck and quickly sailed into San Francisco Bay to sound a distress alarm. The steamer *Active* was dispatched to the site immediately, reached the Farallones at 2 P.M., and spent a couple of hours evacuating 148 passengers. The *Trent*, a small ship attached to the *Lucas* and cut loose hastily when the general uproar started, took away another thirteen. An unidentified fishing boat transported another four to San Francisco, for a total of 165 rescued and fifteen to twenty passengers lost, perhaps more. It took the hungry and grief-stricken survivors only a few hours to run through most of the lighthouse-keepers' quarterly provisions of food and drink.

Insured for $3,000, with no coverage on her cargo, the 700-ton *Lucas* was a complete loss. An *Alta* reporter visited the wreck site on the following morning and offered a poignant testament to her rapid disintegration:

Wreck of the Ship Lucas on the Farallone Islands—One Hundred and Seventy Passengers on Board—Between Ten and Fifteen Lives Lost.

The ship Lucas, of this port, Capt. Dagget, bound from Victoria for San Francisco, with passengers and freight, was totally lost on the morning of Wednesday last, on the Farallone Islands, off the Heads. The Lucas was an American ship, of about 700 tons burthen, and owned by Captain Daggett, who commanded her, and Leonidas Haskell, of this city. She was insured by Richard S. Haven, Agent for Underwriters for $3,000. Nether the cargo nor freight were insured.

Early yesterday morning, some Italian fishermen from the Farallone Islands, came up to the city and reported the ship Lucas ashore on one of those islands. Immediately on the receipt of the news the U. S. Surveying steamer Active, went out in search of the wreck, and shortly after, orders were given to get the steam tug Goliah ready. Capt. Pease, of the Revenue cutter Marcy, also made arrangements to proceed to the scene of the wreck, but the

> Occasionally a long smooth rounded, skow-like [sic] object, of a bright green color floated up and sunk again almost as

SAN FRANCISCO *DAILY ALTA CALIFORNIA*, NOVEMBER 12, 1858

instantly, and so continued re-appearing and vanishing. This was the bottom of the wrecked *Lucas*, the only single article pertaining to which that was not in a damaged or ruined condition, was a large anchor, the stock of which projected on the sunken bows, above the balance of the wreck. Nothing more could be ascertained by a visit to the spot.

While the Farallones had long been known as an outpost of foul weather and seas, the *Lucas* was reported to be the first major wreck occurring within the island chain.

1860

The *NORTHERNER* Disaster

Where: Near Humboldt Bay
Details: Thirty-eight passengers and crewmen lost

One day out of San Francisco, on January 5, 1860, the steamer *Northerner* had pulled parallel to Cape Mendocino, a dozen miles south of Humboldt Bay. As Captain William Dall stood in front of the wheelhouse with his first officer, Arthur French, they felt a jolt under their feet and quickly had the same thought. Captain Dall asked French to go below to the engine room and investigate the trouble. French returned with bad news. The ship's hull appeared to have been breached and was taking on water. Captain Dall ordered the officer to put all the pumps in operation, but even then water in the hold was rising at the rate of an inch a minute.

When the engineer reported that the water would be up to the boiler fires in about forty minutes, Dall ordered the ship's cannon fired in a distress signal. He had the steward tell the passengers to get fully dressed and be ready for any emergency. As the *Northerner* moved at full speed north up the coast, toward some sandy beaches just south of the Eel River, Captain Dall fired his distress rockets and ordered all life boats made ready. The powerful wind carried a drenching rain with it, and the sea was roaring with huge waves and breakers. Amid this fury, Captain Dall headed his craft toward the beach. It was dark now, and when the ship stopped on a sand spit, the coast could no longer be seen.

UNITED STATES MAIL LINE

FOR

PORTLAND,

Victoria, Port Townsend and Olympia.

The Mail Steamship

NORTHERNER,

W. L. DALL..................................COMMANDER,

Will leave Folsom street wharf

For the Above Port

on

TUESDAY,.........................JAN. 3, 1860,

At 4 o'clock P. M.

FORBES & BABCOCK, Agents.

For Freight or Passage, apply on board, or to the Agents of the Pacific Mail Steamship Company, corner Sacramento and Leidesdorff streets.
☞ Blls of lading will be furnished by the Purser to shippers of cargo. None others than those so furnished will be received. de30

DEPARTURE NOTICE OF THE *NORTHERNER* IN THE SAN FRANCISCO *DAILY ALTA CALIFORNIA,* JANUARY 4, 1860

The passengers were all wearing life preservers and lined up on deck, waiting for orders. The pounding waves soon lifted the ship

A CONTEMPORARY ENGRAVING OF THE *NORTHERNER* IN ITS DEATH THROES, AS PASSENGER AND CREW STRUGGLE TO GET EVERYONE SAFELY ASHORE. THIRTY-EIGHT DID NOT MAKE IT. *Secrest Collection*

off the spit and carried it down the beach, parallel to the shore. When the captain was assured his ship would not get any closer to shore, he let the anchor go. The wind had increased to a howling gale and huge waves broke over the ship, carrying away the hurricane deck and all light woodwork.

All six lifeboats had been moved to the inboard side of the ship, facing the shore. Captain Dall, hoping to use the ship as a breakwater for safely launching the lifeboats, now ordered French to place all the women and children in the largest boat and make for shore. One woman, a Miss Gregg, refused to go unless her brother could accompany her. Dall argued with her for a time, but finally told French to go. Although breakers were rolling completely over the lifeboat, French and his passengers safely made shore. The next two lifeboats were not as lucky; both capsized, drowning a total of six passengers and crewmen.

On shore, French and his crew had been trying to launch their boat and return to the *Northerner*, but found it impossible. A crowd assembled on the beach, drawn in by the distress signals, and begged the first mate not to try to return to his ship. The brave officer would not hear of it:

"I have got as much to live for as any of you, but my place is by Captain Dall and my life belongs to the passengers."

French and his men did get their boat into the water and out to the battered *Northerner*—only to be drowned in the furious water that surrounded the battered and struggling ship

Captain Dall next ordered the ship's engineer, Thomas O'Neil, to take a rope line from the boat to shore. O'Neil was successful, but was unable to launch his boat in the tumultuous water. Back on the ship, Dall hoped a lifeboat from shore would materialize on the line, but it never appeared. When a huge wave crashed down on the ship, carrying away the stern, Dall knew there was only one hope of survival left. The remaining passengers would now have to go hand-over-hand on the rope and hope they had the stamina to make it close enough to shore.

THERE WERE MANY HEROES THAT DESPERATE NIGHT, BUT CAPTAIN WILLIAM DALL WAS PRAISED BY EVERYONE. HE WAS ONE OF THE LAST TO LEAVE THE WRECK. *Secrest Collection*

The men on shore were pounded unmercifully by the thundering sea, but they bravely stood in the bitter cold waters, trying to do anything they could to help. One of those on the beach was Seth Kinman, a local frontiersman who had gained

ALL NIGHT LONG LOCAL VOLUNTEERS AND THE SURVIVING CREW OF THE *NORTHERNER* BRAVED THE SAVAGE SEA IN AN ATTEMPT TO SAVE AS MANY OF THE PASSENGERS AS POSSIBLE. *Secrest Collection*

wide renown whenhe had gone to Washington and presented an elkhorn chair to President James Buchanan. Kinman, tethered to the shore by a line, was trying to pull in passengers who dropped a ways shy of dry land. A few who were swept away from the ship's line were later rescued after being swept shoreward. The *Humboldt Times* reported:

> Captain Dall, Mr. Barry and the purser were the last to leave the ship. Mr. Barry was positive he could not reach the shore, and was carried away by the first sea that struck him, and was seen no more. The purser reached the shore by the line. Captain Dall was the last to try the line. He lowered himself, and after being washed over by several seas, was thrown from the line and swam to shore.

> There were six passengers who refused to take the line, and, as it happened, the piece on which they stood broke loose, and they came ashore in safety.

Captain Dall and his remaining crewmen were on the beach all night, looking for survivors. Miles of beach were searched, but none were found until some time later. The fate of Miss Gregg and her brother was reported by the *Times*:

> Yesterday morning at low tide, the body of this unfortunate young lady was taken from the wreck. She had been lashed to the wheelhouse by her brother, with her over clothing. There is no doubt they died together. The body of young Gregg had not been recovered.

It was also reported in the *Times* that one man somehow managed to get a horse out of the ship's hold and pushed him into the water. Leaping onto the animal's back, the man then hung onto the animal and both made it safely to shore. Some forty-five bags of mail were recovered, but thirty-eight passengers and crewmen were lost in the disastrous wreck.

LOCAL FRONTIERSMAN SETH KINMAN WAS ONE OF THE HEROS OF THE INCIDENT, ALSO. THE STEAMSHIP COMPANY AWARDED HIM A BIBLE AND FREE TRAVEL FOR THE BALANCE OF HIS LIFE. *Peter Palmquist Collection*

Today, on a bluff overlooking the tragic beach, a large cement cross marks the grave of many of the survivors of the *Northerner*. It was a sad, but heroic, day in California history.

1861
When the *McCLELLAND* Blew

Knight's
Landing

✳

Sacramento

cisco

Where: Sacramento River
Details: Some fifteen scalded or drowned

The steamboat *J.A. McClelland* was making good time, heading north up the Sacramento River on its regular run to Red Bluff. Owned independently by its captain, C. Mills, the *McClelland* plied the river in opposition to the mighty California Steam Navigation Company. The boat had left Sacramento early that morning and, by 1:30 that afternoon, was just a few miles south of Knight's Landing. Besides a load of cargo on its decks, it was also towing a light barge carrying a quantity of barrels and boxes. It was too hot to be inside, and a dozen or so passengers were gathered on the forward deck, chatting and seemingly enjoying themselves. It was a warm and hazy Sunday afternoon on the river this August 25, 1861.

"The first intimation I had of anything wrong," recalled Sheldon Baldwin, who was steering the boat, "was that the boat blew up and I found myself in company with two other men, who were in the pilot house with me at the time, going up into the air. How far up I went it is impossible to say, but I know the thought occurred to me several times that I was going so high that when I came down I should be dashed to atoms."

Baldwin landed with considerable force in the cavity vacated by the boiler. In the following moment, he was covered with splintered wood and other debris. Crawling out of the wreckage, Baldwin saw engineer Jim Bowman also getting up from behind a pile of rubble. When he tried to assist some of the injured people on the boat, Baldwin realized he was seriously injured and had to sit down. As he looked around, he realized the horror of what had happened:

> It was a terrible sight; pieces of the boiler were thrown hundreds of yards, and fragments of the wreck and freight were scattered on both banks. The boiler went out on the starboard side of the boat, and a portion of it or the fire-box was driven high up on shore, carrying with it the two firemen, or portions of them; one of the firemen struck a pump on shore and was cut in two; when the *Gem* came along and took us off, the bodies in the river had not been taken out, and there were legs and arms and mangled remains left on the river banks; there were only four who fell down on the boat after the explosion, James Cox, Champion, Flynn and myself; the others all fell in the water, and everybody was screaming for help, while some shouted "murder!"

Everyone on the boat, except one, had been killed, mortally wounded or seriously injured. Israel Champion had been in the pilot house with Baldwin and the others, and when he climbed out of the rubble he cut the two skiffs loose, jumped in one and began rescuing those in the water so that none of the wounded would drown. Captain Mills had been scalded and was eased as gently as possible into the boat. James Morrow, a passenger, was also taken from the water, but he was terribly burned. When the air hit his body, he began to writhe in pain.

SHIPPING NOTICE THAT APPEARED IN THE SAN FRANCISCO *ALTA CALIFORNIA*, AUGUST 25, 1861, JUST PRIOR TO THE FATAL TRIP. *Secrest Collection*

As the rescue work began, several small boats put out from the shore to help. A farmer, who had seen what happened, mounted a horse and rode for Knight's Landing to summon D. L. Pickett, M.D. The physician later recalled:

> I happened to have my horse in my buggy when Mr. Simmons came after me and probably reached the scene within twenty minutes after the explosion. There is no doubt that as many as fourteen were killed—possibly two or three more—and seven were seriously wounded. Only one person on board escaped injury of some sort, and that was the steward, who happened to be in the water closet. When I arrived the wounded had been nearly all brought on shore. They were groaning and crying out with anguish, and most of them had suffered severe shocks of the nervous system. The scene was

probably not unlike that of a battlefield. One peculiarity I noticed was, that every man was bleeding at the nose, which may have been caused by the concussion of the explosion, which must have been very hard. They had got a plank out and helped the wounded on shore and into two houses near by. None of the wounded died, but one or two of them probably will not recover.

Joseph Arcega, a Mexican wood dealer who lived in Sacramento, was one of the fatalities. He was a colorful character who had been

General Zachary Taylor's interpreter during the Mexican War. He belonged to several lodges in Sacramento and was quite wealthy. When the explosion happened, he was returning to join his crew and his own steamboat for another wood-cutting expedition. Arcega's body had not been found when his own steamboat, the *Henrietta*, arrived from Knight's Landing. Two men named Keys and Harris could not be located, and it was feared they too were dead, but since the passenger list had been lost there could have been others.

DR. JOHN F. MORSE, ONE OF THE SACRAMENTO PHYSICIANS ATTENDING THE McCLELLAND VICTIMS. *California State Library*

All of the injured had been moved to the deck of the *Henrietta* when the steamer *Gem* arrived from Colusa, on its way to Sacramento. By this time it was 4:30 in the afternoon. Two of the injured men were lodged in a nearby house while the six other wounded victims were moved from the *Henrietta* to the deck of the *Gem*. Dr. Pickett accompanied his patients to Sacramento. E. D. Wheatley, one of the *Gem* passengers, was shocked to watch as his good friend, Jim Morrow, was brought aboard. He stayed by his side during the trip to Sacramento, took him to Bininger's Hotel there, and was with him when Morrow died of his burns. His

AN 1870 VIEW OF THE SACRAMENTO WATERFRONT WHERE THE VICTIMS WERE BROUGHT FOR MEDICAL ATTENTION. *California State Library*

last words were that he was sorry he had ever gotten out of the water.

The next day a coroner's jury was empaneled, and testimony was taken from survivors and other witnesses as to how James Morrow had died. The testimony was graphic, but no one had any suggestions about just why the tragedy had occurred. The verdict read that "James Morrow came to his death by being scalded and mutilated by the explosion of the boiler of the steamer *J.M. McClelland*."

For those who were interested, however, James Bowman told his story to the *Sacramento Daily Union*. As engineer of the steamer, Bowman was in charge of the boat at the time of the explosion. His fireman had consulted with him just prior to the explosion, and the pressure in the boiler seemed normal. But there was more:

> It is true that the boiler was in rather a shaky condition; I would like to have a correct statement made about that. I put the boiler in myself last winter and we tested it for one hundred and fifty pounds, and I made three trips to Marysville with it, and then quit to come on this boat, the *Visalia*. I had applied to go on the *McClelland* again; the Captain told me he wanted some one he could trust, that his engineer was young and rash. I saw the boiler was not right and supposed it had been strained by racing. It had raced with the Red Bluff boat, and had been to the Bay [San Francisco]. But I do not think it had been hurt by salt water. If I had done right, I suppose, I should have insisted on a test, but if a man should do such a thing here in California he "would be called an old fogy, and they would say he was scary." I could not afford to get such a reputation. Besides, Baldwin told me he had seen her carrying 140 pounds of steam, and I thought if she had done that I could trust her with 80 or 90.

It was a bad mistake. A "scary" reputation could conceivably be repaired after some time on the river. However, the fifteen or so scalded , mangled and dismembered victims could never be brought back from the dead. We can only wonder if they haunted Bowman's dreams for the balance of his life.

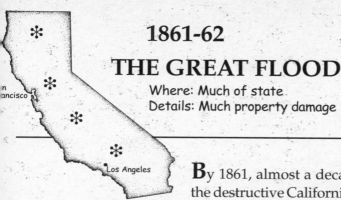

1861-62

THE GREAT FLOOD

Where: Much of state
Details: Much property damage

By 1861, almost a decade had passed since the destructive California floods of 1852-1853. With the gold rush excitement having peaked, the state was settling into calmer times, and it had been several years since the last comprehensive disaster—the Fort Tejon earthquake. However, the winter of 1861-1862 once again jolted the citizens out of their complacency—and headlong into a series of high-water calamities that, if anything, were worse than anything else the Golden State had yet experienced. City and countryside endured what would later be called "the Noachian deluge of California Floods."

As the state prepared for Christmas on the week of December 4, 1861, the cold chill and overcast skies of the season were transposed into black, billowing storm clouds. By Friday, December 6, a heavy rain was coming down from the north, as noted in Marysville lawyer Charles De Long's diary. "Storming terrifically today and tonight—reminds me of '52." By Sunday the storm was raging unabated, as again noted by De Long:

CHARLES DE LONG. California State Library

Sun. 8—The day one continual storm the river up as high at dark tonight as it was at its highest point last year—and still rising whilst now nearly midnight the rain still pours in torrents played cards in my office—came out over $100 ahead Dr. Mitchell owes me $120. The flood is upon us and must I judge submerge Sacramento and ruin thousands of farmers and others in this state.

Mon. 9—Was awoke and sprang up to the alarm of the fire bell ran down & found that the Merchant's Hotel and several large brick buildings had fallen in and the inmates narrowly escaped destruction—the river raised about four inches higher than in 1852, and the whole town was nearly submerged great excitement horrid news coming in from the country of the loss of human life and property.

Like other residents of the city, De Long was reading the news accounts from the Sacramento and San Francisco press. Floods were occurring everywhere at once. Bridges were washed out as far north as Trinity and Shasta counties. Roads between Shasta and Yreka were nearly impassable, and stagecoach travel was rapidly coming to a halt. The December 6 *Nevada City Democrat* reported the rain falling in torrents:

> We are in the midst of another unusually heavy rainstorm, which has continued without interruption for the last twenty-four hours, and as we go to press there is no appearance of the storm abating. The great fall of rain has caused a sudden rise in the mountain streams, and an overflow of the Sacramento is anticipated.

The warning came too late. In Sacramento, the breaking of the levee at several points resulted in many one-story homes being submerged, while cattle were reported swimming in the streets as buildings collapsed and houses floated down the river. Livestock and poultry of every kind were drowned,

A SACRAMENTO STREET SCENE DURING THE TUMULTUOUS FLOODS OF 1861-62 WHEN YOU HAD TO HAIL A BOAT TO CROSS THE STREET. *California State Library* or struggled helplessly in the muddy waters. John Isaacs sent his family to safety just before his large house on Fifth Street was ripped from its foundation. With his house cocked at an angle, Isaacs told rescue boats to rescue women and children in the vicinity first, then later jumped into a boat just as his house lurched loose and began its journey in the swollen current. Thousands were homeless in the area. A farm boy, living some five miles south of Sacramento, later recalled the time:

> When we retired one quiet night, it was with the bright moonlight gliding the hilltops and deepening the shadows in the meadows all about us. When we awoke, we were upon an island with the astonished sun darting his rays across a sea of turbid mountain water that was swirling on every hand. The Sacramento and American Rivers had overflowed their banks and flooded the country for many miles around their point of confluence.

Throughout the mining country, from the north down through Tuolumne County, the rains continued, with only brief intervals of relief. The *Yreka Journal* reported "water rushing down Main street the water surrounded our office and rushed in swift currents between the houses and barns back of us." Nearby Scott Valley was reported to have the appearance of a great lake.

At Camptonville, in Sierra County, a private letter noted: "It has rained one steady shower for over eighty hours, without intermission." Over at nearby Downieville, the north fork of the Yuba River carried away most of the bridges. It was a bleak Christmas, as intermittent rain and overflowed rivers and creeks made traveling and family gatherings next to impossible.

The storm was still continuing during the first week of the new year. The San Francisco *Daily Alta California* noted that, though the rain had been steady, "the town has not floated away, and we have hopes that the rainy season has spent its fury in the impetuosity of the storms and floods we have endured." But this was wishful thinking. The same January 9, 1862, issue announced that another major storm had hit the city. Basements around town were filled with water, and fire companies were kept busy draining them. Water rushing down the city streets caused the collapse of several brick buildings. In the mountains to the east, rain and snow was reported coming down for the past two days.

By January 12, the *Alta California* headlined another "Terrible Inundation"throughout much of the state. On the Stanislaus River, most of the town of Knight's Ferry was swept down the river, and over on the San Joaquin River, much of the town of Millerton was swept away by logs and debris that came hurtling out of the mountains. Thousands of dollars in goods and property were lost. In San Joaquin County, one of the Deering brothers was drowned while crossing Sullivan's Creek. The brothers lost some $33,000 when their two stores were swept away.

Many deaths had been reported during all this time, but homeless, starving and stranded settlers, along rivers and in the outlands were suffering terribly and becoming a primary concern. While San Franciscans were generously sending money and supplies to Stockton and Sacramento, boats ventured into vast flooded areas to search for the stranded and dead. At San Francisco, the United States steam revenue cutter *Shubrick* left on January 18 and anchored overnight at Benecia. Writing later from Sacramento, a crew member detailed their activities:

> At Daybreak, got under way for Rio Vista [where the whole village had been swept away], and supplied the people there with provisions, and then took our way up the old river to Georgiana slough. Here we supplied provisions and took on board seven men, one woman and three children. Five miles above we rescued three men and two women. Twelve miles further on we rescued three men and three miles further picked up a woman and three children. It is dreadful to look upon the suffering along the river—the poor cattle lying dead along what were the banks

At Snelling, in Merced County, the river changed course and swept through town, carrying away Hall's Hotel and many other structures. Charles Bludworth, who lived at the Snelling House, lost $2,000 in his safe when the building was carried away.

Strewn along the riverbanks were small houses, furniture, clothing and dead livestock. A traveler reported that on a high spot on the Norris Ranch along the American River he saw "Timber of huge dimensions, mining machinery of all kinds, lots of furniture and not a few billiard tables ."

A dispatch from Sacramento on January 12 indicated the city was again under water: "Every valuable dwelling or storehouse in the city had its first floor covered and very few had less than a foot and a half water in them. In every house occupied by human beings, somebody, if not everybody, was sleepless during most of the night. It was necessary to make frequent examinations to see whether the water was rising, and determine whether the residents should flee."

To counter this devastation, much of the city was raised some eight feet, building by building, using hundreds of screw jacks and manpower. The cost in money and effort was staggering. It was a monumental achievement.

The southern and coastal regions of the state were not spared during the throes of the great storm of 1862. In the San Bernardino and Los Angeles vicinities, the Santa Ana River became a raging torrent and anything along its banks was destroyed, including vineyards, orchards and grain fields. Steady rains in January caused the San Lorenzo River, outside of Santa Cruz, to jump its banks, destroying dams and carrying barns, sawmills, a paper mill, and a tannery away and out to sea.

None who lived through the mighty deluges that winter of 1861-62 would ever forget the grief and hardship they had experienced. In overall magnitude, it was perhaps the greatest series of floods ever endured by the state.

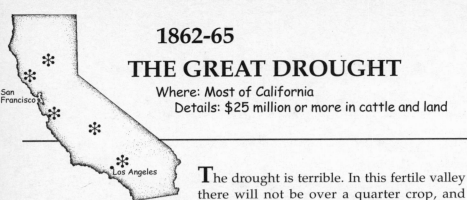

1862-65

THE GREAT DROUGHT

Where: Most of California
Details: $25 million or more in cattle and land

The drought is terrible. In this fertile valley there will not be over a quarter crop, and during the past four days' ride we have seen dead cattle by the hundreds....The hills are terribly dry, totally bare of forage, parched and brown....Dust fills the air—often we cannot see fifty yards in any direction—it covers everything. We cook our dinner, but before it can be eaten we cannot tell its color because of the dirt that settles on it. Our food is gritty between our teeth, and as we drink our cups of tea we find a deposit of fine sand on the bottom. Dirt, dirt, dirt—eyes full, face dirty, whole person feeling dirty and gritty.

So wrote William H. Brewer of the California Geological Survey, as he and his party made their way from San Jose to the San Joaquin Valley in the late spring of 1864. By that time California had been in the grip of a two-year drought which would eventually stretch into a third, kill approximately half of the state's cattle, and ruin a large number of those involved in the industry. Most of this disaster's casualties were animal rather than human but, as would eventually be seen, its consequences were far-reaching and profound.

After California suffered under the immense deluges of 1861-1862 (see previous chapter), the following fall and winter seasons represented an extreme climatic reversal. Very little rain fell, and the cattle barons—who depended on a ready supply of water and foliage for their herds—became quite jittery as spring came, and dryness predominated. In a letter to southern California's most prominent cattleman, Don Abel Stearns, C. R. Johnson depicted an ominous set of circumstances in February 1863: "We have had no rain yet, there is no grass and the cattle are very poor; your Rancho men report a great many dying. Should we have no rain your cattle buyers will get nothing but hides and bones."

As the year wore on, ended and turned into another, there was no relief in sight. There were some slight rains in 1864, but drought soon set in again, and a beleaguered cattle industry resorted to desperate survival measures. With many of its operators in debt, contracted during the flush post-Gold Rush era, the steady decimation of their herds caused most of them to totter financially. Some went bankrupt, unable to sustain loan debts and property taxes. Stearns was forced to sell some of his best specimens to investors in San Francisco for a low eight dollars a head, and in at least one instance, the price sank to an absurd thirty-seven cents per animal.

DURING THIS GREAT DROUGHT, HERDS OF CALIFORNIA CATTLE WERE DRIVEN GREAT DISTANCES TO FIND FORAGE, BUT THE STOCK LOSSES STILL PUT MANY RANCHERS OUT OF BUSINESS. *Secrest Collection*

For the more stubborn denizens of the business, it was often necessary for them to send cattle far afield—up to the Mojave River, down to Baja California, and even across the Sierra—in search of water and food. Many herds on the coast were doomed, as they were too far away from alternative grazing lands, and could not survive the harsh trip to reach them. Those making the attempt failed frequently. For years afterward, it was reported that vast numbers of cattle skeletons were strewn throughout California's pasturages and watering holes, the unfortunate animals falling wherever their flimsy trails of sustenance ran out.

Since no law required cattle to stay behind fences during this drought, the bovines frequently resorted to self-help in the incessant search for food and water. The results, as related by historian J. M. Guinn, could be cruel and heartbreaking: "In the long stretch of arid plain between San Gabriel and Santa Ana there was one oasis of luxuriant green. It was the vineyards of the Anaheim colonists kept green by irrigation. The colony lands were surrounded by a close willow-hedge, and the streets closed by gates. The starving cattle, frenzied by the sight of something green, would gather around the inclosure and make desperate attempts to break through. A mounted guard patrolled the outside of the barricade day and night to protect the vineyards by incursions by the starving herds."

Losses continued to mount as the drought stretched into 1865. The records show that Los Angeles County's cattle population dropped by nearly half, and some other places were even harder-hit. In Santa Barbara County, the 1863 assessment rolls showed 200,000 head, a likely underestimation; by 1864-1865, only 5,000 had survived. With the industry ruined, and livestock accounting for a goodly portion of the state economy, the financial ripples were felt widely. Land, now being vacated en masse by the cattlemen, was available—yet very few wanted to buy it and pay the property taxes, since money was

LARGE TRACTS OF LAND WERE ACQUIRED IN TOWNS SUCH AS LOS ANGELES (SHOWN ABOVE IN THE LATE 1860S), JUST FOR PAYING OVERDUE TAXES. *Los Angeles Public Library*

so tight. In his *Sixty Years in Southern California*, businessman Harris Newmark offered a dramatic example of this phenomenon :

As an illustration of how a fortunate plunger acquired property now worth millions, through the disinclination on the part of most people here to add to their taxes in the time of drought, I may mention two pieces of land included in the early Ord survey, one hundred and twenty by one hundred and sixty-five feet in size— one at the southwest corner of Spring and Fourth streets [in Los Angeles], the other at the southeast corner of Fort and Fourth— which were sold on December 12th, 1864, for *two dollars and fifty-two cents* [emphasis author's], delinquent taxes. The tax on each lot was but one dollar and twenty-six cents, yet only one purchaser appeared!

A precise total for the number of cattlemen and estates driven out of business by the drought has never been ascertained. What is known is that enough were forced out to result in the purchase of vast land tracts, principally in southern California, by a host of speculators able to pay the tax bills. In turn, these properties—secured for bargain-basement prices—were resold at reasonable rates to farmers and agricultural enterprises who benefited through the increasing practice of irrigation and maintenance of reliable water supplies, all of which were unknown during the Gold Rush era and afterward. The drought had, therefore, set off a chain reaction of events that forever transformed the Golden State.

Assessing the exact financial impact of this drought is difficult, and perhaps impossible, owing to the precipitous price fluctuations in animals and property. Only one other nineteenth-century California dry spell (1876-1877) approached its severity, and the total losses in that time frame were said to reach $20 million. Assuming that the 1862-1865 drought was worse by a third, in dollar terms it might well be the greatest California disaster preceding the 1906 earthquake. Even more significant is the fact that it signaled the end of the state's lazy pastoral days, and the beginning of its rapid rise as an economic superpower.

1863
The *ADA HANCOCK* Tragedy

San Francisco

Los Angeles

Where: Southern California
Details: Nearly 50 died in explosion

Harris Newmark, an enterprising native of Prussia who found his fortune in the Golden State and later became one of its prominent memoirists (see previous chapter), arrived in Southern California in late 1853. He had letters of introduction to Captain Phineas Banning and was surprised when the founder of the port of San Pedro was pointed out to him. Expecting to meet an army officer or at least a well-dressed businessman, Harris greeted a large, stout man in shirt sleeves and bright suspenders, wearing ill-fitting trousers and clumsy brogans. Banning was a local rancher who had built wharves and established freight lines operating out of San Pedro and Los Angeles. Despite his appearance, "Captain" Banning was a hard-working leader of the community. In time, Banning acquired a genuine rank when he was appointed a general of militia. His ranch and stagecoach line, along with lucrative freighting and shipping contracts, made him a wealthy and prominent man.

PHINEAS BANNING, A DETERMINED MAN WHO ONCE LED A LYNCH MOB TO HANG THE KILLER OF HIS BROTHER-IN-LAW. *Secrest Collection*

In 1863 Banning was preparing to build a palatial home at his ranch. He had purchased a small twin-screw steamboat to haul passengers and freight to the larger steamers plying the coastal trade. He had named the craft the *Ada Hancock*, after a local army officer's wife. The small steamer soon proved a lucrative addition to his growing business empire. At the same time Banning was also considering changing the name of San Pedro to Wilmington, after his home town in Delaware. (Both names still apply to the area.)

On April 27, Banning, his wife, and young son Willie boarded the *Ada Hancock* with a group of passengers bound for the steamer

Senator, at anchor in the bay. Among those accompanying the Bannings were his mother-in-law; his partner and brother-in-law, William T. H. Sanford; and Thomas W. Seeley, captain of the *Senator.* The Bannings

A PASSENGER TICKET FOR THE SENATOR. Secrest Collection

and others were escorting Sue Wilson, the daughter of Benjamin D. Wilson, out to the *Senator.* Some eighty others were passengers also bound for the *Senator,* and filed aboard as the sixty-foot craft prepared to leave for the five-mile trip to where the larger steamer was anchored. It was just after three-thirty in the afternoon.

As the *Hancock* moved out of a narrow inlet and away from shore, a brisk wind came up. Most of the passengers were on deck and sought shelter on the leeward side. As the small steamer listed to one side, below decks the boiler water shifted to one side as well, exposing some of the flues on the opposite side to the fire. As the boat began to turn north and righted itself, water came in contact with the overheated iron—and an explosion took place.

Captain Seeley was talking to a group of women when the explosion occurred. A chunk of iron ripped across his neck, just below his ear and severed his jugular vein, killing him almost immediately. Joseph Bryant, captain of the ship, was likewise killed. Most of the craft's superstructure was blown to bits and the boat sank immediately, leaving debris and scattered survivors struggling in the water.

The explosion was seen over a wide area, and boats from shore and the *Senator* were dispatched immediately to the scene. The *Ada Hancock's* engineer was seen holding Captain Seeley's head above water,

SAN PEDRO BAY, A FEW MILES NORTH OF WHERE THE ADA HANCOCK TRAGEDY TOOK PLACE. *Secrest Collection* obviously not realizing he was dead. Phineas Banning was discovered crawling on his hands and knees on shore, having been flung some distance through the air. Stunned briefly by the blast, he escaped with only a few abrasions. A newspaper noted his family's close call:

> Two children of Mr. Banning were also on board, one of which received a slight scald. Both of the children were saved from the wreck by a colored servant girl of Mrs. Banning, who displayed undaunted courage and calmness and rendered great assistance to numerous others. During the whole excitement, she remained perfectly calm and was the means of keeping several of the ladies' heads above water after the vessel went down.

Sanford, Banning's brother-in-law, was killed, and his mother sustained several broken limbs and was seriously injured. Mrs.

THE *SENATOR*. California State Library

Banning was bruised about the head, but otherwise unharmed. A rescue crew from the *Senator* told of a gray-haired man "who acted like a hero":

> He was standing on the wreck, holding a wounded person's head above the water, and when asked if he was hurt, said no—not half as much as others about him. After rescuing those around, they took the old gentleman into the boat, and found that his leg was broken. He had, with the consciousness of his own injuries, helped all about him, only to be relieved when the rest had been picked up.

Those in the boat could hardly believe it possible his leg was broken, from his coolness and desire to help those worse off than he was.

There was considerable money on the *Hancock*—a Wells Fargo shipment of ten thousand dollars was partially recovered, although William Richie, the agent, was mortally injured. Fred Kerlin, a nephew of prominent Californian Edward F. Beale, was killed in the explosion. The thirty thousand dollars he was carrying on his person disappeared, along with the jewelry of several others. "It was concluded," commented Newmark later, "that, even in the presence of Death, these bodies had been speedily robbed."

In later years it was suggested that a plot existed between Richie, the Wells Fargo messenger, and another passenger named Louis Schlesinger. The two had absconded with some $125,000 of Wells Fargo funds, rather than the $10,000 initially reported to be in transit. Since the funds were only retrieved in part, this may just be a legend connected to the noted disaster. Regardless, both Richie and Scheslinger were dead.

Nearly fifty of those aboard were killed or later died of injuries, but a complete accounting was difficult to assess because of the many people accompanying passengers to the *Senator*. As with so many other disasters that befell frontier California, there was, in the end, no way to know with complete certainty what had happened, or means to calculate the exact loss of life and property.

1864

EXPLOSION of the *WASHOE*

Where: Near Rio Vista on Sacramento River
Details: More than 80 persons killed and injured

If ever there was a steamboat destined for disaster, it was the *Washoe*. Built in San Francisco at the Owens' shipyard in late 1863, the vessel was put into service on the river between the bay city and Sacramento. It was an "opposition" boat, set to challenge the monopoly of the California Steam and Navigation Company by offering fast service and lower fares. Soon after its launch it was discovered that, although the engines worked perfectly, all of the ship's boiler flues were defective. Not wishing to tempt fate or crank up a rumor mill, Captain G. W. Kidd ordered repairs made immediately.

In a little over a month the *Washoe* was back on the river, where Captain Kidd found himself in vicious rivalry. At different times, when she competed for berthing space at Benecia with the *Yosemite* and the *New World* (both owned by the California Steam and Navigation Company), collisions resulted. In the former, a deck hand had his leg injured so badly that it had to be amputated, and in the latter, a *Washoe* passenger was killed and the vessel forced to run aground

OPPOSITIOI

For Sacramento,
TOUCHING AT INTERMEDIATE PO▨

THE NEW AND ELEGANT STEAMER

WASHOE,
G. W. KIDD,...........................Comman
Will leave Pacific street Wharf,
On MONDAY, WEDNESDAY, and FRID▨
AT FOUR O'CLOCK P. M.

Passage—Cabin...........................One D▨
Passage—Deck...........................Fifty ¢
Freight—Per Ton...........................Two Do
au15

A NOTICE IN THE SAN FRANCISCO *ALTA* I▨ AUGUST, 1864. *Secrest Collection*

in shallow waters. She was later pried loose, repaired, and once again set afloat.

On September 5, 1864, the *Washoe*'s luck—such as it was—ran out when the boat engaged in an impromptu race up San Francisco Bay and into the Sacramento-San Joaquin delta. She left her San Francisco berth soon after four o'clock in the afternoon, with 150 to 185 passengers aboard. Captain Kidd commented that he would wait until after the other steamers left to avoid any chances of another collision, but soon after leaving dockside, the *Washoe* was spotted ahead of the *Chrysopolis*, *Yosemite*, *Antelope* and *Paul Pry*. Further into the

competition, the *Chrysopolis* (much larger than the *Washoe)* pulled ahead and maintained a steadily-growing lead of several miles. The *Antelope,* heavily loaded with freight, lagged several miles behind the *Washoe.*

At about twelve-thirty the following morning, the *Antelope* appeared downriver from Sacramento. Blowing its whistle, the steamer stopped opposite R Street on the levee, instead of at its regular wharf berth. Various curious people gathered to see what was happening, and soon fire bells were clanging throughout the city. Word spread quickly that the *Washoe*'s boiler exploded while the vessel entered the slough above Rio Vista, and many survivors were aboard the *Antelope.* A Sacramento newspaper dispatch gave the awful details:

> The scene on board [the *Antelope*] was such as has rarely been witnessed on the Pacific Coast. The floor of the cabin and portion of the deck were covered with the dead and wounded. The mattresses and bedding of the boat had been brought into requisition and some forty sufferers were stretched out; some of them enduring great agony and others too badly injured to be conscious of their condition. Most of the physicians of the city had been sent for and promptly responded, rendering all the aid within their power. Among the seriously injured were three women, two of them sisters, who died after being placed on board the Antelope. The other, Anna McGee, had a leg broken and was otherwise injured. The other sufferers were men who were, almost without exception, badly scalded about

the head, face and hands, and many of them over large portions of the breast and body.

A thousand people were now on the levee, some seeking friends and relatives from the *Washoe*, and others aiding in the care and disposition of the wounded. Several had died during the trip to the city, and others after they had landed. H. H. Stephens, chief clerk of the *Washoe*, described the scene:

> There were 153 passengers on board the *Washoe* leaving San Francisco, but others came on board at Benecia and Rio Vista. The *Antelope* brought up, killed and injured and uninjured, about 80, leaving some five or six dead bodies and three or four injured persons at the locality of the wreck. The number blown overboard, or killed and remaining in the lower cabin, cannot of course be at present ascertained. The passenger list was lost. The lights were of course extinguished by the shock. The report of the boiler was followed by the crashing of the fragments of the boat, and the groans and cries of the wounded. Some called for help in one form, and some in another; some asked for light, some for water, some desired to be thrown overboard, and others jumped overboard. Some who

THE *CHRYSOPOLIS* WAS THE PRIDE OF THE CALIFORNIA STEAM AND NAVIGATION COMPANY. *Society of California Pioneers*

> were enabled to get on shore did so, and ran into the bushes in vain in search of relief.
>
> I had just laid down in my berth, about fifteen minutes to 10 o'clock and the boat was going rapidly. My first impression was a burst or whiz of steam, sounding like tearing something; immediately shutting my mouth and putting my hand over my nose I rushed for the door. Went on to the starboard quarter of the boat… Think the aft head of the boiler went first and

threw the fires forward, as the boat was on fire in three places forward. The steering gear was ruined, but she took a shear and having headway enough ran ashore. The *Antelope* arrived about two hours after the explosion. Capt. Kidd was in the pilot house with Baldwin and Easton, pilots, and all escaped uninjured. The scene on shore was awful. A fisherman brought a sack of flour and a bottle of oil and did everything he could to alleviate the sufferers.

Mark Twain, then a reporter on the *San Francisco Call* and an old steamboat pilot himself, was uncharacteristically subdued and terse in his report of the disaster:

HEADLINE IN THE SAN FRANCISCO *ALTA* OF SEPTEMBER 7, 1864. *Secrest Collection*

One man, who was scalded from head to foot, got ashore, and in a nude state stood and screamed for help, but would not allow any covering to be put on him. A woman in a similar condition was brought up on the *Antelope*. The steamer carried only the wounded to Sacramento. A large number of the slightly wounded, who could walk or ride, were taken to the rooms of the Howard Association. The Association hired the Vernon House for a hospital for the sufferers.

Flags were set at half-mast throughout Sacramento on that terrible day. It seemed that poor iron in construction of the boilers was a likely cause of the explosion, and was generally agreed that all concerned in the wreck had behaved nobly. Captain Kidd had stayed with the remaining dead and wounded until they were picked up, and contributed $1,000 to a fund established to benefit the victims.

Terrible as the *Washoe* tragedy was, the steamboat era was not yet over in California—and there were many more mishaps yet to come on the state's waterways.

1865

The Wreck of the *Brother Jonathan*

Where: North California coast, near Crescent City
Details: Only nineteen survivors of shipwreck

Constructed in New York at a reported cost of $190,000, the steamship *Brother Jonathan* was launched in November 1850 and put into service between Panama and New York. She was a sturdy, good-sized ship with two thirty-three foot paddlewheels, a 400-horsepower steam engine and two masts of sail-power, later increased to three. She later ran regularly between Nicaragua and San Francisco. Owned initially by Cornelius Vanderbilt, she was sold in late 1857 and commenced regular travel between San Francisco and ports in Oregon, Washington and British Columbia. Her name was then changed to *Commodore* and, with up to 300 passengers paying between $25 and $50 a ticket, became very profitable. In 1860 the California Steam Navigation Company bought the steamships *Senator* and *Brother Jonathan* for a reported $200,000 and in 1861 overhauled the *Brother Jonathan*, which was well-worn by overloading and frequent use. She stayed on the northern route, with occasional detours south to Santa Barbara and San Pedro.

FOR PORTLAND AND VICTORIA

The California Steam Navigation Company's Steamship

Brother Jonathan,

S. J. DeWOLF,................................Commander,
Will leave Broadway Wharf,
FOR THE ABOVE PORTS,
ON FRIDAY,..................JULY 28, 1865,
AT 10 O'CLOCK A. M.

Bills of lading will be furnished to shippers, and none others signed.
For freight or passage apply on board, or at the office of the California Steam Navigation Company on the northeast corner Front and Jackson streets.
jy21   J. WHITNEY, Jr., President.

SAILING NOTICE IN THE SAN FRANCISCO
DAILY ALTA CALIFORNIA, JULY 26, 1865.
Secrest Collection

In late July 1865, the *Brother Jonathan* was being loaded at San Francisco's Broadway wharf for a trip north to Portland and Victoria, British Columbia. Captain Samuel J. DeWolf was keeping a wary eye on his vessel. During her previous trip to Portland, the *Brother Jonathan* had collided with another ship while being guided down the Columbia River by a river pilot, as was customary. Necessary repairs were made to the hull and deck, but DeWolf wanted to put the ship in drydock for further servicing. He also noticed that the ship was sitting too low in the water, and was obviously too full of cargo. Complaints to the California Steam Navigation Company, which profited handsomely from overloaded ships during these war years, went unheeded. Further, DeWolf was told that if he did not wish to take out the steamer, he would be replaced with another captain. Unwilling to surrender his command, he decided to tough out the situation and press forward.

One of California's best seamen, DeWolf must have been queasy as his passengers boarded. Many were prominent individuals: General George Wright, the new commander of the army in the District of Columbia, and his wife; the newly appointed governor of Washington Territory, Anson Henry; and James Nesbit, editor of the San Francisco *Bulletin*. A good deal of money was also loaded on board—Wells Fargo funds, army payroll and banking capital.

On Friday, July 28, 1865, the *Brother Jonathan* left its berth with 185 passengers. Still riding low in the water, she headed north into strong headwinds and choppy waters. As she attempted to pass Crescent City two days later, the weather and seas became increasingly rough. DeWolf decided to dock in port and wait until the storm passed. The wind was so violent that less than half the cabin passengers came to breakfast. Even fewer were present at noon.

At 5 A.M. on Sunday, July 30, a fisherman on the Crescent City wharf was surprised to see a small boat with eleven men, five women and three children come around Lighthouse Point, and land. Soaked by the heavy seas, they began relating the terrible story of the *Brother*

SAMUEL J. DEWOLF, THE ILL-FATED CAPTAIN OF THE *BROTHER JONATHAN*, WHO WENT DOWN WITH HIS SHIP WHILE AIDING HIS PASSENGERS. *Secrest Collection*

Jonathan's wreck. They were the only survivors. The men were all officers and crew of the ship, and one of them reported:

They had returned seven or eight miles and were eight miles due west of Point St. George, when without warning the steamer struck with full force upon a sharp ledge, which at the lowest ebb, projected about a yard above the surface. The bottom of the steamer went to pieces with a crash. In three minutes says the wheelman, the large fragments of the bottom and a part of the rudder were afloat alongside.

Captain DeWolf ordered the lifeboats filled, but the extremely rough water made this difficult. James Patterson, the third officer, heard DeWolf's last words as he was lowered into the one boat that got away: "Tell them that if they had not overloaded us we would have got through all right, and this would never have happened." All the other craft were swamped while being lowered into the huge waves of the sea.

Now fifteen minutes since the crash, the ship was breaking up fast. The sea was so violent that no one wanted to launch the two lifeboats remaining on board. It was later said that General Wright's wife had refused to leave her husband, and they were last seen holding on to each other. Boats were dispatched to the scene immediately, but none got closer than six miles to the wreck. By mid-afternoon, only a few fragments and buckets had washed ashore, but bodies soon began washing up along the northern coast, most of them wearing life preservers.

GENERAL GEORGE WRIGHT. *West Point Military Academy Archives, N.Y.*

Various unusual stories soon emerged from the tragedy. It was reported that a survivor was located on a piece of the wreckage, but was killed and robbed by Indians who reputedly pillaged the other victims that were found. One of the crew members, John Clinton, had earlier served on the ill-fated *Washoe*, where he had been injured yet survived; this time, his luck ran out. Even stranger was a story reported in the San Francisco *Morning Call*:

When Mrs. Brooks and her sister left the ranch at Napa for San Francisco for the purpose of taking passage to Portland, little Charlie Brooks, who was kept behind, was kept in ignorance of his mother's intended departure from California and made to believe that she was merely coming on a visit to San Francisco. On Sunday, July 30th, little Charlie, being still at the ranch, and utterly ignorant of his mother's real whereabouts, seemed all at once seized with a paroxysm of grief and stood transfixed, having told his grandmother who was sitting by him that he had just seen "Ma and Aunt Mary" go down into the water in a ship. A few days afterwards came the dreadful tidings of the loss of the Brother Jonathan, with nearly all on board, the day and hour exactly corresponding with the singular vision—or whatever it was—of little Charlie.

In the aftermath of the tragedy, a lighthouse was constructed at Point St. George, to better guide ships in the vicinity; new maritime laws were enacted to prevent ship overloading; and a succession of salvage operations, continuing well into the twentieth century, recovered much of the treasure that went down with the ship.

1866

Deadly Explosion in San Francisco

Where: Central San Francisco
Details: A dozen dead and many injuries

This disaster had its roots in the year 1846, when the Italian chemist Ascanio Sobrero added glycerol to a mixture of concentrated nitric and sulfuric acids. An oily, toxic liquid in its raw state, it was the most explosive and dangerous material devised up to that time. Sobrero, fearing the damage his discovery could cause, reportedly destroyed his notes—but word of his concoction, dubbed "nitroglycerine," eventually became general knowledge. The mixture was very sensitive to shock, as a number of unsuspecting San Franciscans were to discover some twenty years later.

On April 14, the Pacific Mail steamship *Sacramento* docked at San Francisco with crates marked "merchandise"from Hamburg, Germany. Three of the containers were taken by train to Dutch Flat, where the Central Pacific was slowly hacking tunnels out of the rock-choked Sierra Nevada Mountains for the developing transcontinental railroad. Black powder and hand tools then being used were doing the job, but the pace was much too slow. By April 16, Charles Crocker and James Strobridge were testing this new shipment of nitro-glycerine, discovering that the new material could improve the speed of digging through rock by 50 to 75 percent.

One of the "merchandise"crates still on the wharf, which had been shipped by Wells Fargo, was leaking a peculiar, oily substance. It was decided to move it to the company office to determine the amount of damage. William Haven, freight agent for the steamship company, joined Frank Webster, a Wells Fargo clerk, and several others to dismantle the box in the express company's yard on California Street. Gerritt W. Bell, who operated an assay office next door, was just leaving on a trip, but was called over to see if he could identify the leakage. These five men were all working on the crate when the explosion occurred and smoke, dust and debris filled the air. The *Examiner's* late afternoon edition of April 16, 1866, could only give a brief account of the mysterious blast:

> Several persons are already dead, and a large number are horribly cut and bruised. At the early hour we go to press it is impossible to ascertain the loss of life or the extent of the damage. The building in which the explosion took place is completely gutted. The street in the vicinity presented immediately after the accident the appearance of a field of battle. Several men were carried into the neighboring chemists, mangled and mutilated in the most terrible manner. Many who were still alive when we went to press will it is to be feared, succumb under the dreadful injuries they have received.

THE SCENE OF THE EXPLOSION IN THE SAN FRANCISCO WELLS FARGO OFFICE AS PHOTOGRAPHED BY CARLETON WATKINS. STUNNED SIGHT-SEERS ARE SHOWN WANDERING THROUGH THE WRECKAGE IN THIS VERY EARLY EXAMPLE OF NEWS PHOTOGRAPHY. THIS IS HALF OF A STEREO VIEW.
Courtesy William Jaeger Collection

A more detailed account in the San Francisco *Alta* better captured the moment's horror:

> The consternation which seized on the passers in the vicinity of Wells, Fargo & Co.'s was terrible, and men, women and children, horsemen, pedestrians, drays and express teams without drivers came charging pell-mell down the street in unextricable confusion. As soon as the first noise began to subside there was an immense rush toward Wells, Fargo & Co's building and the streets were in a few seconds so blocked that it was almost impossible for the fire engines to be brought into position to check the flames which it was thought were about to break out.

Blood was visible in many places, and men with heads and hands cut by the falling glass or timbers, were running back and forth in frantic searching for missing friends. The brick rear walls of Wells Fargo & Co.'s building, were terribly shattered while fragments of doorways and window sashes only remained in place throughout the building. Two fine horses attached to the ruins of Wells, Fargo & Co.'s express wagons lay in the agonies of death in the area.... .

A piece of human vertebra was blown over the building on the east side of Montgomery street, and a piece of skull was picked up on California street, east of Leidesdorff, with other fragments of human remains, and a human arm struck the third story window of the building across the street.

The Union Club, situated above the Wells Fargo offices, was also destroyed, and several of the nine bodies recovered from the rubble were dead club employees. Others died later from their injuries, while some fourteen other casualties were hospitalized with their wounds, most being Wells Fargo or Union Club employees.

The blast was promptly attributed to the nitroglycerine. Police Chief Martin Burke was directed by the board of supervisors to seek out any other supplies of the deadly explosive in the city and destroy them. A local firm identified itself as the only agents for the explosive in the city and took out an injunction to restrain the chief in his actions. Bandmann, Neilson & Co. maintained that the only supply of the material, which they called "Nobel's Patent Blasting Oil, or Nitro Glycerine," was in an isolated building some three miles distant from any thickly-settled portions of the city.

By mixing the deadly oil with silica and other materials, Alfred Nobel invented dynamite—patented in 1867. While high explosives never made countries too fearful to engage in war—as Nobel had hoped—at least dynamite was much more stable to handle than nitroglycerin, and the increased safety factor likely saved many lives. Unfortunately, this advance came two years too late for those who perished in the great San Francisco blast of '66.

1868

Oakland Ferry Disaster

Where: Oakland wharf
Details: At least ten died

Oakland
sco

It had been a wonderful weekend of Fourth of July celebrations around the San Francisco bay area. The weather was beautiful. A large festivity at Oakland had been attended by many San Franciscans, who had crossed the bay via the ferry *El Capitan*. At the Oakland pier they boarded cars of the San Francisco and Oakland Railroad, which delivered them to the celebration. After the festivities, most re-boarded the train and reversed their journeys. At the end of the line, the pier was extended conveniently into deep water, where passengers could board the ferry directly from the train. Recently a new gangplank, or "apron," had been installed at the end of the pier. Put into place with hinges, cog-wheels and a ratchet, the apron allowed quick transfer from train to ferry.

It was close to 4:30 on the afternoon of July 4, 1868, when the train stopped at the pier's end. The passengers bound for San Francisco began crowding onto the apron, which abutted the ferry's bottom deck. "Suddenly," reported a newspaper account, "as the crowd on the apron was the densest, quite a number of passengers having already got on board, there came a crash, and those who had reached the deck on looking back were horror-struck to see the draw hanging at a right angle with the wharf and the water filled with men, women and children struggling for life." The ratchet holding the apron level with the pier had failed.

THE NEW AND MAGNIFICENT
LOW-PRESSURE STEAMER

EL CAPITAN !

IS NOW RUNNING BETWEEN

SAN FRANCISCO AND OAKLAND.
jy2-2p1w

SAN FRANCISCO AND OAKLAND

RAILROAD.

TIME TABLE FOR JULY 4, 1868,

ADVERTISEMENT FOR THE *EL CAPITAN* IN THE JULY 2 EDITION OF THE *ALTA CALIFORNIA*. *Secrest Collection*

As shouting men, women and children splashed and screamed in the water, horrified commuters on the *El Capitan* and the pier began rushing around, trying to find some way

A PAINTING OF "COHEN'S WHARF" WHICH WAS BUILT IN 1864 AND WAS THE SCENE OF THE TERRIBLE DISASTER WHEN A HINGED GANGPLANK GAVE WAY, DUMPING FERRY PASSENGERS INTO THE BAY. *California State Library*

to rescue them. Mothers screamed for their families while ropes, planks and life preservers were heaved into the water. A small boat was quickly launched from the ferry, but in the haste to get it into the water, it was smashed against the side of the larger craft. Although the smaller craft was filling rapidly with water, the two crewmen helped several women and men into the boat, then onto a ferry paddlewheel, from where they were assisted onto the deck.

A group of Italians, mostly fisherman members of the Garibaldi Guard, had participated in the Oakland celebration and happened to be at the pier. Several of them hurled themselves into the water and began saving the swimming victims by lashing them to the wharf piles until they could be rescued. They stayed at work until no other victims were seen. One of the Italians, Allessio Ferrero, was also drowned, but it was not known if he was a survivor or rescuer. There was no way to know the precise extent of the fatalities.

A CRUDE WOODCUT FROM THE SAN FRANCISCO *POLICE GAZETTE* GIVES A GOOD SENSE OF THE DESPERATE EFFORTS TO SAVE THOSE STRUGGLING IN THE WATER. *Secrest Collection*

At least one man died while engaged in rescue efforts. Carlo Sonognini, a Swiss, rescued four persons before exhaustion caused his own demise. "This man," noted a newspaper account, "was standing on the steamer when the accident occurred, and jumped in and rescued five or six persons, but his humanity cost him his own life, as he was in the end drawn under by some person who was sinking, and drowned. He was found grasping the body of Mrs. Sanders, and it was apparent that the last effort of his life was to preserve a fellow creature. So tight was his grasp upon the one he would save, that they were drawn to the surface together."

ALTA CALIFORNIA NEWSPAPER HEADLINE, JULY 6, 1868. *Secrest Collection*

Euphemia Sanders was the wife of architect George Sanders, who had his wife on one arm and a sister on the other when the apron gave way. Sanders and his sister survived the accident.

When it seemed all had been saved, the *El Capitan* got up steam and pulled away from the wharf heading for San Francisco. The next morning the Italian fishermen returned to the scene, as reported in the January 6, 1868 San Francisco *Daily Alta California*:

> Yesterday morning, the Italian fishermen, to whom unbounded credit is due, went to work with energy to recover the bodies of the victims. Two men in the employ of the Railroad and Ferry Company, with a boat, also aided in the search. The Italians during the day recovered eight bodies, and the others two more, making ten in all.

In the confusion and excitement, at least two children and three adults were thought to be missing. The *El Capitan* had continued its ferry operations on the bay, its churning paddlewheels undoubtedly scattering the remaining victims over a wide area. Another victim was claimed when, after being rescued, the young daughter of the drowned Italian Ferrero, died on the way home. Mrs. Ferrero was so distraught at losing both her husband and daughter that she tried to throw herself off the top deck of the *El Capitan* on a return trip to San Francisco. The funeral was held on July 6 and, according to the *Alta*, was a sad and curious affair:

Under the circumstances, it is to be regretted that there were not other mourners besides the Italians; that there was not some formal indication of the general sentiments of the community regretting the lost and sympathizing with their surviving comrades. Occasion should be taken to do proper honor to these brave Garibaldians.

An inquest into the apron's failure was inconclusive. It was ruled that lives had been lost through the "gross neglect of A. A. Cohen," president of the San Francisco and Oakland Railway, who had accepted the faulty iron work and failed to provide safety chains that would have prevented the accident. Few, if any, expected any official action against Cohen or his company. The *Alta* muttered:

Thousands upon thousands of lives have been sacrificed in this country either by the incompetency, gross carelessness, or rapacity of the persons engaged in the business of transportation, and we have yet to hear of the infliction of the first adequate punishment upon those who were guilty of these wholesale slaughters.

1868
The Great Hayward Earthquake
Where: Hayward
Details: Some deaths and much damage

'**G** reat Earthquake, People Killed and Wounded, Immense Destruction of Property, Water Gushing up in the Street!"

These were the headlines in a Stockton newspaper on October 21, 1868. First reports of the quake indicated fifteen to fifty dead and destruction in widely scattered areas, but gradually more accurate assessments were being received. It was not as horrendous as the early reports suggested, but it was bad enough.

The shock had its origin on the eastern side of San Francisco Bay, along the Hayward Fault, roughly parallel to and some eighteen miles east of its San Andreas twin. As the extent of the quake became known, damage reports came in from such widely separated towns as Petaluma, Napa, Sacramento, San Jose and San Francisco. It quickly became apparent that the town of Haywards (now Hayward), in Alameda County had been hardest hit, as reported in a letter in the October 22 San Francisco *Daily Alta California*:

> One of the most alarming and destructive shocks of earthquake ever felt here since its settlement by whites occurred this morning at about ten minutes before eight o'clock. The direction of the shock seemed to be from the southwest to northeast, and so severe was it that in a number of places the ground opened from six inches to two feet, through which water and quicksand, in considerable quantities, was forced to a height of from one to three feet. The amount of damage sustained here at present cannot be estimated.

When an accounting had been made, Haywards had indeed been hit hard. An eyewitness wrote that he did not see a structure in town that was not damaged in some manner. The flouring mill owned

Stockton, October 22, 1868

THE GREAT EARTHQUAKE !
San Francisco Terribly Excited.
THE PUBLIC SCHOOLS AND STOCK EXCHANGE CLOSED.
Business Generally Suspended.
Great Damage in the Lower Part of the City.
SEVERAL LIVES LOST.
NO DAMAGE ON THE HILLS.
No Properly Constructed Buildings Injured.
Partial List of the Casualties and Disasters.

STOCKTON *DAILY EVENING HERALD*

by Sheriff Harry Morse was destroyed, as was a huge grain warehouse. An open crack that ran through the town was said to be nine miles in length, and a large damage estimate was assembled. Hardly a chimney in town was standing. There was no loss of life in town, but a cook

A DEJECTED HAYWARDS PROPERTY OWNER IS PROBABLY WAITING FOR THE NEXT SHOCK TO COME. *California State Library*

at the Washington Hotel had his leg badly broken. A young girl's letter from Alameda gives some sense of the terror experienced by everyone in the area:

October 23, 1868 —We have scarcely slept for two nights. Of course, you will see by the papers long before this reaches you all about the terrible earthquake we had on the 21st

I knew in a minute what it was and rushed out the door. It was the hardest shock that has ever been felt in California and lasted too long for an earthquake. It was perfectly frightful to see the large trees swaying all about and to hear the rumbling noise. I expected all the time to see the ground open. It did open at Haywards, twelve miles from here. Éthe shocks still continued, with a little time between. After a while we ventured into the house, and tried to fix things up a little, but it was very slow work, for we had to run out about every ten minutes. We kept all the doors open.

An Oakland carpenter named Thompson was at work on the top of the Baptist Church, on Fourteenth Street, at the time of the earthquake. "The top of the spire is one hundred and fifty feet from

SHERIFF HARRY MORSE'S FLOUR MILL IN HAYWARDS, WAS TOTALLY DESTROYED DURING THE QUAKE. *John Boessenecker Collection*

the ground and swayed to and fro in a fearful manner. Mr. Thompson maintained his position until the earthquake subsided." San Leandro was also hit severely, and few buildings escaped damage. The courthouse was practically demolished, with County Clerk J. W. Josselyn losing his life in the wreckage. Undersheriff Peter Borein and several others in the building narrowly escaped death. Five prisoners in the courthouse jail were yelling and praying to be let out, but Borein could not find the key in the rubble. Finally, the jail door was broken open, and the prisoners transferred to the Alameda city jail.

PETER BOREIN HAD A NARROW ESCAPE IN THE COLLAPSING SAN LEANDRO COURTHOUSE. *John Boessenecker Collection*

San Francisco sustained spotty yet considerable property damange, confined mostly to the eastern portion of the city and the land-filled portions of the bay. The October 22 San Francisco *Morning Call* reported:

> Yesterday morning San Francisco was visited by the most severe earthquake the city ever experienced. The great shock commenced at 7:45 A.M. and continued nearly one minute, being the longest ever known in this region. The oscillations were from east to west, and were very violent. Men, women, and children rushed into the streets—some in a state of semi-nudity—and all in the wildest state of excitement. Many acted as if they thought the Day of Judgement had come. For a time the excitement was intense, and the panic was general.

City Hall, the former Jenny Lind Theater, was badly damaged, and the prisoners also had to be removed to the county jail. Although none of the local schools sustained much damage, the children were given the day off, and by 10 A.M. all business in the city was suspended. The *Alta* commented:

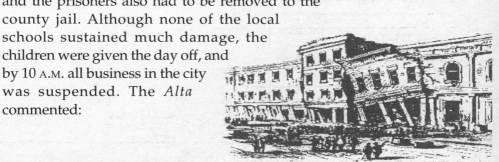

THE RAILROAD HOUSE AND ROSENBAUM'S TOBACCO WAREHOUSE IN SAN FRANCISCO WERE BOTH SERIOUSLY DAMAGED DURING THE QUAKE. Harper's Weekly, *November 28, 1868*

The great shock of 1868 produced a wholly different affect on buildings, from that of 1865. In October, 1865, glass was broken and shivered to atoms in all the lower part of the city by the perpendicular oscillation, while comparatively few walls were shaken down or badly injured. The earthquake of yesterday broke very little glass in any part of the city, but the damage by the falling of cornices, awnings and walls was immense.

Amelia Ransome Neville, in her recollections, also paused to compare the '65 and '68 quakes. She was attending church when the former quake struck. At the first swaying of the building, Reverend Easton urged his parishioners to be calm. Mrs. Neville stuck it out through several of the pastor's urgings, but when a third shock set the walls to "grinding on their foundations," she bolted out into Powell Street—only to find the good reverend already there. "The shake of '68,"she recalled, "that did much damage to buildings on 'made ground,' the section where shallows of the bay had been filled in, seemed less severe to me, but we spent most of that day out-of-doors."

The damage at San Francisco was estimated at $350,000, with the East Bay area undoubtedly sustaining much greater property loss. A trotal of thirty persons were reported killed, with the most distant of the shocks felt as far away as Virginia City, Nevada.

1869

Alameda Locomotive Collision

Where: Alameda County
Details: Fifteen dead and many injured

A Western Pacific train pulled out of the Oakland station at 8:30 on Sunday morning, November 14, 1869. This was the normal departure time and, although it was foggy, the train proceeded normally on its southern course. About five miles down the tracks, the train slowed down at Simpson's Station, the rail junction where the Western Pacific tracks curved eastward to serve the trains between Hayward and Alameda. If the Hayward train had not yet arrived, a switchman would advise the Oakland locomotive to wait until the other train had passed. Switchman Bernard Kane waved the Western Pacific engineer on, and Engineer Edward Anderson increased his throttle and chugged south down the tracks at about twenty miles per hour.

The Western Pacific locomotive was pulling a tender, an express car, a baggage car, a smoking car, two passenger cars and a sleeping car. As it cut through the fog, Anderson was horrified to see another train approaching about ninety yards away. As he pulled on the brakes, he yelled out a warning and one of his firemen jumped off, but Anderson and the other fireman were still in the cab as the two locomotives collided in a grinding crash of metal and hissing steam. "The one engine," later wrote a reporter, "was driven into the other, and both were smashed to pieces. The boilers were thrown to the right side, the smoke stacks being thrown to the left. The Alameda train consisted of six cars, including the baggage car which was thrown up almost perpendicularly."

As people began crawling and spilling out of the cars, it was noticed that the Oakland train's smoking car

THE NEW PULLMAN PASSENGER CARS WERE STATE-OF-THE-ART AND QUITE COMFORTABLE. THE FLIMSY, WOODEN CONSTRUCTION, HOWEVER, MADE THEM DANGEROUS IN A WRECK. *California State Library*

had been telescopedinto the front end of the first passenger car. The force of the collision was such that the smoking car had jammed a crushed and mangled mass of humanity inside the passenger car, to a point where a mere six feet of space was left. Moans and shrieks of pain issued from the wreckage as stunned passengers wandered amid what remained of the train. Some checked themselves for injuries, then began walking from the scene. Others were too dazed to do anything and stood looking at the tragedy, unable to comprehend what had happened. George Cadwalader, a survivor of the flattened passenger car, later recalled the terrible scene:

> I was thrown completely to the rear of the car amid a pile of seats. All the persons who were killed on our train were in the same car with myself. The smoking car was shot into our car so far as to confine all the killed and wounded in a small space in the rear. Judge Baldwin, who was killed, was in the water-closet, at the rear of the car. I found myself after the collision on top of a pile of dead and wounded. I cannot tell exactly how many were in the car, but I should judge about thirty. There were no ladies in the car with us.

The second passenger car on the Oakland train was comparatively undamaged. When it was realized what had happened to the first car, uninjured passengers forced an entrance , but gasped in horror at the scene before them. Several became ill at the sight and staggered away. Others took their place and began the hideous job of untangling the bodies and separating the living from the dead.

Farmers and others from the surrounding area were soon at the scene, bringing axes and other tools. One horribly mutilated man begged to be shot to end his suffering, but died in about three minutes. J. F. Kapp, another seriously injured man, was wedged tightly in the rubble. Another man's arm was torn off, and he was soon dead from shock. The San Francisco *Daily Alta California* reported:

> Mr. J. F. Kapp, who was the first one taken out and laid on the ground, behaved himself in a most commendable manner, though he was suffering with intense pain, his legs being crushed. He gave orders to those about him to go and attend to the others, even giving directions how to carry the injured out and dress them.

One passenger had an uneasy premonition that something was going to happen and moved to the rear of the train. He was uninjured, but badly frightened. There were fewer passengers on the Hayward train, which resulted in fewer casualties.

Many of the injured aided in getting others from the wreck and, by 11 A.M., all the bodies had been removed to the Oakland Insane Asylum for treatment, since the city had no hospital. Worried friends and relatives began showing up to identify the dead and injured. A preliminary count showed some fifteen dead and thirty injured. The Oakland *Transcript* reported:

> The dead, as they lay in the [corn field] stubble, with their faces toward the skies, whither their spirits had so suddenly been called, presented a great variety of appearance. Some showed the marks of horror, while others bore a strikingly peaceful countenance...

> There were some very remarkable escapes, and strikingly so with the lady passengers. There were two ladies seated directly in front of Mr. Boulet, and though he was killed, they did not even receive a scratch.

It was about an hour before physicians began arriving. A coroner's inquest was held the following day at nearby Alameda under Justice of the Peace W. B. Clement. One of the witnesses was Bernard Kane, the switchman who had waved on the Oakland train. A tall, spare Irishman, he had been hired by a man named Adams, roadmaster of the Western Pacific. Adams told Kane he would get back to him with instructions on how the switch worked, but never did. Transportation Superin-

TERRIBLE ACCIDENT
ON THE ALAMEDA ROAD !

Collision Between the Western Pacific and Alameda Trains.

FOURTEEN KILLED AND TWENTY-THREE WOUNDED.

BOTH ENGINES SMASHED TO PIECES.

THE CARS ARE DRIVEN INTO EACH OTHER.

HORRIBLE SUFFERING OF THE WOUNDED.

A Man's Leg Hewn off with an Axe.

Judge Baldwin of Nevada, Among the Killed.

LISTS OF THE DEAD AND WOUNDED.

Incidents of the Tragedy.

We have, this morning, to record a most

HEADLINE FROM THE *OAKLAND DAILY TRANSCRIPT, NOVEMBER 15*, 1869. *Secrest Collection*

WORKING INTO THE NIGHT, FARMERS AND OTHER VOLUNTEERS FRANTICALLY SEARCHED FOR SURVIVORS, CHOPPING AND PRYING THEM OUT OF THE WRECKAGE. *Harper's Weekly*

tendent J. Stevens gave Kane further instructions and a timetable. There was only one problem: Kane was illiterate. At breakfast, when a gravel-carrying train had passed, Kane had assumed it was the Hayward train ahead of schedule. When the Oakland Western Pacific train arrived, Kane signalled for it to proceed, thinking the Hayward train had already gone by. One of the most catastrophic train wrecks of nineteenth-century California had happened, not because of a malfunction or a misunderstanding, but due to a callous indifference and ignorance between an employer and its employee.

Alameda Sheriff Harry Morse arrested Bernard Kane on November 20, but anyone familiar with the investigation must have thought the railroad officials were at least as culpable as the illiterate Irishman. Apparently, the courts found no good reason to make Kane take the rap. On December 2 he was released and cleared of any responsibility for the disaster.

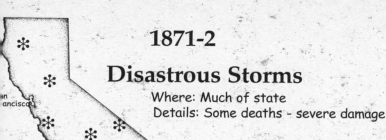

1871-2

Disastrous Storms

Where: Much of state
Details: Some deaths - severe damage

If the winter of 1861-1862 in California set a new standard in inclement weather for the state, it can be fairly said that the corresponding season in 1871-1872 at least equaled that record. Accounts of the latter season show remarkable turmoil and ruin not just throughout the whole state, but through the Pacific coast as a whole—with a seemingly endless procession of bridges washed out, ships going adrift, acres of towns and farmland flooded, and unlucky people drowned and frozen to death.

The early '70s had been a period of drought throughout the Golden State, with its citizens wondering when the heavens would open up and water the long-parched ground. By the middle of December 1871, the weather patterns had made a sharp reversal. Rain and wind began pounding their dual fists against San Francisco, and the gales were said to be the most powerful felt there in years. Ships on the bay were smashing into each other and into the wharves, sustaining everything from light damage to complete breakups. Ferries were unable to make their usual runs, and traffic throughout the entire region was paralyzed. The stateliest buildings in the city— such as the Hibernia Bank and Loan headquarters, and Grace Church—were having their windows cracked and blown out from the heavy gusts. According to the San Francisco *Daily Alta California*, the rain was so hard that it "was dashed almost horizontally into the faces of pedestrians," and this stinging deluge served to keep most pedestrians off the streets.

East of the Bay Area, Stockton was enduring a heavy deluge at the same time, with half the city going underwater. The December 20 *San Joaquin Republican* described the scene: "This morning the people awoke to find lakes and young seas where last night was dry land. The volume of water is not really so great but that it would pass off were it not that its natural channels have been so obstructed by gradings and fillings that the water is diverted and thrown out over the level surface." In the adjoining Sacramento-San Joaquin River delta, the "gradings and fillings" were contributing to a similar disaster. Roads and railways in the area were frequently impassable, and much of the soil lay submerged.

Due north and northeast, the situation was scarcely different. A reporter for the Sacramento *Record* climbed atop the state capitol's dome, looked around for an approximate twelve-mile radius, and saw a large-scale panorama of wreckage and flooding. The bulk of Yolo County was described as a vast inland sea; farmers, however, were more exultant than discouraged, as the moisture was needed to replenish their dried-out acreages.

The citizens of Santa Cruz were especially hard-hit by the December downpours. Swollen by the continuing torrents, the San Lorenzo River jumped its banks and flooded the town's lower portion. The Mission Bridge, next to the nearby California Powder Works, was washed away, and travel outside of town was frequently impossible during the following month. The Pacific Ocean, whipped into a frenzy by the bad weather, was said to emit sounds like "heavy ordnance."

Meanwhile, the human toll of the storms and floods was beginning to mount. No precise figures are available, but it seems likely

SANTA CRUZ, SOUTH OF SAN FRANCISCO, DELUGED BY THE SURF AND A FLOODING RIVER. *California State Library*

that several dozen people perished as a result of this uncommonly severe season. At the end of December, a man named Butler Ives was found drowned in the Sacramento-San Joaquin delta, and farther east, two children were frozen to death near the Ophir Grade. The following month brought scattered reports of drownings, all apparently accidental, at the Guadalupe River, the Stockton Channel, Natividad, and other points.

January saw some lessening of the storms, but they had yet to abate completely, and had firmly established the winter as one of

California's worst. At Arcata, the main wharf was first submerged, and a later storm washed away a large portion of it. It was also reported that the tide in Humboldt Bay was the highest it had been since the 1862 season.

Over in Nevada City, rainfall reached an unprecedented fifty-seven inches, and Yreka and Weaverville—like Santa Cruz—frequently found themselves cut off from the outside due to impassable roads.

By the latter part of the month, the record-setting gales had once again returned to San Francisco, creating rampant disarray on the streets and in the water. The *Alta* chronicled a set of odd conditions which transpired on the 24th: "During the heaviest of the blow the sea was very rough and broke over Meiggs' Wharf, which is of very rare occurrence. A few hours sufficed to dry the surface of the earth and dirt upon the streets. Clouds of dust soon followed, blinding the eyes of all who faced the wind." The notion of dust blanketing San Francisco's frequently-damp streets demonstrates the unusual nature of this strange winter season.

HEADLINE FROM THE *SAN FRANCISCO CHRONICLE, FEBRUARY 21, 1872. Secrest Collection*

Perhaps the severe winter season's most notable single disaster was the collapse of a retaining wall perpendicular to Minna Street in San Francisco. A foot thick, it was raised higher than a three-story home being constructed on adjacent ground, and was braced inadequately. When a gale-force wind kicked up on the night of February 20, the wall fell squarely against its other neighbor, a boarding house. Johanna McDonald, a young mother and proprietor of the place, was killed, along with two of her children and a boarder named Mary Logan. The heavy falling masonry rendered the house into a pile of ruins within seconds; all that was left standing was its rear wall.

As winter turned into spring, the trial by rain, wind and flood ended. California's rivers and lakes had been replenished, but at an untold cost to the state's economy and with a considerable fatality count. With the property damage affecting everything imaginable—ships, buildings, farms, railroad tracks, bridges, and more—it is reasonable to suggest that the losses totaled at least seven figures, in that day's non-inflated currency. A disaster of similar magnitude today would no doubt run into billions of dollars' worth of damage.

1872

The Great Inyo Earthquake

Where: Inyo County
Details: More than sixteen deaths, many injuries

Lone Pine

"The dog was howling and the poultry squawking as if something was trying to choke, and they were so badly frightened they didn't seem to know what to do but squawk, and no wonder—it was enough to frighten anyone."

So recalled young Emma Duva, who had been awakened about 2:30 in the morning of April 26, 1872. Her family lived on an isolated farm some twenty miles from Lone Pine, one of the few towns in Owens Valley, on the eastern side of the Sierra Nevada. There had been warnings—minor shocks—of the earthquake to come, but no one really knew just what to do or expect. When the big quake thundered across the valley that early morning few, if any, were prepared.

Owens Valley was populated mostly by Hispanics at this time, and most of the structures in Lone Pine were built of adobe. Nearly every home and building fell apart, according to Josiah D. Whitney, leader of a scientific party that arrived some time later:

> At Lone Pine we found ourselves in the midst of a scene of ruin and disaster—giving a vivid idea, even after the lapse of two months, of the distressing scenes through which the inhabitants had passed. The town contained from 250 to 300 inhabitants, living almost exclusively in adobe houses, every one of which, and one of stone— the only one of that material in the town—was entirely demolished. Twenty-three persons were either killed outright, or found dead when disinterred from the ruins; four more were so badly injured that they have since died, while sixty others were more or less seriously hurt. Sixteen

BETWEEN LONE PINE AND INDEPENDENCE, THIS GAPING FISSURE IN THE EARTH IS A RELIC OF THE GREAT QUAKE OF '72. *Secrest Collection*

of the victims with no known next of kin were buried in a local mass grave, while other bodies were interred by relatives.

Eva Shepherd, not quite nine years old at the time, had spent the night with school friends at their home near Independence, some eighteen miles north of Lone Pine. It was a bitter, cold night and the three children huddled under their warm quilt in the sod house. "We must have awakened as the sod walls of the little house collapsed during the initial shock," Eva later recalled, and offered these added details to her account:

> No words can express the terror I went through in the next few minutes. Under our feet the rubble was rolling and shaking, while those sod walls were still crumbling and crashing around us. I thought the end of the world had come.

YOUNG EVA SHEPHERD WAS A WITNESS TO THE GREAT QUAKE. *Secrest.Collection*

> To this day I don't know how I managed to crawl out of the ruins of that house. At last, I found myself outside with the Rogers family around me. The ground was heaving and shaking so we could hardly stand. Only one of us was injured. Mrs. Rogers had been caught by a section of wall before she could get out of bed, and two of her ribs were broken. Again and again the ground shook and heaved under us, and we heard a deep, mysterious rumbling.

The nearby, mostly-adobe army post of Camp Independence was nearly destroyed, but suffered only two injuries within its boundaries, a private soldier and his wife. Soldiers sent out to scout the area reported ragged, gaping fissures in the ground, as well as scarps showing large chunks of land pushed upward by the fault's heaving motions. Legs and tails of cattle protruding from cracks showed where the poor beasts had been swallowed by the earth on which they stood. The wide-ranging damage suggested it was a miracle there had not been more deaths and casualties.

Damage from the quake was reported at Indian Wells, some sixty-seven miles south of Lone Pine, as well as far to the north. From Independence northward, where lumber was more widely used in building, damage to wooden structures was minimal. Most of those interviewed agreed that the epicenter seemed to be in the Sierra, west of the area between Owens Lake and Lone Pine. It was

further reported the shocks had been felt over much of California. The stage station operator at Desert Springs, between Los Angeles and Owens Valley, wrote that his "house rocked to and fro like a ship in a storm":

> The shelves discharged their contents, and the furniture was upset by the violence of the shock. In the store room there was a large pile of grain standing in sacks. These sacks were thrown about the room. In the morning, it was discovered that an immense volume of water had been thrown out of the well near the house, and at the time of writing, a large body still continued to pour forth. The stream is very muddy and is strongly impregnated with sulphur.

At the Little Lake stage station, closer to Lone Pine, a stagecoach and eleven wagons and teams were camped for the night. The teamsters were asleep in their wagons. When the rocking became violent, one of the drivers leaped onto his wagon seat and began cursing his mules who, he surmised, were causing the trouble. One of the other drivers yelled at him: "You damned fool, t'aint the mules, it's an earthquake!"

Los Angeles, nearly two hundred miles southwest of Lone Pine, was seriously rocked, but suffered no visible damage or casualties. "Buildings were well shaken," reported the *Los Angeles Daily News* of March 27, "but none, so far as we have been able to learn, suffered any injury. In

many cases the houses were very hastily evacuated by their tenants, without regard to the apparel worn at that untimely hour."

Los Angeles merchants derived much business from the Inyo County mines, and promptly called public meetings to solicit aid for the stricken area. "In extending relief to them," lectured the *News*, "we are aiding ourselves."

The towns of Visalia and Porterville, due west of Inyo, were considerably shaken also, but damages consisted of few fallen chimneys, cracked walls, and damaged shelf goods. In Yosemite Valley, naturalist John Muir rushed from his cabin upon being awakened by the initial rumblings. "The shocks were so violent and varied," wrote Muir, "and succeeded one another so closely, one had to balance in walking as if on the deck of a ship among the waves." Taking cover behind a large tree, Muir watched as mighty Sentinel Rock, which he had just recently been studying, collapsed in an avalanche of mighty boulders.

In San Francisco, the quake was recorded by a weather observer, although most residents of the city felt nothing at all. Shocks were still being felt in Owens Valley in late May, and

THE GRAVES OF THE QUAKE VICTIMS. *Secrest Collection*

the quake is generally thought to have been the most severe to have hit California during recorded history. Only the absence of any large population east of the Sierra and in central California kept both fatalities and property loss low.

1875

BLACK POWDER TRAGEDY

Where: San Francisco wharf at Rincon Point
Details: Several deaths and injuries

It was a typical day on the wharves at San Francisco's Rincon Point. Square-rigged ships and steamboats were loading cargo onto wagons, and stevedores were storing crates in several nearby warehouses while sailors maintained their ships. Farther out, in the water, John Risdon was slowly removing (via explosives) a rock ledge that had long imperiled bay traffic. For the past eighteen months, his working headquarters had been in the same neighborhood, next to Fred Haase's Eureka Saloon on Harrison Street. A blast was scheduled to take place at four o'clock this afternoon. A recently-discharged soldier stood talking to the bartender at Haase's place, while across the street, at John Taisen's saloon, the owner and some friends were engaged in a friendly game of cards.

George Green, a local blacksmith, stepped into Risdon's warehouse and office for a chat with foreman Clark, who was in charge of Risdon's operation. A former employee of Risdon's, Green chatted with Clark and Joe Corran, his assistant, while Clark made up powder charges. Green later recalled:

> He took the loose powder out of a box filled with powder and put this powder into tin cans with a wooden scoop through a hole about one and half inch large. He had filled one can and placed that on the table and placed two empty cans near the box and commenced filling them. The box with powder was standing on the floor from which he filled the cans. He then lighted his pipe and sat down on an empty box alongside the powder. He was crossing his legs which jarred his pipe in his mouth, from which dropped some fire into the box of powder. He then tried to extinguish this spark of fire with his finger pressing on it, when after a moment the powder in the box blazed up, on seeing this I ran out to a distance of about 50 feet, when I heard an explosion take place.

All accounts state that the explosion occurred at 3 P.M.

William Cornell, superintendent of the Harrison Street wharf, was walking towards the bay when it took place, and recalled it vividly:

> It appeared to me that I saw a sheet of flame about twenty feet wide go out from this little shanty where the giant powder was, and go right across the street in a body like the flash of a thousand cannons fired at once. I was confused by the shock for a moment, but was not knocked down. The fire went towards the shanty on the opposite side of the street and seemed to sweep it down by the force of the flame rather than by the concussion of the explosion. Then I saw the bricks and splinters flying in all directions. Immediately after that house went, down all the rest fell together. There were a number of men in the saloon. I don't

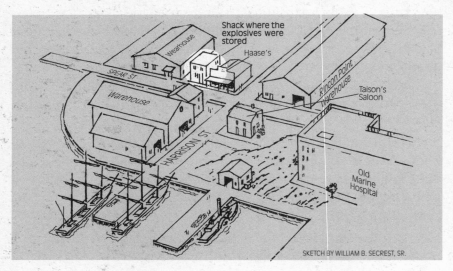

SKETCH BY WILLIAM B. SECREST, SR.

> know how many, but I helped to get out three. One of them was a little burned and the fire was within two or three inches of their feet when we got them out. Everybody was afraid to go in among the ruins at first because it was said that there was more powder in the warehouse and there would be another explosion, but they soon got over this. I ran around to the dwelling house of Haase, immediately opposite the saloon, and saw some one in the ruins and with the assistance of Mr. Cook, the engineer, we got out Mrs. Haase and her little boy. The boy was not much hurt, but his mother is very badly injured.

THE MARINE HOSPITAL LOOMS OVER THE TAISEN SALOON IN THIS LATTER DAY VIEW OF THE EXPLOSION SITE. SPEAR STREET RUNS IN FRONT OF THE SALOON WHILE THE TWO WAGONS ARE IN THE FOREGROUND. *Albert Shumate Collection*

A teamster with a four-horse team was unloading at the wharf when the explosion occurred. He was knocked senseless for a few minutes, and when he recovered, he found his horses dazed and turned completely around in their tangled harness. His wagon was covered with timbers, bricks and other debris.

Tales of miraculous escapes were numerous. George Taylor and his young son were sitting before a window in his office two blocks away from the explosion. "He and the boy," reported the San Francisco *Chronicle*, "were sitting beside the window when a volley of missiles flew across the street, knocked the door from its hinges, demolished the window and littered the room with fragments... but neither of the occupants were injured."

Several smaller explosions rocked the Risdon warehouse, which helped spread the fire raging through the shattered area. Swamped momentarily by alarms, it took firefighters a half hour to reach the scene, only to discover insufficient water pressure by the time they got there. Interviewed later about the problem, Fire Chief David Scannell commented: " It is the fault of the water company that only four-inch mains are laid in that section of the city. They should be eight inches. I called attention to these mains in my last report." The firefighters waged a lengthy battle against the flames, sometimes jumping into the bay to escape them, and evacuated a total of fifteen injured—several of whom later died from their injuries.

Huge crowds of people were now gathered on the streets, on rooftops and on a cliff next to the nearby Marine Hospital. Police had to stretch ropes to keep the crowds back, as friends and relatives cried out for word of the dead and wounded. The oldest boy of Fred Haase came home from school to a scene of horror. "The poor little fellow," commented the *Chronicle*, "fell across the body of his father, flung his arms around the neck of the dead and sobbed as if his little heart would dissolve with grief. The sight moved all who witnessed it to tears." His mother also was badly injured. The San Francisco *Alta California* reported on the search for casualties:

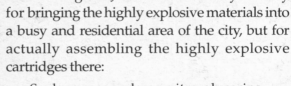

HEADLINE FROM THE *DAILY ALTA CALIFORNIA*, APRIL 8, 1875. *Secrest Collection*

> It was known that the saloon, the coffee-house, a house or two used by a couple of poor families as dwellings, had been occupied and the inmates were missed. After diligent search in the vicinity of the spot where the explosion was said to have occurred, a ghastly human form, black, charred and smoking, was brought forth—a horrid sight, that chilled and sickened the thousands of people who had assembled. The body was that of a man, but so begrimed and burned out of all semblance to anything as to be unrecognizable. It was placed in a wagon, but before it could be removed the cry went up that still another body had been found. It was a steaming and noisome mass of roasted and shapeless flesh.

An editorial in the *Chronicle* castigated John Risdon severely not only for bringing the highly explosive materials into a busy and residential area of the city, but for actually assembling the highly explosive cartridges there:

DAVE SCANNELL, THE LONG-TERM SAN FRANCISCO FIRE CHIEF. *Secrest Collection*

> Such compounds as nitro-glycerine, hercules and giant powder, dynamite and all kindred substances, should in their manufacture, storage and handling be driven beyond the boundaries of the city, or at least outside of its inhabited quarters.

Unfortunately, loose local ordinances and standards persisted and California would see a number of similar mishaps occur before the nineteenth century's end.

1876

CHINESE THEATER TRAGEDY

Where: San Francisco
Details: Nineteen dead with many injured

In 1876, San Francisco's Chinatown was a cramped world of narrow, lantern-lined streets and alleys, shops, restaurants and theaters. Scarcely a quarter-century old, it had arisen during the gold rush as the business and cultural center for Chinese who flocked to the mines. It had become an insulated world, infrequently visited by whites (many of whom loathed the presence of any Asians in the United States), and often ignored by the rest of the city.

The theater provided a means of escape from the sense of isolation that often pervaded Chinatown. In San Francisco there were two Chinese theaters, with the Chinese Royal Theater at 622 Jackson Street, near Dupont, being the most popular. Across the street was the Chinese Thespian Temple. Chinese plays were rather dull affairs to the American eye, but the Chinese enjoyed them. Usually they were representations of historical events—a consecutive nightly presentation that might last three months. In the traveling companies, only men could appear on stage and any female parts were played by a male. When a character died on stage, after giving his last gasp, he simply got up and walked off stage rather than bringing down the curtain to signal the event. In fact, there was no curtain.

The Chinese theaters were unusual in other aspects, too. The stage was simple, sets were minimal and, aside from a few boxed seats, the audience sat mostly on benches. An orchestra consisted usually of five or six musicians playing gongs, drums, oriental fiddles and other assorted instruments. There was no shouting or yelling by the audience, as in the American theater. The Chinese patron was content to merely nod or sigh in reflecting emotion.

SCENE IN A SAN FRANCISCO CHINESE THEATER ABOUT THE TIME OF THE DEADLY STAMPEDE OF 1876.
Secrest Collection

Special police were employed by the Chinese—white men who were members of the police force, but paid by Chinese property owners. They kept order in the "Quarter," and did what they could to hold down vice, but frequently were compromised to overlook dozens of gambling and opium dens, as well as the bordellos of Chinatown. The theaters could also be trouble spots. There had been several recent near-riots in a Chinese theater, when individuals wanting free admission would yell "fire" in a theater window. In the resulting exodus they either purloined a ticket, or re-entered unnoticed with the returning crowd of regular patrons. The San Francisco *Chronicle* reported:

> The terror-stricken audience, not delaying to look around and determine the truth or falsity of the cry, would rush for the door over the benches and in the greatest confusion. The policeman who was watchful would quickly swing open the closed doors and, drawing his club, push his way in until he reached a bench where he would stand frantically waving the crowd back and applying his club vigorously to the ones in front. The sight of the officer would immediately allay the fears of the Chinamen in the rear and lead

them to look around to see whether there was really any fire. In a few moments the entire audience would be reseated and the play would be continued in its shrieking way. The men who had rushed out in the beginning of the excitement would return and among them would be the "check grubbers" who had caused all the excitement to secure free seats.

On the evening of October 30, 1876, the Jackson Street Royal Theater was playing a benefit, and the house was full. The capacity of the place is not known, but accounts state that nearly two thousand Chinese were enjoying the performance. When someone noticed a seating box near the stage smoldering, the "fire!" cry set off a wild stampede for the exits. The raised gallery was at street level, but the exits from the auditorium below led through tight passageways to even narrower stairways before reaching the gallery above. As the crowds fled the gallery, they were assaulted by hordes, pushing and screaming, up from the stairways below. Where a doorway opened to a short flight of stairs to the street, those from below collided with those fleeing the gallery in a crowded, clawing mass of humanity. When the large door was accidentally closed, the mob pushed it from its hinges, down upon the crowd on the other side. As the exodus continued, the door and the hapless Chinese underneath it were trampled.

POLICE CAPTAIN WILLIAM DOUGLASS.
Secrest Collection

Amazingly, the players on the stage were unaware of these ghastly events and went on with the performance. The San Francisco *Alta* reported:

> The police, under Captain Douglass, were speedily on the ground and took measures to control the affrighted Chinese, and to receive the dead and wounded. Twenty-eight bodies were carried out from the doorway. Of these nineteen were dead, seven were seriously bruised and dreadfully wounded, two of them probably fatally. One Chinaman's leg was broken. One of the badly injured was a little boy. Several of the wounded were taken to Chinese houses in the vicinity.
>
> The scene in front of the theater was ghastly, as the dead and dying lay on the street and sidewalks, the dying, groaning and struggling, and a stream of chattering and appalled Chinamen poured out, hopping over bodies.

On the sidewalk, a hoodlum asked if any white men had been killed. When he was assured that only Chinese had died, he replied, motioning with his foot toward the many bodies, "Good, it don't matter about these."

The dead were all laid out at the coroner's office on Sacramento Street. A huge crowd of curious whites attempted to view the bodies and, finally, it was announced that only Chinese would be admitted to identify the nineteen victims. The verdict of the coroner's jury was that the theater deaths were accidental, but it was recommended that the grand jury look into "the construction of said theater as regards its means of egress."

The bodies were placed in express wagons and taken to various homes, while others were prepared for shipment back to China. As Chinatown mourned, the rest of San Francisco fast lost interest in the tragedy and went back to work.

1879

STOCKTON STEAM EXPLOSION

Where: Stockton
Details: At least 15 dead, many injured

A large crowd gathered at the El Dorado Street bridge, crossing over the Stockton Channel, on the cold winter day of February 22, 1879. It was just after two in the afternoon, and various large steam riverboats were tied up at the warehouses that lined the south bank of the waterway. The crowd milled about along Channel Street and along the west side railing of the bridge, waiting to see the demonstration of a new vertical water pump. Many of the people had practical reasons for witnessing the event, while others were merely curious about the new invention. Others had stopped to see why the crowd had collected. Several hundred had gathered in a short time and now watched as Emory F. Avery, the inventor, placed the pump in the water with the help of several other men.

It is not clear just how large the pump was, but apparently several men could handle it adequately. There was a chute coming off the top of the pump to illustrate the volume of water it could generate. The engine, driven by a steam boiler, was placed a short distance away and connected to the pump with a belt. It was ordinarily utilized

THE EXPLOSION OCCURRED FURTHER ALONG THIS WHARF, AT THE EL DORADO STREET BRIDGE. *Secrest Collection.*

to operate a threshing machine and weighed nearly three thousand pounds. The steam boiler utilized chunks of wood for fuel. R. A. Meyers, a local engineer who had worked frequently with Avery in the past, now aided him as the boiler was stoked with wood and the gauge scrutinized for pressure. Meyers later recalled:

A PORTABLE STEAM ENGINE SUCH AS THIS WAS RESPONSIBLE FOR THE TERRIBLE EXPLOSION. *Secrest Collection*

> The blow-off [valve] began leaking very suddenly, and the water gauge burst; told Avery he had more steam than he thought that the gauge did not indicate, and told him to jar it and see if it moved. He got up and pounded on it; it indicated 25 or 30 pounds, I could not say which, and after striking it raised five pounds. After that it never moved. He had been with me so much I thought he understood his business and was deceived by the gauge. I think he was so confused by the many demands made on him that he did not consider how much steam should be generated by the fires he had on. I walked off a short distance and turning, saw him screwing down the valve. It is my impression he thought there was not sufficient steam to run his engine, being deceived by the gauge. I assisted in moving the engine and stepped back a few feet.

Avery seemed confused and he now screwed down the safety valve, thinking the boiler was not generating enough steam. He was watching the pressure gauge when a flash of light and a deafening explosion shattered the immediate area. In that split second, pieces of the steam engine, bodies and body parts were flung through the air in a wide circle. A ten-pound chunk of metal struck the wall of the nearby *Stockton Independent*'s office, and a reporter was quickly on the scene to report the instantaneous demise of fifteen people:

> In an instant the street was strewn with horribly mutilated corpses and with wounded and crippled victims of the terrible disaster. The sight was enough to appall the stoutest heart. Of the

fifteen bodies, all but one or two were unrecognizable by their most intimate friends, and were only identified by their clothing or by papers found upon their mangled remains. Some had portions of their heads blown off and their brains scattered in all directions; some were disemboweled; others had their limbs torn off; and while blood, fragments of flesh, torn and gory clothing, and the inanimate bodies of men, that but a minute before were full of life and vigor, lay thick around within a narrow space.

Many were moaning as others struggled to their feet or attempted to sit up. Those who could walk went off to seek medical attention. Edwin Severy, struggling out from under several dead bodies, was amazed to find he was unhurt. W. H. Van Vlear, a local gunsmith and partner of Avery, was close by the machine when it exploded, but only suffered a scald on his leg. Avery himself was blown across Canal Street, his corpse mutilated horribly. George Norton, another of Avery's partners, had a serious head wound, his face scalded, a thigh broken and other injuries, but declined any aid until the more seriously injured were attended. Young West Mahoney was scalded and his face pitted with sand and gravel. Since some of the wounded wandered off, the number of injured was uncertain. Newspaper accounts reported they numbered between twenty-five and forty.

THE WEBER FIRE COMPANY STATION WHERE PART OF THE STEAM ENGINE LANDED. *Haggin Museum*

There were many close calls in the area. A young boy riding along El Dorado Street had his velocipede blown out from under him, though he was unhurt. A bank employee named Dean, standing near the engine with his little girl, was slightly injured when struck by a corpse, but his child sustained only a minor injury. A piece of debris came to within three inches of striking a baby in a buggy, causing the mother to faint.

A printer named Jim Balthis was sitting near and directly in front of the engine when it exploded. The boiler was blown directly over his head, landing several blocks away, in front of the Weber Fire Company's engine house. Another, more grisly discovery was two teeth to which a portion of the gum was attached.

The explosion was heard over much of the city, and people gathered quickly to see what had happened, while the coroner began removing the bodies. Mrs. Avery had to identify her husband's mutilated body by his clothes and a mark on his back. A coroner's jury soon began hearing testimony from engineers and various witnesses, while the *Independent* sold out three editions devoted to the horrendous tragedy. Meanwhile, funerals and burials of the victims began taking place, and Stockton's businesses, banks and schools shut down in mourning.

As thousands of people from the surrounding towns and countryside began visiting the site of the tragedy, the coroner's jury finished its review of the incident. A number of engineers agreed that the cause of the explosion was a faulty gauge, and when it malfunctioned, Avery should have shut down the boiler. Meyers, the engineer, suggested in his testimony that Avery was not experienced enough to have been in charge of the demonstration. Perhaps in deference to Avery's widow, the jury's verdict simply put the blame on a faulty gauge, rather than the deceased operator. And why not? After all, no verdict could bring back those fifteen or so mangled bodies.

A DIRE CALAMITY.

Terrific Explosion of a Steam Boiler in Stockton.

Eighteen Killed ---- Twenty - Three Badly Wounded.

CRIMINAL CARELESSNESS THE CAUSE.

List of the Dead and the Suffering-- A City in Mourning.

[SPECIAL DISPATCHES TO THE MORNING CALL.]

STOCKTON, February 22.—One of the most terrific explosions in the history of California occurred at half-past two o'clock to-day, at the head of Stockton Slough, on El Dorado street, in a crowd of more than two hundred people, assembled to witness the trial of a new propelling pump, recently patented by Norton Avery and Van Vlear, of this city.

THE CATASTROPHE.

The pump was set in the slough, and run by a threshing machine engine, the spectators stand-

SAN FRANCISCO *MORNING CALL*, FEBRUARY 23, 1879.
Secrest Collection

148

1879

RAILROAD TUNNEL EXPLOSION

Where: Mountains west of San Jose
Details: Nearly forty Chinese dead or injured

In 1876, the South Pacific Coast Railroad began building south down the eastern San Francisco Bay area toward San Jose. From there it headed west, laying down track to open up the Santa Cruz Mountains and coastal cities to an ever-increasing tourist trade. The cost of building tunnels through this steep, pine-forested range was the highest in California at the time—$110,500 per mile—but company president Alfred E. Davis was equal to the task. By purchasing huge tracts of land, and constructing a succession of buildings, roundhouses and depots, Davis often moved along ahead of his surveyors. Gangs of Chinese laborers, many of them imported earlier to build the transcontinental railroad, did much of the grading and excavation.

By early February 1879, the Chinese workers had completed one of six tunnels for the route, and had bored and blasted some 2,300 feet into solid rock to create Tunnel Number 2. Progress was in inches and feet, but the crews kept up their relentless pace. Tracks were laid into the tunnel so that the rock could be easily removed in small cars. At one point, a seam in the rock was opened by a blast in the tunnel, and the fumes of coal oil became apparent. A ten-ton air pump was installed to minimize the chance of an explosion, and foremen used lighted candles on poles to clear fumes during shift changes. Generally, it worked, but it was a risky method—as events would later prove.

On the night of February 12, a larger than usual quantity of gas accumulated during the crew change, and the usual clearing process turned deadly. The San Francisco *Alta* reported:

WHILE THE SANTA CRUZ MOUNTAINS WERE BEING CONQUERED BY THE SPCRR, STAGECOACHES PICKED UP PASSENGERS FOR SANTA CRUZ AT THE END OF TRACK. San Jose Mercury, November 10, 1879

149

The most terrible explosion followed. The report was heard for miles, and a volume of flame shot through the tunnel and from its mouth to the height of 200 feet in the air. The blacksmith shop, distant about seventy-yards from the mouth of the tunnel, was blown to pieces. A few minutes after the explosion, Hyland [sic], the foreman, groped out of the death hole, and was soon after followed by three or four of the Chinamen, all of them hairless and horribly burned about the heads, necks and hands.

A CHINESE CARRIES TEA TO WORKERS IN A RAILROAD TUNNEL
California State Library

While the crew members had survived, all were terribly seared, several having their eyes burned out. Foreman M. C. Highland, when told by the doctor his hair was all gone, replied: "Well doctor, that will save me having to pay the barber twenty-five cents for shearing for some time." Highland died later, and it was thought only two of the crew would survive their burns.

Despite this tragic setback, the gangs of workers finished the Number 2 tunnel and were soon working on the longest tunnel, Number 3, at Wright's Station. By fall significant progress had been made and, by late November, only some 700 feet remained to complete the tunnel. Unfortunately, the coal oil problem persisted, despite the continued use of air pumps.

On the night of November 18, 1879, a particularly large charge of powder had been detonated in the tunnel at 11:30 P.M. The *San Jose Daily Mercury* recounted what happened next:

> The explosion of the powder seems to have liberated a large quantity of petroleum gas, for it was almost immediately followed by a blaze and an explosion which aroused the whole camp at the mouth of the tunnel, and all the people residing in the vicinity. The Chinamen outside were greatly alarmed for their comrades, and rushed in with their naked torches. Before they had proceeded far they were met by Perry Hinkle, the superintendent, and Thomas Johnson, the car-driver. [Soon] another and still more terrific explosion took place, shaking the ground as by an earthquake, and hurling everything in its path to destruction.

The explosions hurled bystanders and workers into the air, with falling timbers causing a number of injuries. A locomotive engine house, various sheds, the blacksmith shop, and two engines used to pump air into the oil-polluted cavern were blown to pieces. Debris was scattered in a hundred-foot radius around the tunnel's mouth.

The terrible news was telegraphed to San Jose early that morning, and a physician and others were soon on their way. In the meantime, Chinese workers again entered the tunnel and dragged out seventeen of their battered and burned co-workers. It was a scene out of hell. Blackened flesh was peeled from horribly burned bodies. One Chinese had bones protruding from a mangled leg, while another had a foot blown off. Even those with less severe injuries had lungs seared with the deadly gases of the explosions and were in terrible pain.

The wounded were placed in their cabins, located at Wright's Station, until a doctor could arrive—but there would be little anyone could do for many of them. It was reported later that one of the victims was in so much pain that he had hanged himself in his room. Indications were, however, that he had been strangled by his friends to alleviate his misery. By the next day four others of this group had died, while a Chinese hospital in San Francisco took in nine of the victims. According to the *San Francisco Post*, little was done for them:

> Some of them are covered with a dirty, dark brown ointment, which has been spread all over their flame-scorched heads, and which would seem to contain opium in some form, although the cigar manufacturer next door says that it does not. It is evident that the poor creatures are under the influence of some blessed pain allayer, for they lie there motionless and evincing no signs of the terrible agony which they must experience. The hospital is a

THE VILLAGE OF WRIGHT'S STATION, ESTABLISHED AT THE ENTRANCE TO TUNNEL NUMBER 3 OF BITTER MEMORY. THE TUNNEL ENTRANCE CAN BE SEEN BEYOND THE DEPOT AT LEFT CENTER. *Los Gatos Museum*

one story wooden store near Pacific street, on Dupont, destitute even of a washstand, a bedstead or pure air. The unfortunate parboiled heathens lie on sacks or thin mattresses, with no fresh linen or comfort of any kind to alleviate their misery.

Meanwhile, fourteen burned and mangled bodies had been retrieved some 2,000 feet inside the tunnel. There were twenty-seven dead by this time, and several more died later. "There ought to be some stringent restrictions against such careless men," noted the *Mercury*, " but it seems there are not, and con-tractors are not likely to to make them."

A LOCOMOTIVE ENGINE STANDS OUTSIDE THE ENTRANCE TO LETHAL TUNNEL NUMBER 3. *Los Gatos Museum*

Yet they did. When work resumed in December, larger blowers were put into service, safety fuses were used to detonate the gas, and electric lights replaced far less safe kerosene lamps. Still, several other explosions occurred, which caused sixty Chinese to quit and be replaced by Cornishmen from the nearby New Almaden quicksilver mines.

The South Pacific Coast Railroad reached Felton the following year, and a vacation and tourist playground was opened up. Soon forgotten were the laborers who paid with their lives to make it all possible. In Washington, congressional committees worked on anti-Chinese legislation in a country that had decided Asian immigrants took too many jobs away from white citizens.

1879

THE GREAT BODIE EXPLOSION

Where: Bodie, Mono County
Details: Seven dead, nearly twenty injured

Bodie was one of the largest and richest of the California mining camps. Prospector William S. Bodey staked the first claim there in 1859, and the camp was named for him. By late 1862, however, the growing town's name was being spelled "Bodie." Located high on the eastern slope of the Sierra Nevada, the first miners found that placer gold mining was not possible because of a lack of water, but quartz mining by tunneling and shafts showed some promise. Hot and windswept in summer, the barren, sagebrush-covered hills in the area were blanketed in as much as ten feet of snow in winter. Despite these weather extremes, the camp grew steadily in the 1860s, and by the late 1870s there were between 10,000 and 12,000 inhabitants in a town known as one of the wildest in the West. It overflowed with saloons, while a constant stream of promoters and engineers arrived on the twice-daily stagecoaches. During the producing years, the mines at Bodie were said to have generated between ninety-five and 100 million dollars.

In 1879, between five and six hundred miners were toiling on Bodie Butte, looming above the town, and the mines on surrounding

BODIE STREET SCENE DURING THE TOWN'S DECLINING YEARS.
California State Library

hills. The Red Cloud, Mono Syndicate, Summit, and the Bodie were all big producers. The biggest of them all was the Standard. Located originally in 1861 as the Bunker Hill Mine, the operation had many owners, and ups and downs, before it came into its own in the late 1870s. Incorporated in April 1877 with a total capitalization of five million dollars, the Standard built a large mill on the outskirts of town. A tramway carried ore from the mine to the mill, where it was processed.

On the evening of July 10, 1879, the town received a startling shock, as reported in the July 12 San Francisco *Chronicle*:

> At about half past 7 o'clock this evening the town was thrown into the wildest excitement by a deafening explosion in the direction of the Standard mine. The concussion was fearful, shaking the whole town like a severe earthquake, breaking windows, throwing doors open, etc. The streets were soon filled with terror-stricken people inquiring for the cause, when an immense column of smoke hundreds of feet in height was seen rising on the hill followed by a general alarm of fire from the whistles of the different hoisting works. This was taken up by our fire department, and a rush was made for the hill by people on foot, on horseback and in

The Standard Mine where the explosion occurred.

BODIE

154

wagons. The shock was distinctly felt at Bridgeport, 25 miles distant, and citizens at that place telegraphed over for the cause.

The explosion, the shower of rocks and debris on the town, and the giant plume of billowing smoke said it all. Two tons of giant and black powder had exploded next to the Standard Mine, where it had been stored in a magazine dug into the hill. It happened right after William O'Brien and Charles Malloy, the Standard's foreman and a miner, had gone off to retrieve powder from the cache. Friends and family members of miners now raced to the scene, hoping loved ones were not among the casualties. By the time they reached the site, word of the disaster was spreading.

Most of the miners' shacks and boarding houses in the vicinity were now scattered all over the mountain. A Mrs. Allen, who ran a nearby boarding house, was dug unhurt from the rubble of her home. The men underground were startled at the explosion and vibration, but no one was injured. Although there was a great deal of property damage, the mines themselves were hardly interrupted in their operation. There were those who thought the most serious damage was done to the Central Saloon, near the McClinton Mine, where every bottle in the place was broken.

Wagons hauled the bodies down to the Miners' Union Hall, where the dead were laid out and the injured were treated. Merchants in town generously donated supplies to anyone in need. A coroner's jury on July 12 could not establish the cause of the explosion, but noted that O'Brien and Malloy were missing and presumed dead. In closing, the jury proceeded to close the gate after the cow had escaped:

> In view of the recent sad calamity, we would recommend for the future protection of life and property, that all powder magazines be removed at least a mile from town.

A total of seven were dead, several injured dying later. Some twenty, perhaps more, had been injured. Considering the circumstances, the town was fortunate more damage and deaths did not occur.

1879
BALLOON ASCENSION TRAGEDY

Where: San Francisco
Details: Two men killed in accident

Excursions by balloon became commonplace in California soon after statehood was achieved, as a way of entertaining thousands of bored and lonely miners living many miles away from their homes. Large, pear-shaped containers of silk or cotton, inflated with gas or smoke for buoyancy, they were the only means of flight during the nineteenth century and sure to attract a crowd wherever they were seen. A net covered the balloon, slipping over the top, with a rattan basket attached at the bottom for passengers or cargo. A valve above the basket controlled the gas and smoke, and was closed to initiate descent.

By the 1870s, balloon-ing became even more practical with the advent of Woodward's Gardens in San Francisco. The private home of speculator Robert B. Woodward, it was an oasis of trees, parks and ponds on Mission Street. It featured exotic animals, races, circus acts, skating, plays and, beginning in 1873, as-cencions into the sky. Woodward contracted with noted Rhode Island balloon-ist "Professor" James Allen, who used a steam winch to

A BALLOON ASCENSION IN THE DAYS WHEN WOODWARD'S GARDENS WAS THE ENTERTAINMENT CENTER OF CALIFORNIA DURING THE LIVELY 1870S. *California State Library*

take up and return his balloon from a 900-foot altitude above the city. The sensational rides fast became popular attractions, and attracted ever-increasing crowds to Woodward's playground.

Another balloonist, named S. W. Colgrove, embarked from the Gardens on July 4, 1879, with a young woman named Allison. The balloon climbed rapidly into the upper atmosphere, but a sudden gas leak caused the balloon to plummet an estimated 5,000 feet to San Francisco Bay. Brisk winds skimmed the gas bag and its terrified passengers over the water of the bay, with Colgrove and Miss Allison hanging on for dear life. The balloon finally grounded itself on a piling in the bay's mud flats. The exhausted and lucky couple made their way safely to shore.

The adventure should have been a wake-up call for Colgrove. Apparently, however, it only made him eager to try again. By the fall, Colgrove had acquired another large balloon, which he named the *General Grant*. He scheduled another free flight from Woodward's Gardens on October 5, and the usual large crowd gathered in the pavilion on that date. When a reporter scheduled to accompany Colgrove on the flight acquired a bad case of cold feet, he was replaced by a young Wells Fargo employee. An hour prior to the flight, however, the Wells Fargo man backed out also and Colgrove frantically began searching for yet another replacement. When he complained to the Garden's manager, Charles H. Williams, the good-natured Williams agreed to go along.

A stiff breeze had been blowing all day, and as the 3:45 launch time arrived, Williams and Colgrove were watching a man named Abbott who was filling the balloon with gas. When Williams told Abbott he was going up, the manager was kidded about his heavy weight.

"You had better leave your 'paunch' behind," cautioned Abbott as Williams smiled good-naturedly.

"It all goes with me," responded the manager as he and Colgrove climbed into the wicker basket of the giant balloon.

The San Francisco *Chronicle* reported:

> Just before the start Williams shook hands with the reporter and said with a smile: "I suppose you will have an extra column in the *Chronicle* tomorrow on my account." As the balloon arose it sagged heavily towards the monkey sheds, but rose just in time to escape them and swept slantingly towards the northeast, barely missing the smaller of the two windmills on the eastern sheds. On passing the sheds the air-ship was lost to sight.

From the top of the pavilion Charles Eastwood witnessed the balloon's movements, and later described them to a reporter:

> He says that the balloon seemed not to be properly ballasted, and went up and down, diving something after the manner of an ill-balanced kite. This caused it to catch in the telegraph wires, which it tore down, and in the collision the basket was partially overturned. As soon as it was freed from the wires the balloon shot up into the air.

J. Farrell, walking down Howard Street near Fourteenth, saw the rest of the tragedy unfold, and related his story to the San Francisco *Evening Bulletin*:

> He saw the balloon sweep across, and thought it was going to collide with a house. However the balloon rising a little, and swerving to one side, took off the chimneys. The balloon must have torn through the telegraph wires in an instant, as he says he did not know it had struck them till he came under the spot and found the wires broken. The balloon kept rising a little, until when over Folsom street Mr. Farrell estimated that it was between 125 and 150 feet from the ground. Then the car seemed to be connected with the balloon by three or four ropes, all on one side, so that the car hung in a vertical position. Crouching in the bottom he saw the larger man (Williams). Colgrove was up on top of the car with his arms around the ropes. When just over Folsom street Williams shot out from the car and fell on his head and hands. Colgrove a few seconds after came down feet first.

The crowds at Woodward's saw something was wrong, and burst through the tunnels and pathways to get out to Mission Street. Others had already reached the scene of the disaster. A woman physician, practicing in the neighborhood, Dr. M. P. Sawtelle, later recalled the scene:

> I was among the first on the spot. When I reached there Mr. Colgrove was still sensible, and asked to have his head raised. It was proposed to carry him on a wagon, but at my suggestion he was carried on a mattress by twelve men to his room on First avenue. When placed on his own bed he was wholly unconscious and breathed his last in half an hour. His left arm was crushed above the elbow, and the right dislocated at the wrist. The skull was evidently crushed.

Huge crowds gathered quickly to view the terrible scene, and four policemen had to hold back the mob. Williams had been killed on impact, and his body was removed to the undertaker's about five P.M. Both men were young men, Colgrove only twenty-eight and Williams thirty-six, and very popular. A well-attended benefit was held at Woodward's Gardens on October 19 for the families of the dead men. An editorial in the *Chronicle* denounced all balloon exhibitions as "deriving their sole interest from their danger:"

> Regarded from this point of view they are as demoralizing as the old Roman gladiatorial contests or modern Spanish bull fights, and we trust that public sentiment, enlightened and vivified by the recent fearful tragedy, will sternly refuse to countenance them in the future.

THE COLGROVE-WILLIAMS TRAGEDY ACCORDING TO *THE WASP. California State Library*

If the *Chronicle's* comparison was apt, its hopes for an end to ballooning in the country was not. Its popularity continues, even in today's era of manned flight—though more reliable equipment and better regulations have lessened the danger factors significantly .

1880

Santa Cruz Excursion Train Disaster

Where: Santa Cruz mountains
Details: Ten or more dead with thirty injured

Its origins steeped in a series of 1879 construction tragedies (see earlier vignette), the narrow-gauge South Pacific Coast Railroad continued a run of bad luck in the following year, when it finally reached Santa Cruz and began attracting a continuing stream of vacationers from the San Francisco Bay area.

On Sunday, May 23, 1880, the new railroad brought a fourteen-car excursion train over the mountains. A collection of various Bay Area social groups, including the San Francisco Bohemian Club, the Alameda Harmonie Verein and the Independent Rifles, had commissioned a locomotive and three flatcars to carry 150 people to the Felton Grove of Big Trees, a scenic and popular mountain spot. The flatcars were fitted with chairs and a four-foot guard railing, and the early morning open-car ride had been a beautiful trip. Families and couples wandered through the giant redwoods, collected wild flowers, fished, or just enjoyed the natural setting. The weather was ideal.

Duncan McPherson, editor of the *Sentinel*, was part of an excursion which had left Santa Cruz by train to explore the grove on this splendid day. The train from the north was on a siding, and its passengers now mingled with those of the Santa Cruz locomotive's group. It was one of those afternoons that everyone hated to see end.

At 3:25 P.M. Bob Elliott, the Bay Area train's engineer, blew his whistle to signal boarding the cars for the return trip to Santa Cruz. His smaller locomotive had pushed the three flatcars to the grove, but he had to back up on the return trip,

LINES OF TRAVEL.

South Pacific Coast Railroad
(NARROW GAUGE.)

——COMMENCING——

Saturday, May 15, '80.

TRAINS WILL LEAVE

SANTA CRUZ (DAILY)

FOR BIG TREES, FELTON, GLEN wood, Wright's, Alma, Los Gatos, Lovelady's,

San Jose,

Santa Clara, Agnew's, Alviso, Mowry's, Newark, Hall's, Alvarado, Mount Eden, Russell's, West San Lorenzo, West San Leandro and Park street, and Pacific avenue (ALAMEDA),

Oakland and San Francisco.

From SANTA CRUZ BEACH at 4:46 and 6:37 A. M. and 12:55 P. M.

ARRIVING IN SAN FRANCISCO at 9:57 and 9:50 A. M. and 6:35 P. M.

A Local Train for Felton will leave Beach at 8:59 A. M. and South End of Tunnel at 9:00 A. M., daily; RETURN-ING, leaving Felton at 8:30 P. M.

A Mixed Train will leave the Beach at 12:55 P. M. and South End of Tunnel at 12:50 P. M., daily, arriving at Felton and Glenwood before the regular after-noon train. THOS. CARTER, Superintendent.

GEO. H. WAGGONER, Gen'l Passenger Agent.

WITH THE RAILROAD NOW A REALITY, THE *SENTINEL* PUBLISHED SCHEDULE REGULARLY. *Secrest Collection*

160

since there was no place to turn the train around. The flatcars would be pulled rather than pushed.

Elliott made a quick check of his engine and, when the conductor signaled all were aboard, he pulled the whistle and began slowly chugging backwards. Howard Antrim, a civil engineer for the railroad, had also joined Elliott and his fireman in the cab. This was Elliott's first trip on the line. Antrim was, however, very familiar with the new road and was along as an advisor. The train began a three-mile ascent to the summit of the forested ridge, from which Santa Cruz would be the next stop.

After reaching the summit, the backing train began a downhill grade, carrying it through a tunnel as the coasting locomotive began picking up speed. Elliott noticed he was going too fast, and signaled for the flatcar conductor to brake. When there was no response he again signaled, then looked behind at the flatcars. The train jerked into a curve and began swaying too much. Suddenly there was a bump, then a series of bumps, as several of the cars jumped the tracks. Elliott was braking now, but he knew it was too late. As the locomotive screeched to a halt, the engineer and his crew jumped to the ground and ran back to the cars.

The passengers were scattered along and on the tracks, amid the overturned wreckage of the flatcars. People had been flung from the cars when the guard rails had given way, and now groans and screams were adding more horror to the scene. Elliott and those with him rushed among the carnage, but there was little they could do.

Ordering the fireman to stay and help the injured, Elliott and Antrim uncoupled the engine and resumed backing the two miles into Santa Cruz. There they obtained medical supplies, physicians, and others to help. Returning to the scene, they found that ten people were dead and five more apparently dying. Some thirty or more were injured. All were taken to Santa Cruz where the Ocean House, the Germania Hotel, Wilkins House, and some private residences were utilized as hospitals. The less seriously injured were weeded out and put on trains back to San Jose and the Bay Area. The railroad paid any and all costs incurred by the accident.

ALTHOUGH INACCURATE IN DETAILS, THIS OLD DRAWING GIVES SOME SENSE OF THE TERRIBLE DEATH TOLL OF THIS HORRIBLE TRAIN ACCIDENT. *California State Library*

A coroner's jury was empaneled immediately to learn why the tragedy occurred. Apparently, the first flatcar had remained on the tracks and the passengers were unhurt. Santa Cruz County Sheriff Elmer Dakan had been a passenger on this car, and testified:

> I was on the rear car. As we were passing through the tunnel, the car seemed to lurch and go forward faster than before. Just before we came to where the track crosses the county road, I heard the whistle. I saw no one holding the brakes, or attempting to reach them. The ties slipped toward the river and away from the bank. Just as we emerged from the tunnel the train lurched forward and came down very rapidly. The speed seemed to be as great as that of the passenger trains anywhere between here and San Francisco. I think that the cars ran off the track toward the river and then the passengers rushed to the bank side of the cars which had the effect to tip up the cars. The racks (rails) struck the bank and were broken. Those who were clinging on the racks were jammed against the bank and dragged to the ground. If the company had put on passenger cars I do not think they would ever have jumped the track.

DUNCAN MCPHERSON, EDITOR OF THE *SENTINEL*, WAS ABOARD THE TRAGIC TRAIN. *California State Library*

Other testimony was in much the same vein. A week of investigation determined that the primary reasons for the wreck were faulty couplers on the cars, no brakes on the flatcars, inexperienced trainmen, and "unforeseen causes." Had they lived, the fifteen dead and several dozen injured probably would have added little to these conclusions. The disaster had just happened too fast.

1883

Tehachapi *RUNAWAY* Train

Where: Mountains near Bakersfield
Details: Over twenty killed and injured

Tehachapi

Southern Pacific train Number 19 left San Francisco on the morning of January 19, 1883, on the regular San Joaquin Valley route to Los Angeles. The valley was mostly a cold and barren prairie this time of year. All that broke the trip's monotony were stops at small, false-fronted frontier towns and occasional cattle-loading chutes. Making an eastern turn at Bakersfield, the train paused briefly at Sumner, then moved on to Caliente where a second engine, or "helper," was coupled behind the main locomotive. With this added power, the train began a steady climb through the Tehachapi Mountains.

The rail line had only been completed to Los Angeles since 1876. This particular stretch of the Tehachapis was unique because of the manner by which the steep grade had been overcome. Since a railroad grade of only 116 feet to one mile was allowed by the government, a series of loops and seventeen tunnels was designed to carry trains through to the summit at Greenwich Station, by then called Tehachapi. The tunnels' contours were such that, at one point, a long train could actually pass over or under itself. Number 19 reached

AN 1882 VIEW OF THE SOUTHERN PACIFIC ROUNDHOUSE AT SUMNER WHERE NO. 19 PASSED THROUGH ON THE WAY TO THE TEHACHAPI STATION. *Secrest Collection*

Tehachapi at just after 2 A.M. and pulled up at the depot. It was a dark, bitter cold night, with a vicious wind blowing. While there, the main engine was uncoupled and sidetracked to the round-table so the helper engine could be detached from the mail car and returned to Caliente. It was a simple routine, hitherto utilized without mishap by every train passing through these mountains.

Meanwhile, the train's rear brakeman, John Patton, escorted a female passenger from the train over to the depot. When Patton returned to the cars, he discovered his train was missing. In the dark, with high winds blowing, he likely failed to hear the train as it

Engine and tender not on runaway train

Sleeper cars

These last two cars were saved

These 5 cars were the ones wrecked and burned

picked up speed and rolled backwards down the grade minus an engine. The brakes had apparently not been set properly—or been set at all! Suddenly, he realized what had happened, and rushed back to the depot to telegraph for instructions.

There were seven cars on the engineless train as it gained speed going backwards down the increasing grade. A day coach filled with Chinese and others who could not, or would not, pay for a sleeping car was in front. This was followed by the smoking car, two sleeper cars, an express car, a baggage car, and the mail car.

Passenger George McKenzie had been talking with conductor Reid on the front platform of the "smoker" when the train pulled into Tehachapi. When Reid left to report to the depot, McKenzie

noticed the car started moving. Having some railroad experience, he quickly realized what was happening:

> My first impulse was to put on the brakes. The brake of the platform on which I was standing I could not make work, I then stepped over to the platform of the sleeping car. I found that brake, too, was out of order, yet by exerting myself, I got it partly set up.

164

Then I immediately started to go through the sleeping car to get at the other brakes, but to my horror and dismay I found the door to the sleeper locked. I then rushed for the other end of the train and got to the brake of the rear platform of the smoking car, which I got to work with good effect. I then went back to the same place I was at when the train first started, where I tried the same brake with no better results. At that moment the sleeping car was uncoupled from the smoking car at the platform where I was standing.

The five coaches behind McKenzie's car were going too fast for a curve and had flipped off the tracks, crashing into a ravine to become a tangled mass of iron and splintered wood. McKenzie managed to get his two cars under control by hitting the brakes, but looking behind, he saw the glow of flames and knew the five derailed coaches were on fire. Howard Tilton, a passenger in the sleeper, awakened just before his car and the four others plunged into the ravine. He later recalled:

> I was hurled from my berth. I was sleeping on the left side of the car, which fell upon the right side, and I was covered to my waist with mattresses, woodwork and debris, but found no difficulty in freeing myself. Smoke passed through the car giving timely token of impending peril. I saw Mr. and Mrs. Porter Ashe. Miss Peterson, the maid, was buried under about six feet of debris. We soon succeeded in pulling her out.

The honeymooning Ashes, their maid and Tilton squeezed through a window after securing some blankets. All were dressed in their underclothes and were shivering, despite wearing blankets.

THE WRECK AS DEPICTED IN *FRANK LESLIE'S ILLUSTRATED MAGAZINE*, FEBRUARY 3, 1883. *Secrest Collection*

165

Several others were seen crawling from the cars as Tilton and another man managed to pull a badly hurt passenger from under the wreck. A minute later, the wreckage burst into flame from the stove and coal oil lamps. An obese woman named Squires was unable to get through the windows and could not be helped. Her screams were terrible to hear as she was engulfed in the flames.

McKenzie and others from Tehachapi began helping the survivors, who were suffering greatly in the cold. Ex-governor John Downey was among the injured, and lost his wife in the disaster. Twenty-one persons were thought to have died in the wreck. but some thought the toll was higher. People had gotten on and off the train throughout the valley, so no accurate accounting could be made. By 9 A.M. a wrecking crew arrived from Tulare, including the district superintendent W. W. Prugh and other railroad employees.

According to the January 27 *Kern County Californian*:

> He immediately assumed charge of everything directing his measures in such a way as to shield the company from blame as far as possible, and monopolizing, or acquiring control of the telegraphs in order that no statements, unless with the proper coloring, could get abroad.

A coroner's jury assigned blame to carelessness on the part of conductor Reid and brakeman Patton. Both were arrested and placed in jail, but were acquitted in late March 1883. Downey wrote a scathing letter to the *Los Angeles Times* condemning railroad policies for the tragedy and, although most agreed with him, little was done. The only agreement among everyone was that the Tehachapi disaster was one of the worst accidents in California railroad history.

1887

THE *PARALLEL* DISASTER

Where: San Francisco coast
Details: Serious injuries and destruction

At 9:30 in the evening of January 15, 1887, residents of San Francisco's western edge were startled to find a schooner run aground close to the world-famous Cliff House. John Hyslop, superintendent of the nearby Point Lobos signal station, went down to view the wreck while others began lowering themselves down the cliffs to reach the accident scene. Adolph Sutro, one of San Francisco's most notable business-men, who resided in the neighborhood, proceeded down the cliff and told Hyslop to report the disabled schooner to a nearby marine rescue station.

Several of Sutro's employees climbed aboard the *Parallel*, which remained in full sails, although her keel was destroyed. When no one was found aboard the ailing schooner, the men returned to the shore. By this time the rescue station men had visited the ship and also found it devoid of the crew, but they picked up a dog found on the vessel. Lacking any stabilization, the schooner now drifted onto the rocks underneath the Cliff House which, incidentally, was one of Sutro's many real estate properties.

Most agreed it was shortly after one o'clock on Sunday, January 16, when a terrible explosion occurred and the *Parallel* was "blown to atoms," as one newspaper expressed it. Two members of the marine station were seriously injured as they stood with their comrades on the cliff, just above the ship. Henry Smith gave a startling account of the incident:

> We were directly over the schooner and could have tossed a pebble on her deck. We were in this position looking down upon her when a blinding sheet of flame sprang from I hardly know where, accompanied by a terrible roar, and I lost all consciousness. When I recovered, which I should judge was about fifteen minutes later, I found myself lying about 200 feet away from where I stood

HUGE CROWDS VISITED THE SCENE OF THE *PARALLEL* EXPLOSION AND VIEWED THE DAMAGE TO THE CLIFF HOUSE AND OTHER HOMES AND STRUCTURES IN THE AREA. *Secrest Collection*

when the explosion occurred, and partly buried with rocks, dirt and splinters.

Amazingly, R. C. Pearson, the lessee of the Cliff House, and his family were in the building at the time of the explosion. He had been tending bar earlier in the evening when the ship was spotted close by. He was just getting into bed when the explosion happened, and later recalled:

> The room seemed to turn around, he was struck heavy blows on the chest and limbs and a stifling odor of plaster filled the air. He was partially stunned and bewildered, but rushed to the window intending to open it and let fresh air in, but his hands encountered only the vacant air; there was no window. Three children in one room were uninjured, although the room was a shambles.

Adolph Sutro reported: "I had been asleep some time when suddenly I woke with a start. I could hear the door rattling loudly and I jumped out of bed. The house seemed to quiver like a living animal for a moment, and then a crash of glass occurred that seemed as though everything in the house had fallen."

ADOLPH SUTRO, THE MILLIONAIRE DEVELOPER AND OWNER OF THE CLIFF HOUSE, WAS ONE OF THE FIRST ON THE SCENE OF THE DISASTER. *Secrest Collection*

Sutro's mansion was severely damaged, with nearly every pane of glass in the building broken.

A quick survey some hours later revealed there no serious injuries other than the two men of the lifesaving crew. It was miraculous that no one died in the disaster.

Even before the morning papers spread word of the calamity, hundreds, and soon thousands, of people began arriving at the scene. "As the hurrying crowds drew near the scene of the fearful explosion," reported the *Alta California*, "the legend 'Bar open,' scrawled in black letters on a piece of board and nailed to the south end of the building occasioned a general smile in more ways than one." Bartender Pearson had quickly, and practically, recovered from his terrifying experience.

Newspaper reporters scouring the San Francisco waterfront soon had the whole story. Peter Hansen and Chris Christensen were located in an East Street saloon surrounded by enthralled listeners. The two *Parallel* shipmates were telling all who would listen of their brush with death. The vessel's minimal crew consisted of Captain W. C. Miller, a mate, cook and four seamen. After leaving port on a routine trip to Oregon, they were blithely told that besides a normal cargo, the ship was stocked with forty-five tons of giant powder, one ton of black powder, one box of caps and fifty boxes of coal oil. A lack of wind had made it difficult to get out of the bay, and this persisted into the Pacific. Despite all the crew's efforts, the *Parallel* began drifting toward shore. The men were afraid to drop anchor because the explosives rested on the ship's bottom. If the craft struck a rock, an explosion might occur.

"Anyhow," related seaman Christensen, "we weren't taking any such chances for thirty dollars a month, and we quickly lowered our small boat, into which all seven of us tumbled, including the

THE EXPLOSION.

Scenes and Incidents in the Cliff House Debris.

Crew of the "Parallel" Land in Safety at Point Bonita.

A Desperate Pull for Life.

Damage Done to the Sutro Mansion and Conservatory.

Miraculous Escapes From Death—Three of the Life-saving Crew Injured—Cargo of the Schooner—A Terribly Wrecked and Shattered Cottage—The Great Crowd Yesterday.

The hour at which the schooner *Parallel* went ashore and blew up, just under the Cliff House, Sunday morning, and the difficulty of reaching that locality afforded but little time for the

HEADLINES IN THE SAN FRANCISCO *ALTA CALIFORNIA*, JANUARY 17, 1887.

captain." Rowing frantically back through the Golden Gate, the men spent the night at a lighthouse, witnessing the explosion from there.

THE RESTORED CLIFF HOUSE AS IT APPEARED IN AN 1893 PHOTOGRAPH. THE SMALLER ROCK, ABOVE RIGHT, IS COV ERED WITH SEALS AND SEA LIONS. *California State Library*

That morning they borrowed money enough to catch the Sausalito ferry for San Francisco.

Although Captain Miller and his crew never had to think twice about abandoning their ship and its dangerous cargo, criticism of their actions soon surfaced. The ship and cargo were insured for $30,000, but so long as no obvious malfeasance had occurred, the claim would probably be paid. "As long as owners of vessels are satisfied with their captains' competency," noted the *Chronicle*, "insurance companies make no objection in covering risks." It seemed the only way to test Captain Miller's case was for the grand jury to indict him for negligence, but this was not likely to happen in a sea-going city like San Francisco. Suggestions were made, however, that the loading of such dangerous materials should be made out in the bay, and not at a city wharf.

If anyone cared, it was never established just how many seals had been killed on the Cliff House rocks by the explosion.

1887

The DEL MONTE HOTEL Fire

Where: Monterey
Details: No deaths, hotel destroyed

The brainchild of Southern Pacific railroad magnate Charles Crocker, Monterey's Hotel Del Monte was one of the most opulent hotels in the country, if not the world. Completed in June 1880, a scant four months after the groundbreaking, the place was set on 126 beautifully-landscaped acres and looked like a hunting lodge used by European royalty. The main structure was four stories high and of Swiss-Gothic design, surrounded by wings and wide verandas. A large lake offered a boat landing, while a clubhouse featured billiard tables, bowling alleys and a bar. At the nearby seaside were heated, glass-roofed pavilions covering salt-water swimming pools heated at different temperatures.

In the first seven years of its existence, the sprawling hostelry hosted some 120,000 guests, 40,000 of whom were from outside the country. Travelers were flocking to the seaside pleasure palace from around the country and across the world.

The day's last trainload of guests arrived from San Francisco on the evening of April 1, 1887. In the billiard room, two young men were still engaged in a pool game at 11:30. A player from Helena,

SITUATED ON MONTEREY BAY AND SURROUNDED BY WALKING PATHS, GARDENS AND BEAUTIFUL FORESTS, THE MAGNIFICENT DEL MONTE HOTEL WAS ONE OF THE SHOWPLACES OF THE WORLD. *Secrest Collection*

Montana had just racked up some points when he stopped to look around. "What's that smell?" remarked his opponent, as he sniffed the air. "It's smoke," replied the Helena man, as both men rushed to the door and threw it open.

A fog of hazy smoke filled the hallway as the two men rushed toward the main office, where fire and smoke were emerging from a lower room. Several sweating and blackened hotel employees were throwing water on the flames, while another struggled to cut a hole in the floor.

"Rouse the house!" shouted the man from Montana.

"No, no," shouted one of the fire-fighters, "you'll create a panic. Keep cool and we'll have it out in no time."

One of the guests, Miss Fanny Crandall, later described the steadily-worsening scene:

> I'd gone to sleep early, and I guess I had slept an hour or more when I was awakened by some one pounding on my door.

> I thought that burglars were trying to get into my room, and I covered up my head and screamed. Then some one outside swore horribly and said the house was burning up. I arose at once and began to dress. Suddenly I saw a flash and a cloud of smoke as I glanced out of the window and that scared me so that I just ran out without putting on another thing. A lot of men laughed at me as I ran down-stairs, and one of them shouted to me to stop. I did stop, and the nasty thing only asked me if I hadn't forgotten to dress myself.

By now the hallways were filling with frightened and shouting people, pushing and shoving each other through the shrouds of smoke. The San Francisco *Examiner* reported graphically on the hysteria that had taken place:

> Women in their snowy night robes, clutching desperately a few valuables in their hands, dashed men in decided deshabille aside and made for the great stairway, only to be lost to view in the clouds of smoke. Naked limbs belonging to members of both sexes could be dimly seen on every side.
>
> Mothers bearing in their arms their little ones, begged for the assistance that few received. Husbands and fathers fought desperately for all they loved on earth. Mad panic reigned supreme.

Manager George Schonewald saw that the fire was rapidly going out of control, and ordered the place flooded. To his dismay, only a trickle came out of the hotel's special water system. "Full force!" shouted the manager, "Full force!"

"It's on full force," shouted an employee.

A hasty examination showed no reason why the system had failed. Sabotage was suspected, but Schonewald quickly grasped that without water fighting the fire was hopeless. "Save the guests," he shouted. "Let everything else go!"

Even before this, however, the hotel's own firefighting company was doing its best to heed Schonewald's order. The *Examiner* reported:

> Ladders had been run up to the broad piazza on which

JUST A FEW HOURS
THE FIRE STARTED,
REAT HOTEL WAS A
ILE OF BLACKENED
RUBBLE, THE TALL
INEYS STANDING AS
MUTE SENTINELS
TO THE TOTAL
DESTRUCTION. *Newspaper sketch from the* Examiner *of April 3, 1887.*

tumbled, stepped and fell frightened men, women and children from every section of the hotel. As rapidly as they appeared they were carried to terra firma and allowed to wander whither they willed. Fifteen minutes after the first alarm was given the grounds presented a curious spectacle.

The flames lit up every foot of space, revealing men, women and children in every conceivable stage of dress and undress. As a general thing the lords of creation were in a condition to appear on Kearny street, but the femininity was most decidedly not.

E. T. M. SIMMONS HAD JU
BEEN DEMOTED FROM
MANAGER AND WAS A PR
SUSPECT IN THE FIRE.
FORTUNATELY, NO ONE W
SERIOUSLY INJURED OR D
Examiner *Special Edition*

As trunks, clothes and mattresses tumbled from the windows, guests could be seen huddled under trees in the glaring light of the huge, devouring fire. Luckily, all the approximately 360 guests and employees were saved from the deadly conflagration.

In a few hours, the mighty edifice was a smoking pile of blackened ruins. Hotel officials promptly offered all the aid needed to their distraught guests. Anything they had lost was replaced, and return tickets to their homes was provided.

Suspicions of arson began when the water system failed. A recently-demoted Del Monte manager named E. T. M. Simmons was promptly isolated as a suspect. He reportedly had a prison record, and was very upset when he was replaced by George Schonewald. Detectives were quickly shadowing the suspect and when enough evidence had been gathered, he was held in the Monterey jail.

The new Del Monte began arising on the ashes of the old, and re-opened in the fall. Charles Crocker stated that there was no insurance on the hotel and the original cost, including furniture, had been $350,000. Others thought a million dollars was closer to the cost.

The Del Monte burned once again in 1924, and was rebuilt a second time. It was later used as a military training facility during World War II, and continued in that role for a half-century.

1888

The *JULIA* Tragedy

Where: Wharf at Vallejo
Details: Sixteen dead, many injured

Built in 1864 by Captain John North for the California Steam Navigation Company's Stockton route, the *Julia* was a small sidewheel steamer of 503 tons. On the evening of September 30, 1866, as the *Julia* headed across San Francisco Bay opposite Alcatraz Island, the engineer advised the pilot that something was wrong with one of the boilers. While the ship was reversing course, the steam drum blew out, killing five passengers and injuring eleven others—some fatally.

Repaired and restored to service, the *Julia* was shunned as being unsafe for a time. The little steamer picked up its trade gradually, and provided many more years service on the bays and rivers, during a period when the California river trade was easing into its twilight years.

As the Southern Pacific Railroad expanded throughout the Golden State's interior, it began acquiring a fleet of river steamers to consolidate control of the state's transportation. By the late 1880s the *Julia* was purchased by the company and began helping facilitate travel between railroad connections. It had also been refitted to burn oil, instead of coal.

On February 27, 1888, the *Julia* eased away from Vallejo's Georgia Street wharf at 6 A.M., commencing its regular run. Captain George Gedge commanded a ten-man crew. These days the little steamer kept busy ferrying laborers across the Carquinez Straits to the lumber yards, grain warehouses, and iron works at Vallejo Junction. It was cold and foggy this particular morning and, ten minutes later, the steamer had docked at South Vallejo to pick up more morning workers. Captain Gedge watched as the gangplank slammed into place, then walked down and greeted the morning passengers gathered at the wharf's gate. The officer was later interviewed by a San Francisco *Daily Alta California* reporter:

> Captain Gedge says that he was on the wharf as usual collecting tickets from the oncoming passengers when the signal for departure was given. He locked the gate from wharf to gangplank, and then walked slowly down aboard the steamer. He heard the bell from the pilot-house sound for the engines to be started, and then heard the first whistle usually blown just before heading out into the stream. He was just about to ascend the stairs to reach the upper deck and go thence to the pilot-house, when the explosion occurred. He says he felt the shock, and then everything seemed darkened. He reached out his hand and turned up his coat-collar, and that is all he recollects. He was found there afterwards, prostrate, covered with debris, but only slightly injured, beyond the severe shock.

The captain had instinctively turned up his coat collar to protect his head and face from the scalding steam of a boiler explosion. Because of the foggy, cold weather, the passengers were all on the lower deck, gathered around the smokestack for warmth. One of the ship's boilers, right under their feet, had blown up and undoubtedly killed most of these men. The steamer had been literally split in half.

Mrs. Ferrier, wife of a gunner stationed at nearby Mare Island, was the only woman on board and fell from the saloon deck to the berth deck below. As she jumped overboard to avoid the fire, she screamed at everyone to cover their faces, and was soon rescued by a nearby boat. Severely burned on her legs and bruised, she did survive.

The captain of a nearby tugboat from Mare Island was another eyewitness to this terrible incident, and described the scene:

THE WHARVES AT VALLEJO, SHOWN HERE AS THEY APPEARED IN 1895, A FEW YEARS AFTER THE JULIA DISASTER.
National Archives

We were moored to our wharf and were to leave for the city at 7 o'clock. I observed the *Julia* which had just entered her pier at South Vallejo after returning from North Vallejo, which trip she makes every morning, bringing laborers over to the Vallejo Junction side and meeting the overland train from Oregon at the junction. It was just ten minutes to 7 o'clock when I noticed a blinding flame shoot up through the smoke-stack, which was followed by an awful explosion, and in another moment the *Julia* was wrapped in flames.

We steamed down to the spot and the sight which met our gaze was frightful. The burning oil was thrown up and out and fell all about the spot. The wharf caught immediately and was soon enveloped in smoke and flame while the steamer burned as rapidly as if it had been tinder. The air was filled with the shrieks of the wounded and dying, and the mad struggles of those who were caught in the boat were heart-rending to behold. The heat was so intense that it was impossible to approach near the scene. One of the unfortunates was caught in one of the wheels and it was only by superhuman efforts that he succeeded in extricating himself from his position, and he dragged himself on the deck and he was lost from our sight in the smoke. The deck was literally strewn with the dead and wounded.

The explosion caused the oil-burning *Julia* to splatter volatile fluid all over the wharf and the railroad sheds which lined it. Several large vats used to refuel the *Julia* now caught fire also. The huge and fast-spreading blaze now threatened to engulf the nearby Starr Flouring Mills, but a Vallejo fire company managed to save it.

Meanwhile, nearby boats had rushed to the scene and rescued anyone found in the water. When the boat exploded and split in half, the roof collapsed and many of the passengers were trapped beneath it as it sunk and burned to the water line. In the midst of this holocaust, relatives and friends had gathered around, calling out names and trying to locate survivors. Some sixteen bodies were recovered. An equal number were missing and thought to be crushed or drowned under the fallen top deck. Most of the eighteen injured were scalded to some extent, and several were not expected to live. Many were hurt by falling timbers or cut by fragments as they flew through the air. There was no passenger list as many bought weekly tickets in advance, but it was thought there were at least forty on board the craft. Many of the ship's crew were also injured severely.

SKETCH OF THE *JULIA* BURNING AT ITS BERTH ON THE SOUTH
VALLEJO WHARF. San Francisco Chronicle, *February 28, 1888*

A coroner's jury was empaneled late that afternoon to determine the blast's cause, while a day of mourning was declared and burials of the dead were scheduled for the following day. When it was discovered that the boilers had just recently been checked, attention was diverted to the new oil tanks. These were exonerated as a cause of the trouble, since divers reported they were still intact. The cost of all the damage was set at $250,000.

The explosion of the *Julia* was the last of California's great paddle-wheel disasters. The decreasing use of steam engines, and the continuing encroachment of the railroads, spelled doom for this long-standing method of transportation—but, at the same time, the disuse of defective and often unsafe boilers ushered in an era of improved safety for the state's waterways.

1889

BAKERSFIELD's Trial by Fire

Where: Bakersfield
Details: Business district of town destroyed

Bakersfield

At noon on the Sunday afternoon of July 1, 1889, someone noticed smoke and flames at the rear of the newly-constructed home of N. E. Kelsey on Bakersfield's Twentieth Street. Soon, clanging fire-bells were heard in the distance. A crowd began attacking the blaze with buckets and small hoses but, for some reason, pressure in the water mains was weak and those congregated were unable to accomplish much. To make matters worse, the steam fire engine experienced similar trouble when it arrived, and could not work adequately until twenty minutes had passed.

Then, as now, Bakersfield was the largest city in the southern end of the great San Joaquin Valley. Crops from large and small farms scattered in the area were shipped out of the city, which was located on one of the Southern Pacific railroad's main routes. Stock

ranches raising horses, cattle and sheep were also plentiful, and likewise helped fuel a bustling local economy. The San Francisco *Chronicle* remarked:

> Bakersfield has probably grown more rapidly in the past six months than any other town in the state. It lies in the center of one of he most productive plains on this coast, where irrigation on dry tracts and drainage in the swamps have converted desert and marsh into a veritable garden stretching away for a hundred miles. It has three newspapers and its estimated population last year was 2,000, which has probably doubled within the year.

> Until recently most of the surrounding land was held in large tracts, but it has now been put upon the market in small tracts and a prodigious increase in population has been the result.

FURNITURE IS STILL PILED IN THE STREET AMID THE RUINS OF THE CITY'S BUSINESS DISTRICT. *Bakersfield Public Library*

Thanks to this new-found wealth, Bakersfield was no longer a rickety, false-fronted frontier town. It boasted a variety of recently erected, beautiful structures of stone and brick, with accompanying bric-a-brac decoration to rival that found in San Francisco. It was a wonderful time as Bakersfield and Kern County were being eased into the Gay Nineties, but the threat of fire could still instill terror into the heartiest soul. As recently as June 29, 1889, the *Kern County Californian* newspaper had published a long, front-page article extolling the importance of fire companies. Just how important they were was about to become evident.

The fire had made rapid strides in those deadly minutes, while all nervously waited for water pressure to build in the hoses. By the time substantial streams were secured, what had been a relatively small fire had been magnified into a blazing inferno. The fire now spread to Kelsey's furniture store, along with the Hayden & White shop, and was closing in on the *Echo* newspaper office—all in the same block as the Kelsey residence on Chester Avenue. Burning shingles were now sailing through the broiling air and igniting nearby buildings. The Union Stable caught fire in this manner, which established a new center for the raging conflagration. The fire was now jumping streets, and the heat was so intense that firefighters were forced to retreat constantly.

When the *Echo* office was reduced to ashes, the firefighters concentrated on saving the new Southern Hotel—"our pet, our pride and our glory," as one firefighter described it. While tenants desperately began trying to save what they could of their belongings, a steady stream of water was concentrated on the building. To seemingly mock this determined effort, a wind blew up and whipped the flames into an even more furious inferno. The hotel was surrendered to the flames as the exhausted firefighters turned their efforts toward saving the Masonic Temple and Arlington House. The *Californian* reported:

WIPED OUT!

Bakersfield in Ashes.

A TERRIBLE CALAMITY.

Every Business House Burned to the Ground.

THE SOUTHERN IN RUINS!

$1,018,300 Worth of Property Goes Up In Smoke.

LIST OF LOSSES

What the Insurance Amounts To.

NO ASSISTANCE NEEDED.

The Town to be Rebuilt Immediately.

REMOVING THE DEBRIS!

KERN COUNTY CALIFORNIAN, JULY 13, 1889. *Secrest Collection*

THE FIRE-RAVAGED RUINS OF BAKERSFIELD LOOKED LIKE A BATTLEFIELD, BUT TEMPORARY BUILDINGS WERE QUICKLY PUT UP AND REBUILDING WAS SOON UNDERWAY. *California State Library*

And still the fire swept on until by 2 o'clock 20th street on the north, the alley beyond L Street on the east, 17th street on the south and the alley beyond Chester Avenue on the west marked the boundaries of a fire which destroyed 15 blocks, including every business house, hotel, restaurant, butcher shop and place of supply in the town. In all about 120 buildings, 40 of them dwellings, were destroyed. It was a clean sweep. A quicker, fiercer fire has seldom been seen, and night went down upon a dreary place.

The *Californian* office had also perished, but by July 13 the newspaper had arisen phoenix-like from the ashes, publishing an issue containing extensive details about the fire. It related a long list of destroyed homes and places of business—over a million dollars' worth of destruction in all. As complete as was the tragedy, the following morning trainloads of supplies came in from surrounding farms and towns, ensuring that no one in town would go hungry. The mayors of Los Angeles and San Francisco sent messages asking how they could help in this hour of need. Local citizen meetings, however, agreed that while they were very grateful for the offers of assistance, Bakersfield could help herself—and the citizens would rebuild the blackened city as speedily as possible.

And they did!

1889

The UTICA Mine Disaster

Where: Angels Camp
Details: Seven or more killed, several injured

Angel's Camp

cisco

Named after the New York home town of one of its owners, the Utica Mine near Angels Camp was a fickle producer for several decades. It changed hands a number of times and eventually became the property of Charles D. Lane and four other investors in 1884. Lane, an ardent spiritualist, purchased the property on the recommendation of a San Francisco medium named Mrs. Robinson. She looked at quartz rocks he brought in from the site and predicted it would pay millions. After she repeated the same prediction to several strangers, supplied with different rocks from the same site, Lane was convinced her prediction was correct and purchased the mine.

By the following year, the Utica was paying $200 to the ton. However, when it again seemed to be petering out, several of the owners became disillusioned and sold their interests. Mrs. Robinson continued to encourage Lane and his partners, however, and the mine soon began paying again.

Tempering this streak of luck was a series of problems and accidents, which began to plague the mine in June 1889. Six men shoring up a tunnel with heavy timber frames barely avoided being buried when some supports gave out. Elmer Miller was killed and several other miners were injured. In October, several more men were hurt on the job. "The mine," noted the *Calaveras Chronicle*, "is widely known as an unsafe one, although no serious blame is attached to the owners."

Two miners, L. Lewis and John Revira, refused to work in the mine and quit their jobs. Lewis, with twenty years of experience as a miner, stated that in all his experience he had never seen such a dangerous mine. The grumbling was such that Alvinza Hayward, one of the owners, hired George Williams on the strength of his reputation as being an expert in shoring up mine tunnels. Williams was given full charge of timbering in the mine, and neither the superintendent or foreman could override his decisions.

The end of 1889 saw torrential rains that soaked the ground badly. Local residents looked up at the sky and wondered when it would end. On Sunday, December 22, Williams and a timbering crew of eighteen men prepared to descend into the north shaft to shore up the slope at the three hundred-foot level. All other mine employees had the day off, but Williams saw warning signs in the tunnel and wanted to shore it up before the men went returned to work.

Charles Lillie, foreman of the mine, asked Williams if he thought the mine was safe.

"My reputation is at stake," replied Williams. "I must keep the mine up."

Lillie replied, "Will your reputation save you and your men? Let the mine go. My men don't go into that level."

Lillie then removed his men from working that particular level. Williams, confident and undeterred, led his men on to the elevator and began descending into the dark shaft.

Arriving at the three hundred-foot level, Williams again noticed some leaning side timbers, and strung his men out from the opening and into the tunnel shaft. They had no sooner begun replacing the timbers than the roof of the tunnel crashed down, burying most of the crew. There was no cracking of timbers, no sound that could have alerted the doomed men to flee. Three of the men closest to the tunnel entrance fled the scene, rushing through an opening into the adjacent Stickle Mine.

The three survivors clambered up a ladder and soon reached the

Entombed !

A DEADLY MINE

17 MINERS CRUSHED TO DEATH BY A CAVE.

Angels Camp the Scene of a Terrible Disaster.

Timbers Inadequate to the Enormous Strain Upon Them.

LIST OF THE UNFORTUNATE VICTIMS.

The most fearful and heartrending accident that ever happened in this county occurred at the Utica mine at Angels Camp, last Sunday afternoon,

CALAVERAS CHRONICLE HEADLINE, DECEMBER 28, 1889. Secrest Collection top. Outside, Tom Corbin had a head injury and was bleeding badly. Dan Danielson and August Anderson had escaped unscathed. Everything had happened so suddenly that it seemed certain the sixteen victims had not suffered, but had been crushed to death in a moment. A rescue team was sent down immediately, but upon viewing the mass of rocks, timbers and earth that filled the tunnel, they knew there was little chance for survivors. After digging some eight feet into the tunnel without finding a body, the workers realized further attempts would only risk more lives and likely yield no further survivors. The *Calaveras Chronicle* reported:

> The latest dispatches in regard to the recent terrible accident at Angels Camp say that it is now impossible to tell when the work of hunting for the bodies can be resumed, if ever, as the ground is cracked in all directions and, even by timbering every foot, the work would be dangerous. The large sink-hole on the surface now lets the water into the mine and the pumps are continually at work to try and keep the water out of the north shaft.

Operations at the mine were suspended, and a pall of gloom hung over the community. Nine of the dead men were married and had families. All holiday festivities in town were canceled. It was one of the worst mining tragedies in California history.

It was nearly a year later, in late December 1890, that four of the bodies were finally recovered. A few weeks later, on January 5, yet another tragedy struck the mine. A large load of rock and earth,

THE UTICA MINE IN 1888. THIS SHOWS THE NORTH SHAFT WHERE THE TRAGEDY TOOK PLACE. *Secrest Collection*

together with nearly a dozen men, was being raised to the surface at noon. The skip, or elevator, had reached within one hundred fifty feet of the top when a cable broke, plunging the rock and miners some six hundred feet into a sump at the bottom. Rescue crews promptly began the recovery of the bodies, but the victims were terribly mutilated.

The Utica Mine's highest production was reached in 1896, when it was producing as high as $300,000 a month and employing one thousand men. It was the highest-producing mine in the Angels Camp District, its final production being $17 million. The supreme irony was that Mrs. Robinson correctly foretold the ground's wealth but, apparently, had no inkling of the human tragedy that would bedevil the mine in 1889 and 1890.

1890

Disastrous California Storms

Where: Throughout state
Details: Six known killed, much property loss

Snow, snow, everywhere, has been the complaint of the residents of Siskiyou County since the old year made way for the new. For almost two weeks, with scarcely an intermission, the white feathery flakes came whirling down thick and fast, until the whole landscape seemed wrapped in a mantle of dazzling purity. Beautiful to look upon, but underneath its seemingly innocent exterior, there lurked danger and destruction; so men were kept busy shoveling the "beautiful snow" from the roofs of barns and houses into the streets, where it did not look so pretty, but could certainly do less damage to life and property. The snowfall at Oak Bar is estimated at three and one half feet.

Thus did the February 19, 1890, *Yreka Weekly Journal* comment on the winter storms which caused so much damage and hardship throughout California. Roads were washed out, bridges were swept away, and hundreds of ranches lost buildings and livestock. The ground, still soggy from storms of the previous December, seemed unable to absorb anything more. The yardstick for flooding had always been the great deluge of 1861-1862, but a pioneer rancher who lived on Greenhorn Creek near Yreka, Charley Abbott, insisted "there was double the quantity of

YREKA, SHOWN HERE IN THAT BITTER WINTER OF 1890, FOUND IT DIFFICULT TO COMBAT THE SNOW AND RAGING RIVERS. *California State Library*

water in the creek during the late storm than in '61 or any other year."

In January 1890, a drenching rain in the south washed out roads and held up trains to Los Angeles, while seventy-one inches of rain was reported in the Tehachapi Mountains. In the San Joaquin Valley, Merced had endured eleven inches of rain during the season, with some overflow from the rivers and creeks. Intervals of heavy rain and snow were reported in Napa, Ukiah and the northern coastal counties. In the higher elevations, snow was piling up with no relief in sight. Howland Flat, in Sierra County, reported sixteen feet of snow, while on January 6 a letter from nearby Forest City reported the town had disappeared:

> We are completely snowed in—houses buried and the boys are riding their snowshoes over tops of the buildings. A person coming into town would never know that a building was in the same place. One day last week there was a slide from the roof of the Forest House completely taking the brick chimneys and smoke stacks and giving a general scare to our town and people.

All this was just a prelude to the horrific catastrophe east of Downieville on January 3, 1890. Fourteen-year-old Amelia Ryan was visiting with some friends at the home of Mrs. John Rich in Sierra City. Mrs. Rich's son was thirteen, and her three daughters ranged in age from six to eighteen. It was bitter cold, and there was no school in session due to the heavy snow and blocked passes. Mrs. Rich knitted on the sofa as the children told stories and played games. Amelia had been brought up from Downieville by her father when the road had been briefly opened the previous Tuesday. William Ryan had barely made it back when the roads were again closed by the snow.

About three-thirty that afternoon, Joseph Haitz was shoveling snow from the roof of the Catholic church when he heard a ominous roar emanating from the bluffs above town. Turning to look more carefully, he saw a huge avalanche roaring down a gully and heading straight for town. With a yell, he leaped from the roof and avoided the oncoming slide. At his home, his wife and child barely avoided destruction, although their home was filled with snow. The great white mass tore through the Rich and Mooney homes before crashing through other buildings and dissipating. Immediately men rushed to the scene from every direction, burrowing into the mass of snow and

SIERRA CITY IN THE 1890S. *History of Sierra County*

debris to find any survivors. Mrs. Rich was found dead, with her knitting still in her hands. All the children, except Lillie, were dead. In another home, Mrs. I. T. Mooney and her thirty-year-old daughter were also dragged dead from the ruins.

William Ryan struck out for Sierra City as soon as he received the news. Bringing his daughter back to Downieville for her funeral and burial, Ryan also brought young Lillie Rich back to live with his family, since she was now an orphan. It was a kind gesture in the midst of an overwhelming tragedy.

In Yreka heavy snows piled up on the roofs, causing building rafters to groan. Townspeople were quickly shoveling the snow from the roofs to the street, but this clogged the streets causing other problems. The Scott Valley *News* reported that an old Chinese miner had been found dead in his cabin after the roof fell in on him.

A TERRIBLE SLIDE.

A Snow Slide Wrecks Three Houses in Sierra City.

SEVEN PERSONS KILLED.

The Slide Destroys the Residences of I. T. Mooney, Antone Lewis and Mr. J. Thompson—The Catholic Church, Wm. Merrish, W. Buscomb, and Sykes', Noblet's, Trompetti's and Haita's houses partially wrecked.

Last Friday afternoon between three and four o'clock, an immense slide of snow started about half way up the Buttes and passing over a hollow, which has always prior to this turned the slide to the East so that it could do no damage, and striking the residences of J. Thompson (occupied by Mrs. Rich and family), I. T. Mooney and Antone Lewis totally demolished them. The Catholic Church was wrecked but the steeple and cross left standing. The house occupied by Buscombe was carried about forty feet off its foundation, not materially injuring

DOWNIEVILLE *MOUNTAIN MESSENGER*, JANUARY 11, 1890.

As the snow let up, a heavy and steady rain commenced for nearly a week, which melted the snow and made the rivers and streams rise. When Yreka Creek began threatening a new hospital,

189

blasting powder was used to open up an old channel to divert the water. The hospital buildings were saved, but the blasting choked the creek with trees, brush and other debris, which caused further problems. Foot bridges and railroad grades were washed away by the backup, while a dam was formed at the railroad bridge, sending water coursing into Chinatown. Besides causing a great gully in the main street, seven or eight buildings owned by Chinese were washed away.

All through the mountain country, roads were washed out and rendered impassable by gullies. "Humbug creek," reported the *Journal*, "was higher than ever known before, and J. C. Burgess and D. V. Spencer, on their way to Yreka with teams, were obliged to wait three days before the stream was low enough to ford at the most favorable point."

Scott Valley became inundated, with all its fences rendered invisible and only building roofs peeking above the waterline. All the residents were rescued by boat. The settlement at Fort Jones would also have floated away had the storm continued much longer.

To the southwest, on the Trinity River, a family named Huestis lived on a flat above the river, while the father worked a mining property. The snow storm had passed, and the six days of rain had turned the river into a steadily rising torrent. On the morning of February 3, 1890, the father was away on business, and his wife and their two sons and daughter were enjoying breakfast. Suddenly, Mrs. Huestis stopped eating and looked around. It was quiet. They could no longer hear the river roaring down below their cabin. Stepping to the window and looking out, the woman was startled by what she saw and screamed, "The river is flowing upstream!"

The children joined their mother at the window, and all were terrified at what they saw. Chock full of trees, brush, and lumber from destroyed buildings, the muddy river was indeed flowing upstream. Rushing outside, they realized that a massive slide downriver must have blocked the river's course and forced it to back up.

About two miles downstream was a rocky ridge, towering some eighteen hundred feet above the river. Over many years a fault-crack had developed there, stretching from the base to near the top. The weather and warm rains caused a rupture in the fault, and a large section of the ridge slid down into the river. The Trinity *Journal* reported:

> A whole mountain tumbled into Trinity River, at Dixon's Bar, burying two Chinamen, and damming the river to back the high water a distance of 14 miles. Much property was damaged, and several had a narrow escape from drowning. The occurrence of the slide in daylight prevented the loss of many lives.

The San Francisco *Chronicle's* headline read "A Monster Landslide," and gave additional details:

> The river backed up twelve miles and was dammed for seven hours, forming a vast lake. The water forced its way through but as yet has not cut a sufficient channel. This is the largest slide recorded in Trinity County, and Weaverville people never heard of one in the state to equal it.

The same phenomenon occurred on the Oak Bar wagon road, when the whole side of a mountain slid into the Klamath River, taking the road with it.

Back at the Huestis home, the family began packing while they watched the river rising closer and closer to their door. Just as they were preparing to leave, the water stopped, and began receding.

Some of the ranchers in the mountains lost as many as fifty cattle a day during the storms, and there was scarcely a ferry, bridge or water-powered sawmill left in the northern counties. There were no overall estimates of the monetary losses, but they must have been enormous. Mercifully, few lives were lost. The Downieville tragedy and the great "China Slide," named for several local Chinese miners lost during the unique damming of the Trinity River, remain the most durable symbols of that bitter and disastrous winter.

1890

OAKLAND TRAIN TRAGEDY

Where: Bridge between Oakland and Alameda
Details: Thirteen or more killed, many injured

On the afternoon of May 30, 1890, a narrow gauge train picked up passengers at the Alameda ferry wharf and began its daily run to Oakland. The same trip had been made many times, but with one difference: the regular train crew had been placed in charge of an excursion to San Jose, while the replacement crew usually worked the Los Gatos run. Edward Rerath was the conductor, Sam Dunn the engineer, and Charles O'Brien the fireman. The switch in personnel resulted in dire consequences.

As the train whistle sounded, steam arose and the engine inched forward, heading north to its next station stop. After passing some shipyards at fifteen miles an hour, the train approached the Oakland Creek drawbridge on a wide curve, where the structure was clearly visible. "As we approached the bridge," Fireman Charles O'Brien later recalled, "I rang the bell as usual, put on the blower and replenished the fire. Suddenly Dunn applied the air, threw the engine over, and I looked up, saw the danger signal and the open draw."

Captain Henry McIntire of the yacht *Casco* had just anchored his craft on the west side of the bridge. The ship, owned by the wealthy Dr. Samuel Merritt, had been out for a morning sail. Relaxing on deck, Captain McIntire heard the bell ring, signaling the bridge's yielding to another vessel:

> The bridge was then swung around and the yacht *Juanita* was allowed to pass through. The danger flags had been placed at the ends of the bridge when it was opened and I noticed them flying at the time. As the bridge began to swing slowly back to its place, I

THE APPROACH TO THE DRAWBRIDGE AS SEEN BY ENGINEER DUNN. San Francisco Examiner, *May 31, 1890*

saw a passenger train coming around the curve, and as it did so it slowed down. I was looking for the engine to stop, as it is accustomed to do when the bridge is opened, a few feet distant from the end of the bridge, but was somewhat astonished to see it going right ahead, with the bridge still open. The next sight I saw fairly chilled the blood in my veins—the engine was toppling over into the chasm.

Rerath was in the last car as the engine plunged over the opening in the bridge. When he opened the door of his car he discovered, to his horror, that the next car was hanging over the edge of the bridge. By this time the passengers in his car were panicking, all trying to get out the doors, and he did what he could to ease their anxiety. The engine and tender had plunged into the water, carrying the first passenger car over with them. Only a portion of the car was showing above the water. The second passenger car was poised precariously over the edge, its coupling tearing away as the engine plunged over the edge.

The water was now alive with people struggling out of the sunken car. Frank Finley, a San Francisco Lumber Company clerk, was

SAN FRANCISCO

SAN FRANCISCO BAY

OAKLAND

THE DRAWBRIDGE

ALAMEDA

submerged, and recounted his ordeal to a San Francisco *Chronicle* reporter:

> I was sitting so as to face the engine and when we approached the drawbridge I looked up and it seemed to me that the bridge was open. I watched with much anxiety, and in a few moments my fears were proved to have been well grounded, and a crash followed by a horrible crushing of timber were the first indications I had of

A NEWSPAPER SKETCH MADE FROM A PHOTOGRAPH SHOWS THE DRAWBRIDGE STILL OFF TO THE SIDE. THE TWO SAVED CARS ARE SHOWN MAKING A DRAMATIC SCENE OF THE TRAGEDY. San Francisco Examiner, *May 31, 1890*

> our car's frightening fate.

> I saw a man leap from the engine, and the next thing I remember we were in the water. I groped blindly for the door, and when I reached it I worked my way from the platform to the roof, which at that end of the car rose out of the water. Out of the twenty-five or thirty people which I estimated the car contained, quite a number escaped in the same manner as I did.

Meanwhile, Captain McIntire had sent five small boats, manned by the yacht's sailors, rowing toward the scene of tragedy. People bobbed in the water screaming for help, while others struggled to follow Finley. Frank Hawley got stuck trying to get through a window and, during a desperate struggle, managed to break away:

> When I got through finally I crawled to the top of the car holding on with my arms until rescued by a boat. As the water began coming into the car the scene within was indescribable. The screams and moans were heartrending. As the lower end of the car became submerged the cries ceased. There was no chance for escape and they died like rats in a trap.

The boats rescued all those who escaped, although several in the water were washed downstream and drowned. When some men turned up with an ax and other tools, they got onto the roof of the submerged car, chopped a hole and dragged out more bodies. But no one was found alive in that deadly car.

As wagons and buggies arrived to remove the dead, mobs of sightseers went out of control, and the entire Oakland police force was required to control and disperse them. The crowds then went to the coroner's office, where the bodies were laid out and identified. Here another cordon of police held back the clamoring mob, looking for the corpses of friends or relatives, "and only partially succeeded," according to the *Chronicle*. "Sheriff Hale, who stationed himself at the door, performed the work of three men."

From the beginning, the press had charged Sam Dunn with "criminal negligence" and "recklessness" for failing to stop, and he neglected to appear at a coroner's inquest which formalized these accusations. Sheriff William E. Hale sent inquiries around the state for authorities to be on the lookout for Dunn, who never re-turned to his home at Boulder Creek in Santa Cruz County.

SKETCH MADE FROM A PHOTOGRAPH ILLUSTRATES THE RECOVERY OF THE DEATH CAR. THE RIPPED UP ROOF INDICATES THE DESPERATE ATTEMPT TO RECOVER SURVIVORS AND BODIES.
San Francisco Examiner, *May 31, 1890*

The *Chronicle* penned its own obituary for the hapless engineer:

> It was at first reported that the engineer of the train had paid the penalty of his negligence with his life, and perhaps this is the happiest thing that could have happened to him. To feel the responsibility of having caused the death of nearly a score of human beings will be an inferno such as even the pen of Dante could not portray.

1890

Runaway Train over the Sierra

Where: From Truckee to Cascade
Details: Four dead, others injured

It was some twenty minutes before 4 A.M., on a chilly morning in the high Sierra. After eastbound freight train No. 19 chugged into the Summit station, the engine was uncoupled from the seventeen cars it was hauling, and pulled ahead to take on three empty cars. It was a routine stop on this Southern Pacific railroad. The small mountain community of Truckee was some twelve miles ahead on the road over the mountains to Reno. No. 19 was seven hours behind schedule, and was followed some miles behind by freight train No. 23 and a passenger train. The schedule was for No. 23 to sidetrack at Cascade and let the oncoming passenger train pass the slower freight. There was a telegraph house and 300 feet of newly-constructed snow sheds at the station.

Ahead, at the summit, the No. 19 engine was being positioned for its coupling with the empty cars. Pulling ahead of the switch so it could link the vehicles together, the engineer could no longer see the lights on the main cars of the train it had just left behind. Reversing his throttle, the engineer began backing onto the switch, where he joined the added cars and began moving forward.

THE RAILROAD SNOWSHEDS AT CASCADE LOOKED MUCH LIKE THE SHEDS SHOWN HERE. *California State Library*

Back at the main section of cars, Conductor Frank "Yank" Kingsley was flagging in the rear of the train. It was quite dark, and he was suddenly aware of the wheels of the caboose moving. There was a strict railroad rule not to trust the automatic air brakes on the cars and to apply the hand brakes also whenever the train stopped. Suddenly, Kingsley must have realized that he had not set the hand brakes, and the air brakes were not holding! They were at the summit of the road and, having been parked on a slight grade, the train was now rolling backward and slowly gathering speed. Running to the platform of the caboose, Kingsley quickly climbed to the roof and began frantically applying the hand brake. It was too late. The engineless cars rolled backwards at an ever-increasing speed, and nothing would stop the train now.

A carpenter employed by the railroad, Jacob Schaab, was riding inside the caboose and noticed the train was running away. Kingsley was still trying to apply the brake as Schaab rushed to the platform and looked around, desperately trying to decide what to do. The train had gone about a half-mile when he jumped, but by then the cars were going some forty miles an hour and he was badly injured. The August 23 San Francisco *Chronicle* reported:

> Meantime the runaway was tearing down the grade with a constantly increasing speed, the frantic efforts of the heroic conductor having no perceptible effect in checking her. A track-walker at Summit Valley, three miles from Summit, thought only two cars passed him, and says he only heard a rushing sound and saw the dust.

> The engineers of No. 23, who were on the sidetrack at Cascade, say that the flying train passed them at the rate of 150 miles an hour.

Fortunately, only one rear car and the caboose of No. 23 remained on the main track when the crash occurred, as was noted in the *Chronicle* account:

> There was a mighty roar as of a prolonged peal of thunder, and in the twinkling of an eye 352 feet of new snowsheds and as many feet of railroad track, with the telegraph section and twenty cars, were swept into a broken, confused, indescribable mass, portions of which extended far down the steep bank toward the Yuba River.

> Telegraph Operator J. B. Dorsey was asleep in the rear of the station and awoke to find his house being thrown fifty feet down the bank. A caboose was directly under his bedroom and four freight cars were huddled together in the front of the office. There

was a clear space just large enough to hold him and his bed right in the midst of the horrible debris.

Dorsey climbed out of a rear window and discovered that, except for two crushed toes and a few bruises, he was unhurt. Some 200 carpenters and bridge builders were camped nearby and rushed to the scene, where Dorsey explained what had happened.

The engineers of No. 23 had no idea that their train had been struck. The velocity of the runaway train was such that it had cut like a knife through the last two cars of No. 23, and the rest of the train on the siding didn't even feel the slightest jar. It was incredible that the runaway cars had stayed on the tracks in the seven miles it had traveled. The *Chronicle* article described the terrible scene:

> At the wreck an immediate search was made for the men who were known to be under the debris. The wreckage was piled twenty feet high. Cars were crushed to fragments, and trucks, axles, wheels and steel rails were twisted and broken like pipestems. The strong shed timbers were ground into splinters and freight of every description was mingled through the entire mass.

Rescuers worked as quickly as was considered safe, and soon the bodies of Vic Veara and Oliver Beaver were discovered. Both were terribly mangled. Later, the crushed and lifeless body of William Connelly was found. Beaver and Connelley were both thought to have been in the caboose of No. 23 when it was hit. Connelley had taken the regular conductor's place at Rocklin when George Hurley had been taken ill. The *Chronicle* article continued:

> At 8 o'clock the body of Frank T. Kingsley was discovered. His head was torn entirely off, only the skin of the face remaining. He was about 50 years old and leaves a child in Massachusetts. He was one of the most trusted and popular men on the road, and when it was known that he had voluntarily taken that wild ride to death in order to save his comrades, hundreds of men shed tears over his lifeless remains.

It was determined that, if the runaway had reached Cascade a half-minute later, the path would have been empty and No. 19 would have gone on to collide with the oncoming passenger train. As soon as the tracks were cleared that afternoon, the injured Jacob Schaab and the four dead men were taken to Sacramento.

Southern Pacific General Superintendent J. A. Fillmore received many reports of the tragedy during the day. Before the coroner's jury was summoned, Mr. Fillmore gave his own explanation of the terrible events as published in the San Francisco *Examiner*:

> The company's rules are that when cars are left standing on a grade the hand brakes must always be set. It will not do to trust to air brakes alone as these are sometimes out of order and leaky. If this order had been obeyed, the accident would not have happened.
>
> At Emigrant Gap Kingsley gave the brakeman bills of lading for the way stations. He was not seen after this and there is little doubt that he retired to the caboose and went to sleep, presuming on the safety of the train in the hands of the brakemen.

Fillmore had received reports that Kingsley had been seen on top of the caboose trying to operate the hand brake. These reports had not been verified at the time the superintendent was interviewed, however. Early indications were that the conductor was to be made the fall guy for the tragedy. With few witnesses to the fatal scene, it was not the first time a dead victim would be assigned the blame, rather than the company, for failing to be aware of "sometimes out of order and leaky" airbrakes.

1891

Tragic Wreck of the *Elizabeth*

Where: Pacific side of Marin County
Details: Seventeen or more deaths, others injured

There was nothing to suggest that the *Elizabeth*'s passage from New York to San Francisco was going to be anything other than uneventful. A 1,775-ton vessel with general goods in her hold, she had left port on October 23, 1890, and embarked on what became a four-month journey to the Pacific. Aboard the ship were Captain James Colcord; his wife, son and daughter; and twenty-four or more crewmen. The sole bit of trouble experienced during any part of the trip was the loss of the ship's lower foretopsail to high winds on the following January 15. However, as she neared the finish line, on February 21, events turned quickly toward the ominous.

CAPTAIN JAMES COLCORD
San Francisco Examiner,
February 24, 1891

While attempting to close in on the Golden Gate, a strong gale kicked up from the east-southeast and began to buffet the *Elizabeth*. With wind and seas rough, and several nearby vessels having difficulty navigating, it became obvious that the ship would not be able to sail into port by itself. The February 23, 1891, *San Francisco Examiner* described what then happened:

The *Elizabeth* at this time was just inside the bar and refused to lay her course, owing to the direction of the wind. In the meanwhile the steam tugs *Monarch* and *Alert* were making for the *Elizabeth* with all speed. The *Monarch* reached the vessel first and came close alongside.

"Are you going to tow?" shouted the captain of the *Monarch*.

"Yes; what will you tow me for?" replied Captain Colcord.

THE SCHOONER *ELIZABETH*
San Francisco Examiner, *February 23, 1891*

"Fifty dollars," shouted the captain of the tug.

"No, no; that's too much," responded Colcord, and turned to walk on the after part of the poop.

"Well, what will you give?" demanded the captain of the tug.

"I'll give you twenty-five dollars," said Colcord.

"No," the captain tug replied, and was turning to leave when Captain Colcord shoutedto him, offering to split the difference, and make the fee $37.50.

This proposition was refused by the tug captain, who at once turned and left.

At $12.50, the mistake turned out to be the costliest of Colcord's career. He hailed the *Alert* and a tow line was thrown out, but the turbulence all around soon caused it to snap in two. A second effort proved fruitless, as the violent winds began pushing the *Elizabeth* ahead of the tug. While frantic efforts continued to put the *Alert* in the lead, the vessels were nearing Tennessee Cove, on the Marin County coast. The inlet's name came from a steamer that had run aground there on March 6, 1853. No lives had been lost in the previous disaster. This time, worse fate was to prevail.

Heading fast toward shore, and sensing that disaster was only seconds away, Quartermaster Joseph Taken told Colcord that he should lower a boat and at least manage to save his family. At this point, the situation was so grim that Colcord's son, Bertie, was almost carried away by a wave, and the boat was smashed so badly upon meeting the sea that its rudder flew off.

Colcord then ordered Taken and fellow crew members George Hanna and Bernard Johnsen into the precarious craft, hoping the men could stay close and let his wife and children get aboard. It was filling fast with water, being pitched about violently, and was in imminent danger of breaking up—along with the *Elizabeth* herself.

Quartermaster Taken described the desperate scene in the February 23, 1891, *San Francisco Call*:

> We made our way back [to the ship] again and again, until once we were driven way out by a stronger undertow than before.

As we came in we acci-dentally got too near the port counter and the heavy billow that raised the stern so high, just previous to our last strain at the oars, that we were crushed by its returning as the undertow rushed out. Our little boat was broken into three or four parts, and we were

THE WRECKAGE OF THE *ELIZABETH*, BASHED INTO KINDLING ON THE ROCKS OF TENNESSEE COVE. San Francisco Examiner, *February 24, 1891*

submerged under the stern. The returning billow raised the stern, and we floated out with the next undertow. The sea claimed, then disclaimed and then reclaimed us, and we were washed a dozen times against the vessel's side before each of us had caught hold of the broken boat. We held on by the keel.

The situation had now reached a point of complete desperation. Colcord had a dinghy lowered containing his family, First Mate Charles Barclay, and two other crew members. Amid great difficulties, the boat managed to make it to the *Alert*, leave the Colcords there, and then Barclay returned with his men to the *Elizabeth*, finding the captain badly injured but still in command. When a large wave hit the ship, Colcord was flung against the deck and killed. The remaining men jumped in the water and began swimming frantically for shore.

As news of the *Elizabeth*'s afternoon peril spread around San Francisco Bay, the Fort Point life-saving crew struck out for the north and soon met with its own series of disasters. Setting forth in a lifeboat, pulled by none other than the *Alert*, the crew was pitched and tossed so badly by the rough waters that its captain, Charles Henry, was flung overboard. His corpse later resurfaced in the bay. Once the men had crossed the bay and reached Sausalito, they had no luck in obtaining a horse team to reach

FEARFUL DISASTER,

The Ship Elizabeth Goes Ashore on the Rocks Four Miles North of the Heads.

Twenty-six Lives in All Probability Lost in the Wreck and but Six Known To Be Saved.

The Captain of the Baker's Beach Life-Saving Station Is Also Drowned.

The Lifeboat Men Make Gallant Efforts to Reach the Doomed Ship.

THE STATEMENTS OF THE SURVIVORS.

Frantic Efforts of the Captain to Launch His Boat in the Raging Sea—How His Wife, Son and Daughter and Three Seamen Were Saved—The Tugs Could Not Handle the Ship, Lines Parted Like Twine and the Elizabeth Drifted Unerringly to the Jagged Rocks—The Life Boats Are Landed at Sausalito and Will Have to be Carted Overland to the Scene

SAN FRANCISCO EXAMINER, FEBRUARY 22, 1891

Tennessee Cove, and had to pull their life-saving equipment over there by themselves. Henry Schmidt, one of the rescuers, described the scene in the *Examiner*'s February 23 issue:

Then I saw a lot of broken stuff on the beach and went down to it. I saw the whole vessel was broken up like match-wood. The pieces of the ship were so thick in the water that I could walk out on them a ways, as though it were a raft. There was any quantity of coal oil, candles, claret, thread, brown paper and general merchandise lying along the beach. Our trip was useless so far as employing our life-saving apparatus went. There were no lives to save and no ship left except in the form of splinters.

Miraculously, the men who went into the rudderless boat were all saved, and five others—Barclay, Charles Sievert, Olav Eide, Luis Marie and Fred Granholm—also made it to shore, along with the Colcord family. Everyone else aboard the *Elizabeth* perished, along with its cargo and its $70,000 value. The crew later defended the captain and his bravery to all who would listen but, in retrospect, one must wonder if the tragedy could have been prevented had a less thrifty man been at the helm.

1892

Mare Island Naval Explosion

Where: Across from Vallejo
Details: Fifteen sailors killed, others injured

One of the most horrible and sickening casualties ever recorded in California occurred at 11:30 o'clock this morning at the location of the Government navy-yard on Mare Island.

And so began an article in the San Francisco *Call* about men and explosives in nineteenth-century California. As has been shown previously, it was an oft-repeated and all-too-familiar kind of story.

On June 13, 1892, the U.S. naval cruiser *Boston* was sitting in her Mare Island drydock, from which she was soon to be released for active service. The ship had arrived from Chile in late May for some standard maintenance work. On that morning, a troop of fifteen *Boston* sailors marched down the gangplank and proceeded to the south end of the island, where the powder magazines were located. It was an isolated part of the island, opposite the wharves of south Vallejo. Here, where buildings were few and none were inhabited, extensive damage or fatalities in the event of an accident were unlikely. Also, in its thirty years of service, there had never been a fatality from an explosion at this sprawling naval station.

MARE ISLAND IS IN THE FOREGROUND WITH THE CITY OF VALLEJO IN THE DISTANCE ACROSS THE NAPA RIVER. *National Archives*

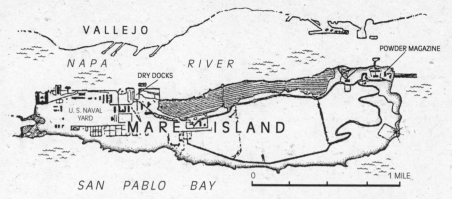

VALLEJO

NAPA   RIVER

DRY DOCKS

POWDER MAGAZINE

U. S. NAVAL
YARD

M A R E   I S L A N D

SAN   PABLO   BAY

0   1 MILE

Arriving at the powder magazine, gunner in charge George Hittinger set his men to their task. Regulations dictated that all worked in their stocking feet or wore soft slippers. The men stood and worked on a screen so no spilled powder would be underfoot. Tools were made of copper or wood. The job consisted mainly of measuring the powder carefully, pouring it through a funnel into the top of the shell, then attaching the head of the shell. These were six- and eight-inch shells, used in the big guns of the ship. It was a routine, and boring, job.

Captain G. C. Wiltse, commander of the *Boston*, was standing on the stone drydock surrounding his ship when he heard the explosion. A cadet standing nearby shouted and pointed toward the south end of the island. Wiltse looked and saw a huge cloud of smoke in the distance, with other explosions continuing. Everyone could see that the magazine had exploded. The officer shouted to have his launch readied, and had Lieutenant Moore take a crew to the scene immediately. As the launch tied up at the dock adjacent to the flaming and smoking powder house ruins, shells were still exploding. Lieutenant Greaves, the watch officer of the *Boston*, leaped ashore and looked around:

> When we reached the scene we beheld one of the most sickening sights that it is possible to describe. The magazine building had been blown to pieces and the debris was blazing fiercely with the charred remains of some of the unfortunate men who had not been blown outside the confines of the walls in the midst of the flames. But the crew did not pale at the sight. They set to work and worked gallantly

I want to say that all of the men did noble work and are entitled to great credit for the bravery which they displayed while the heated shells were bursting all around them.

Only three of the fifteen-man crew were still alive. Seaman second-class John Briscoe was found at the water's edge, where he had been blown fifteen or twenty feet through the air. The young sailor was naked,

SITE OF THE TERRIBLE MARE ISLAND EXPLOSION. HITTINGER'S BODY WAS FOUND C THE ROOF WHERE THE "X" IS MARKED. San Francisco Examiner, *June 15, 1892*

his blackened, raw flesh scalded and still smoking. A naval officer asked him what had happened.

"I don't know," he gasped out. "I was loading an eight-inch shell when there was an explosion."

When he was being lifted into a wagon, the pain was more than he could bear. "For God's sake, shoot me and rid me of this pain," he cried. "I'm burning up. Oh, this pain is terrible. I can't bear it. Shoot me boys; please shoot me ; it will be an act of mercy." His skin had been scorched away, leaving all the charred tendons and nerves in the man's body exposed, and the least touch caused him intense agony. Two other seamen, R. Reniche and J. H. Hulton, were horribly injured and also hurried off to the hospital, but all three died eventually.

SEAMAN F. O. LEGAT, ONE OF VICTIMS OF THE EXPLOSION. San Francisco Examiner, *June 15, 1892*

Rescue parties from Vallejo, the *Boston* and other nearby ships and the island barracks were soon looking for survivors. George Hittinger's headless body was found on the roof of a nearby building. While some sought to control grass fires before they could spread to an even larger powder magazine, others dug frantically through the ruins, finding only body parts. Dismembered bodies were scattered everywhere.

Captain Heath, of the ferryboat *Amador*, was in the water between Vallejo and Vallejo Junction when the explosion occurred. He received permission to go over and render what assistance he could, and reported thus:

> The scene when I got there was horrible beyond description. There were seven mangled bodies laid out side by side under a bank at the side of the hill. They were so burned they looked like roasted mutton. Pieces of arms, legs and bodies were strewn about the side of the hill and men were going about picking them up. It was the most terrible sight I ever saw.

A prompt inquest was held but, aside from minimal agonized statements from seamen Briscoe and Hulbert, nothing could be learned about the explosion's cause. Some insisted that the real villain in the case was a recent naval directive that sailors, rather than professional explosive handlers, fill the shells for the big guns. An unnamed naval officer was quoted in the San Francisco *Examiner*:

THE CAPTAIN AND CREW OF THE FERRY *AMADOR* DID NOT HESITATE TO RUSH TO THE AID OF THE VICTIMS OF THE TERRIBLE DISASTER AT MARE ISLAND. *California State Library*

> Why, it is a disgrace to the Navy Department, with a ship in dry dock to send its ordinary seamen to load six and eight inch shells. Those men have been engaged for a week past, in regulation shoes, working with powder, percussion caps and fulminates, loading shells, when that duty should have been performed by experts in rubber shoes, and the first thing that has happened, as a natural consequence, was this dreadful explosion.

1892

Los Angeles Columbus Day Explosion

Where: Southern part of city
Details: Seven killed, many injured

San Francisco

✳Los Angeles

For the 400th anniversary of Columbus's discovery of America—October 21, 1892—the Italian community of Los Angeles sponsored a massive celebration. This event took place in a large vacant lot, near a power station and the Santa Fe Arcade train depot. After the various speeches and events had been concluded that afternoon, the evening entertainments began, consisting primarily of a fireworks display that began at dusk. In another part of the city, an evening dance was being held at a large pavilion as part of the celebrations.

There were over a thousand spectators gathered that evening for the fireworks display, always a great crowd-pleaser. Many children, with and without their parents, were of course present .

A large circle, defined by stakes and a wire rope, was in the middle of the lot. William Wilson, manager of the Los Angeles Fire Works, and his assistant, Herman Kammert, began setting up the

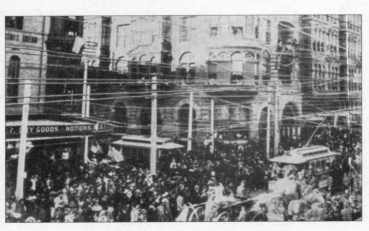

1892 COLUMBUS DAY CROWDS ON THE STREETS OF DOWNTOWN LOS ANGELES. A TERRIBLE TRAGEDY WAS JUST A FEW HOURS AWAY.
Secrest Collection

evening's display. They carried their supplies into the center of the circle, with scattered crowds gathering around. There were forty mortars, as they were called, and a large supply of shells, Roman candles and powder. The shells were different sizes, from four to ten inches, with powder and a fuse at one end. The mortars were merely a two-foot length of pipe, welded to a stand that held it in a vertical position. To the cheers of the crowd, the colorful displays were soon lighting up the area. Wilson later described what happened:

> We had fired all the shells except a few that we had saved for the final salute. We went to another part of the grounds to fire the salute, and, after we had fired it, we looked back and saw shells and fireworks flying in every direction. Myself and my assistant, Kammert, ran from the set piece, where we had fired the final salute, to where we had left the shells, fireworks and powder. This was about 100 yards. We tried to beat back the crowd, and so keep them from destroying the shells and fireworks, but we were powerless.

> They had broken down the wire rope which had been put up to keep them back, and I even tried to beat some of them back with a stick, but they rushed in over the rope in such large numbers that we were powerless. Near some of the shells was three or four pounds of powder in a cigar box; there could not have been more for the box was only about half full when I left, and when I got back it was all gone; some of the crowd then fired three or four shells; then, as nearly everything had been destroyed, I said to Kammert, who works for me, "Well, as there are only three shells left, we might as well get rid of them."

Wilson then fired off several shells as Kammert lit the fuse and dropped one of the remaining four-inch shells into the mouth of his mortar. Wilson's story continued:

> He (Kammert later) said it did not go to the bottom, but exploded as he put it in the mortar. The explosion was so terrific that I knew something was wrong; some of the crowd must have put some of that powder into the mortar. If they had not done so, there would have been no accident; I fired this mortar about 20 times during the evening; if a mortar is properly handled it will not burst and there is no danger.

There was a roar and a blinding flash as Kammert's mortar exploded, sending chunks of shrapnel ripping through the crowd. After the flash there were screams and shouting, but it was pitch black by now, and no lights were on the lot. No one knew just what had happened, but in a few moments people began running from the scene. A bystander rushed to the nearby depot and secured aid by obtaining headlamps from engines parked on the track. The men lit the lamps, rushed over to the field, and illuminated a macabre tableau. The *Times* described what they witnessed:

> The dead and wounded were scattered around the burst mortar for a distance of thirty feet. Men with their legs torn off, and little boys and girls with legs horribly mangled, and several children with their stomachs literally ripped wide open so that the intestines protruded.

At first it was thought there were only wounded, but soon lifeless bodies were being found about the field. Frank Ford, a mortally wounded fourteen-year-old newspaper boy, was discovered and his body removed. Soon six- year-old Lillian Rapp's body was taken from the field, along with that of twelve-year-old Louis Oden. The corpses of two adults, Antonio Highetto and Victor Cassino, were also located. A total of twelve injured—some critically—were taken to the receiving hospital at the central police station.

The station was a madhouse of groaning and screaming patients, sobbing women looking for family members, and the grating sound of bones being sawed away from mangled flesh. Over a dozen physicians were laboring over the torn and lacerated bodies. Fourteen-year-old Gilbert Christian had his right leg blown off, and his companion limb badly lacerated. He was seen consoling his mother, who was weeping uncontrollably.

"Don't cry mother, it is nothing much. I'm all right. I have had lots of good doctors, and I am feeling fine." Strong men turned aside and wept at the scene. The boy was given little chance to survive.

On the next day visitors mobbed the lot to see the sixteen- by nine-foot excavation created by the explosion. William Wilson was held at the police station after Chief Glass had questioned him, and suggested he never should have fired those last few shells with the crowd all standing around. It was even suggested that a frustrated Wilson had overloaded the exploding mortar in his anger at the crowd.

After over sixty witnesses were interrogated during an investigation that lasted nearly a week, Wilson was exonerated of any blame in the tragedy. It was determined that members of the crowd had dumped powder into the mortars, resulting in two of them exploding. Wilson and Kammert's diligence and care in setting up the display had been trumped by a cruel prank. It was a tragic day, compounded by the fact that some common sense would have prevented it from ever happening.

1894

Austin Creek Train Disaster

Where: Near Fort Ross
Details: Five men killed

When the North Pacific Coast Railroad was pushing north from Sausalito in the late 1880s, its Sonoma County terminus was established at Cazadero—Spanish for "hunting place." The small village was owned by a wealthy San Franciscan named George Montgomery, a two-fisted drinking man who acquired religion in 1890 and tried to make his resort a temperance town. The hunters, railroad men, loggers and others who frequented the place, however, never quite took to this idea.

THE RAILROAD STATION AT CAZADERO AS IT APPEARED SOME YEARS AFTER THE TRAGEDY IN 1907. *Courtesy Gary Rodgers, Cazadero historian*

A roundhouse and other railroad structures at the settlement were augmented by company employees' cabins and a hotel operated by Frank Hart and his mother. Located on Austin Creek, some eleven or so miles from the coast, Cazadero was in the heart of beautiful redwood and pine forests. Besides providing train service to the Bay Area for travelers, the railroad also serviced the many sawmills in the area.

On Sunday evening, February 14, 1894, a group of railroad employees were having their evening meal in the Cazadero Hotel. The heaviest storm seen since the 1890-1891 winter was the major conversation topic, and rapidly rising rivers and streams were discussed in relation to train schedules. The No. 6 engine was set to leave at five o'clock the following morning. Conductor William Brown insisted on taking out the engine to determine the road's

safety, as trestles spanning Austin Creek were being pounded mercilessly by logs and debris hurtled downstream. Engineer Arthur C. Briggs was less eager to go into the driving rain, but argued with and reluctantly consented to join Brown.

Briggs coached the engine out of the roundhouse, and Conductor Brown positioned himself on the cowcatcher on the front of the engine, keeping an eye on the tracks in the beam of the locomotive's powerful headlamp. Five local residents crowded into the cab with Briggs and his fireman, Tom Collister. Hotel owner Hart was one of them, along with hotel bookkeeper William Bremmar; Cazadero postmaster Thomas Gould; Joseph Sabine, the station agent; and railroad employee John Rice. Allowing so many into the engineer's cab was strictly against the rules, but Briggs likely permitted it as the trip was expected to be brief.

Three-quarters of a mile down the road, the first bridge came into view. Brown signaled for a stop. The water in Austin Creek was almost twenty feet higher than normal, and level with the tracks.

ENGINE NO. 11 ON THE ELM GROVE TRESTLE IN 1890. THIS IS THE EXACT SPOT WHERE THE TRAGEDY OCCURRED THAT STORMY NIGHT FOUR YEARS LATER. *Courtesy Gary Rodgers, Cazadero historian*

Briggs and Brown discussed what to do next. Much debris was clustered around this first bridge at Elm Grove, but it looked stable enough. Brown later recalled:

> We agreed finally that I should go over the bridge on foot and walk to the next trestle, taking time to thoroughly examine both structures. Our idea was that if the second bridge had been washed away or was in a dangerous condition, it would be folly to cross the first bridge. Briggs was to wait on the Cazadero side of the trestle until I returned with my report.
>
> I crossed and examined the bridge carefully. Although I did not like the looks of things I thought I would go on to the next bridge and examine the first one again upon my return. Never before have I seen Austin Creek so turbulent. Even during the terrible storms of four years ago the water did not rise so high nor did it rush down the mountain with such resistless velocity.

Conductor Brown made a cursory inspection of the first bridge and then moved on, planning to check it again on his return to the engine. He kept walking and, when down the tracks a mile or so, heard a terrible scream off in the distance. He continued his story:

> I heard a sound that will ring in my ears till my dying day. It was a long, loud scream, the death cry of the seven men who went down in No. 6. For a moment I was paralyzed, my blood seemed to freeze in my veins and I lost control of my legs. Through the awful darkness and the torrent of rain I could see absolutely nothing. When my senses returned I ran with all my might back to the bridge.

Frantically rushing about and calling out to any survivors, Brown heard only the rushing water and banging of the debris against the broken trestle. The conductor tried to walk back to Cazadero, but became lost and spent the night in a logger's cabin. Early the next morning he reached the authorities, and work and rescue teams quickly made their way to the bridge.

When Joseph Sabine's son heard the news, he leaped on a horse and galloped to the bridge, where he plunged into the water and searched fruitlessly for his father. He was swept away and almost drowned himself, but horse and rider were pulled safely to the creek's other side. Strangely enough, a local Indian lit a candle on a board and placed it upstream in the water. It was later found in a tangle of brush and debris—along with Sabine's body.

As the water finally began to recede, parts of the locomotive began to appear. It had fallen on its side and taken its human cargo with it. All the bodies were recovered from the wreck, with the exception of Frank Hart's. His vest was recovered, and it was thought he had floated down the river and perhaps out to sea.

Brown blamed the tragedy on engineer Briggs, who proceeded across the bridge before getting word from the conductor. This, however, conflicted with testimony from diners in the restaurant, who had overheard Brown arguing with Briggs. Whether Brown said anything to cover his own trail will never be known, since he was the only survivor. What is known is that a coroner's verdict labeled the tragedy an accident.

SKETCH MADE FROM A PHOTOGRAPH ILLUSTRATES THE ENGINE IN THE WATER AFTER THE CREEK WATERS HAD RECEDED. San Francisco Examiner, *January 17, 1894*

But this was not the whole story. It was learned later that a group of men had been drinking that evening at Cazadero's Lonesome Cottage Saloon, and ran out of liquor in that temperance town. They coaxed engineer Briggs to take them on a short jaunt, south to Duncan's Mills, to restock their supplies. The newspaper stories pub-lished right after the accident were slanted by locals to protect the railroad. Having experienced financial problems in its recent past, the railroad could ill-afford a series of lawsuits and damage liabilities. Eventually, the full tale—vouched for by those in the know—was published in an issue of the Salvation Army's magazine, *The War Cry*.

Tragedy Strikes the *Blairmore*

Where: San Francisco Bay
Details: Six men drowned

"**T** HE BLAIRMORE TURNED TURTLE," read the headline in the April 10, 1896 *Los Angeles Times*, describing one of the rarest of marine disasters—a 1,767-ton ship listed on its side, then capsized and sunk, all in the space of five minutes. The article noted but two other instances of this happening to a large vessel in California waters—the *Julia Castenar* in 1859, and the *Earl of Dalhousie* in 1885. Of these, the *Blairmore*'s mishap was the most unusual of all, for its sheer rapidity and the fact that several hundred tons of ballast should have kept it aright. The unfortunate *Earl* carried no stabilizing weight at all, and took a while to sink, while the ballasted *Blairmore* succumbed in no time at all.

A square-rigger built in Glasgow during 1893, the *Blairmore* was a charter ship that featured extra-large dimensions for its size class— 261 feet long, 39 feet in the beam, with tall steel masts. She was thought to be a clumsy, cranky vessel by her crew, bucking to have a misfortune of some kind befall her. She docked at San Francisco during February 1896 uneventfully enough, to unload a cargo of coal, but was stuck in port for several weeks afterward because the

THE *BLAIRMORE* ROLLING OVER AS DEPICTED IN THE SAN FRANCSCO *CALL*, APRIL 10, 1896.

charter boat market went flat. While waiting to set sail on a new voyage, she was anchored at Mission Bay, close to San Francisco's southeast side and the Union Iron Works.

At seven o'clock on the morning of April 9, a heavy wind struck from the southwest and, coupled with a swift tide, knocked a fast blow to the *Blairmore*. Captain John L. Caw explained what happened next in the April 10, 1896, *San Francisco Examiner*:

CAPTAIN JOHN L. CAW, OF THE *BLAIRMORE*. *Secrest Collection*

> It was a hard combination for a ship to battle against. We had no chance whatever, and the whole thing happened so quickly that none of us realized until it was almost too late what was in store for us. I was standing on the poop-deck when the first of the squall struck us. The vessel laid over considerably under the blow, but not enough to alarm me. I felt sure that she would right herself readily, although it was one of the most vicious squalls I have ever encountered during all my experience at sea, and I have been pretty well all over the world.
>
> When the vessel listed a number of flower-pots which I had placed on the poop-deck toppled over and began to roll about. I was afraid they would go overboard, and began to scramble after them. I caught two of them just as the ship righted herself, and was starting for the others when the squall seemed to increase in its fury, and we began to go over again. This time our ice rail went under water, the spars dipped and, after hanging in that position for a few seconds—it seemed like an age to me—the ship went clear over. I was tumbled off the poop deck and into the water—just how, I don't know.

Unmentioned in Caw's account was the fact that a nearby tugboat, the *Active*, offered its assistance as the *Blairmore* made its first precipitous dip into the bay. Figuring that the ship would soon be upright, Caw declined assistance. When he was proved wrong, the nearby tug *Alert*—which figured so heavily in the *Elizabeth* shipwreck (see earlier chapter)—headed toward the capsized ship, along with the British ships *Cromdale* and *Yeoman*. The last-mentioned rescued Caw, his dog, the second and third mates, and five other crew members.

Less fortunate were six men working inside the *Blairmore* at the time of the accident. Sighting the tragedy from the iron works, superintendents John T. Scott and James A. Dickie were fast to assemble a rescue team and board the tug *Rockaway*. Within a few minutes, the men were trying to cut a hole in the ironclad bottom of the ship, hoping to free the imprisoned sailors. Scott recounted the desperate scene in the *San Francisco Call*'s April 10 issue:

> When we began to hammer at the hull we heard the groans and shouts of the men inside and these spurred us on to hasten their deliverance. The air kept gushing out of the ventilators making the water boil around them and the rising tide was closing in upon us. I tell you we worked with a will, for it was a race between our chisels and the threatening water.
>
> Then came the critical moment, and we prepared to break the piece in with our heavy sledge-hammers. The tide was beginning to lap over the plate which we had pierced, and in a short time it, too, would be beneath the water.
>
> Then we struck together. Two good, sure blows and the piece fell in—and my God, I shall never forget what then took place.
>
> The air seemed to heave itself out of the vessel in a solid body, and the hull dropped, I might say, right out from under us. The water rushing in through the gaping hole would meet the ascending force from below and be driven upward fully ten feet with a tremendous roar.

One can only imagine the rescue team's despair at having unleashed this geyser and hastening the remaining crew's condemnation. Those lost were First Officer Thomas Ludgate; Steward Samuel Kenny; Seaman Henry Clark; Sail-Maker T. Renebaum; Appren-

THE ILL-FATED RESCUE ATTEMPT OF THE TRAPPED *BLAIRMORE* CREW. *San Francisco* Call, April 10, 1896

tice Roland Emil Siegel; and Watchman H. Synstrand.

While it was probably not the best practice to keep a relatively low ballast on the *Blairmore*—estimates run between 260 and 400 tons—Caw was ultimately cleared of any wrongdoing by an inquiry panel, fully cognizant of the freak conditions which would have made survival difficult even for a solidly-weighted ship.

Since the *Blairmore* sank in an area with heavy maritime traffic, it was necessary to patch and raise her, recovering the sailors' bodies in the process. She was towed to the docks of the Pacific Rolling Mills, where a weird sequel to the tragedy unfolded. Reports began to surface of banging noises issuing from the ship—made by the sailors' ghosts?—and of strange lights sighted in her immediate vicinity. One watchman, investigating a nighttime clamor, had the flame of his lantern blown out suddenly—and went scrambling out of the vessel in total terror.

Refitted, sold and renamed on several occasions—first as the *Abby Palmer*, later as the *Star of England*—the *Blairmore* cotinued to ply the Pacific waters until she was finally reduced to the role of a sawdust barge in British Columbia.

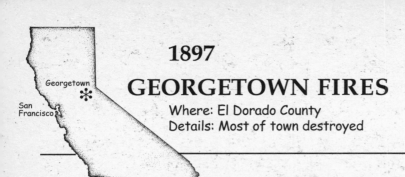

1897
GEORGETOWN FIRES

Where: El Dorado County
Details: Most of town destroyed

As word spread of a fire in Georgetown's midst in June 1897, people ran out of their businesses in the old minng camp, looking for tell-tale smoke in the air. Although wind was dispersing the growing black cloud, the source was seen to be the Tahoe Saloon. While men rushed to that scene, the blaze spread rapidly to adjoining structures, and people began moving furniture and personal effects into the street for safety. By noon, all the frame buildings in the business district were smoking piles of ashes. The Georgetown *Gazette* chronicled succeeding events in its June 17 issue:

> The interior of Jackson's store was soon discovered burning. Soon a regular fusillade of cartridges began, which resembled a sham battle, and then a slight explosion which took the roof off the building. Flames leaped high in the air and once more the hotel was in danger. Next, from Jerrett's, Sornberger's and Shepherd's stores, supposed to be fire-proof, smoke was seen emerging. People had already commenced to move back their things to the houses that were spared, when an explosion of sporting powder in Sornberger's lifted the roof off the rear of the store. Dynamite was known to be in the place. As to how much no one could tell, but there was not more than three 10-pound boxes of giant and a portion of a 25-pound keg of sporting powder in the store. Cartridges commenced to explode, and it was said by men accustomed to handling giant powder, that there would likely be no danger unless caused by concussion.

It began raining about two o'clock, and many of those watching the conflagration crowded onto the porch of a residence to see the dynamite go off. They were not disappointed. At 2:15 there was a blinding explosion when Sornberger's store blew to bits, followed by a huge cloud of dust and smoke shutting out the daylight. Screaming men and women ran in every direction as bricks, glass and other debris rained down on them. A flying iron door from Sornberger's was hurled across the street, and demolished the residence of a Mrs. Crawford. Mrs. Nancy McLain and H. B. Newell were struck down and instantly killed by flying bricks. A young man named Clinton Hurlbert, while watching the fires, was struck in the hip by a flying object and seriously injured. Heavy flying debris sliced trees in half, and the whole area looked like a battlefield. Windows were broken all over town, and debris and belongings were scattered in a four-mile radius around the scene. The American Hotel was one of the very few buildings that survived the holocaust, but there was much additional damage. Some fifteen business houses were gutted or destroyed, at an estimated loss of between $150,000 and $200,000.

Residents could only be thankful that more casualties had not occurred. It was reported in the *San Francisco Chronicle* that: "the insurance was not heavy on account of the high rates that are charged because of the lack of fire fighting facilities." As a result,

A PORTION OF THE BURNT OUT GEORGETOWN AFTER THE 1897 CONFLAGRATION. *Talisman Press Collection*

most losses sustained in the disaster were total. It was inexplicable why Georgetown was not better prepared to cope with fires. Certainly, the past had given the residents warning enough.

Georgetown was founded in 1849, and in December of that year the San Francisco *Alta* reported the town had some five thousand miners working in the general area. The original village of shakes, logs and canvas was scattered along Empire Canyon, with little room to grow up the steep sides of the gorge. By 1852, the town had a post office and connections to a stagecoach line.

When a local miner named Eber Thomas died in July 1852, friends suggested a portrait be made of the dead man and sent home to his family. This released an unfortunate set of chain reactions, as the San Francisco *Herald* was later to report:

Coloma, July 14, 1852 — About two thirds of the flourishing village of Georgetown, twelve miles east of this place, was burned to the ground this morning, between the hours of 9 and 12 o'clock. As near as we can learn, the fire originated in a canvas tenement known as the "Round Tent." A Daguerrean artist who was operating in a portion of it—taking the likeness of a dead person—suddenly in the midst of his labors, discovered the curtains that he used, together with the side of the tent, in flames; a sudden breeze springing up accelerated the work of destruction, and in two hours the largest portion of the buildings in town were reduced to ashes.

After this fire Georgetown's old site was considered impractical for rebuilding, and a new location for the town was selected atop a nearby ridge. Miners from miles around aided in clearing the ground and, soon, the forest was echoing to the sound of hammers and saws as a new Georgetown came into being. The new town flourished, but protection against fires was still not considered a priority. However, many in the community were uneasy about this lack of foresight.

In March 1856, the local Georgetown *News* published a long letter warning of the fiery sword of Damocles that dangled over the town residents' heads. Signing his warning "Aquarius," the writer warned that Georgetown's only defense against fire was water, and that water could only be obtained from wells thirty to forty feet deep. Depending on such a slow source would be the same as no protection at all! "Aquarius" suggested building cisterns at strategic positions around town, that could easily be kept filled by the local fire company. "Something should be done," insisted Aquarius, "and that immediately."

The editor heartily endorsed the writer's ideas, but nothing was done—with the inevitable result. On July 7, 1856, another fire broke out and, once more, Georgetown was destroyed. "Last night not a six horse team of provisions could be found in the place," reported the Stockton *San Joaquin Republican*, "the goods saved having been carried off on the backs of owners who fled. Destruction complete." On July 11, however, the

FIRE AND DEATH AT GEORGETOWN.

Famous Pioneer Mining Camp Meets With Disaster.

Two People Instantly Killed by an Explosion of Giant Powder.

One Business House Left Standing Loss Over One Hundred Thousand Dollars—A Blaze at Monrovia.

Special Dispatches to the "Chronicle."
PLACERVILLE, June 14.—Georgetown, located about eighteen miles northeast of this city and in the early fifties one of the most noted mining towns of California, was almost totally

same newspaper published a testimonial to the dauntless spirit of the community:

> Fire at Georgetown—A correspondent of the *State Journal* says: A load of lumber was delivered in the town two and a half hours after the fire commenced, when cheers were given by the crowd, and the American flag was hoisted on the top of the trees which once decorated the main street of the village.

This was far from the end of the town's fiery history. On August 17, 1858, the Sacramento *Daily Union* noted: "Georgetown is burning. It is impossible to get any particulars this evening." Again, most of the business portion of the town was consumed, with only the two brick buildings, Glassman & Company, and Steinfels & Company, saved. Much property was saved, thanks to fireproof cellars built underneath many of the houses, and the total loss was thought to be about $50,000. Once again, "with undismayed energy," the citizens began to rebuild.

On April 19, 1859, all the east side of Main Street was hit by fire. Ten years later, on May 28, 1869, five residents lost their lives in another large-scale conflagration, and much of the business district was again destroyed. That was the last great blaze, until 1897, to hit the town.

In October 1934, Georgetown again sustained heavy damage when eleven buildings were destroyed by a $100,000 fire. Rebuilding took place once more and today, to the great credit of those dauntless if careless townsfolk, the village still exists in the golden hills east of Sacramento.

1898

Santa Cruz Powder Plant Explosion

Where: Santa Cruz
Details: Eleven killed, many injured

Early California, like the rest of the nineteenth-century United States, depended heavily on gunpowder and related explosives. They were used in percussion pistols and rifles of the period, and were needed for blasting out roads and tunnels, mining operations, and various other construction or demolition purposes. Long sea voyages tended to weaken powders so, soon after its creation, the Golden State developed an extensive home industry for explosives of all kinds. As the previous chapters have shown, this planted the seeds for many a manufacturing tragedy. Of these, the last of major importance happened just before the century's end, near Santa Cruz.

In late 1861 the California Powder Works was incorporated by John H. Baird of San Francisco. The company was headquartered in the beautiful San Lorenzo Valley, a mile and a half north of the coastal village of Santa Cruz. The site was along the San Lorenzo River, a beautiful and isolated area where there would be no danger to anyone except those who worked there. Just as important were the surrounding forests. The local trees included oak for barrel staves, used to package the powder; hazel bushes, for barrel hoops; and madron, oak and alder could be burned to make charcoal. Power was supplied by the river.

John Simes, whose paper mill was a half mile below the site, was given the construction contract. Twenty-one powder mills, ten shops, six magazines and stores, and thirty-five other buildings were constructed. It was a million-dollar project, with Simes taking some of his payment in stock. The first powder was manufactured in 1864 and, by 1865, 150,000 twenty-five-pound kegs of powder had been produced. This new and burgeoning industry employed between 150 and 275 workmen.

Naturally, the powder works was a dangerous place, although

every precaution was taken to protect the employees. Buildings were constructed with concrete walls and breakaway roofs, so as to direct the force of any explosion upward. There were explosions and some deaths over the years, but there was little trouble attracting new workers, and a small village of workers' homes grew up on what was called Powder Mill Flat. In time, the sprawling facility would

THE CENTER OF THE SANTA CRUZ POWDER WORKS COMPLEX, WHERE THE EXPLOSIONS OCCURRED. DESPITE THE DESTRUCTION, PRODUCTION SCHEDULES WERE MAINTAINED. *San Francisco* Chronicle, *April 27, 1898*

also become a tourist attraction. When Simes died in 1871, his paper mill property was purchased by Baird, who then expanded his powder works even more extensively.

Originally, the kegged powder was taken in wagons to a Santa Cruz wharf for shipping. When the railroad came through in 1880, the powder was shipped direct to San Francisco. By this time California was producing its own powder, independent of the eastern powder manufacturers.

The Santa Cruz powder plant was very successful at the time Colonel Bernard Peyton took charge as superintendent in 1898. The Spanish American War was in progress and, except for the Du Pont plant in the East, the Santa Cruz facility was the only factory in the country producing smokeless powder. In late September 1897, there was an explosion of 100,000 pounds of powder in one of the plants. It occurred at two o'clock in the morning and no one was injured, but the cost was $20,000.

In April 1898, the company was busy filling an order for 3,000,000 pounds of smokeless powder, made by the United States armed forces. Governor James Budd was concerned about sabotage at the coastal facility and offered to send two troops of cavalry to patrol the perimeter of the sprawling powder complex. Colonel Peyton felt their own force of guards was adequate for policing the operation.

On the afternoon of April 26, 1898, the employees at Powder Mill Flat were looking forward to their six o'clock quitting time. Without warming, their reveries were interrupted by a succession of vicious blasts. In later years Mrs. Phyllis Patten, then a young schoolgirl, recalledthe scene:

> The whole town shook with the force of the explosions. I was sitting by a window in the school looking out. It was a quarter past five in the evening. All of a sudden there was that terrible explosion, then a stream of sparks flew past the window—almost like lightning.

Young Phyllis and many other Santa Cruz residents rushed from their homes toward the beach. A man dashed down the street on a horse, yelling that the main powder magazine was about to explode next. People were standing on the streets everywhere as several more explosions reverberated in the hills to the north, and great plumes of smoke rose in the distance. Family members and friends of workmen began running toward the smoke, hoping to meet someone with news. But only dribbles of information were being received. The first explosion had been in the nitroglycerine factory, blowing the building to bits and shaking the city like an earthquake. As fire spread from this first explosion, blasts took place in the guncotton plant, the dryhouse, and several smokeless powder buildings. Flaming bits of debris caught trees and grass on fire, which soon spread to where the workers' homes were located.

Naval Reserve members were quickly on the scene to fight the fires as were many men from town. However, several of the homes and boarding houses on Powder Mill Flat burned before the fires there were brought under control.

The body of one young man, Guy Fagen, was so mangled and burned he had to be identified by his teeth. He was only sixteen years old and had been hired the previous day. Luther and Ernest Marshall were brothers who were both killed in one of the explosions. Ed Gilleran had just gotten off work and was walking home when the first blast occurred. A large rock hit him in the head, killing him instantly. In all, eleven men died as a result of the disaster.

There was some talk of Spanish sabotage, which was dismissed by the local police. The explosion was thought to have been more likely caused by spontaneous combustion. About $75,000 worth of destruction had taken place. All the wrecked buildings were concrete and simple wood structures, built at little cost. Fortunately, most of the damage was restricted to the facilities manufacturing rifle and shotgun powder. The prismatic powder factory that made the powder for cannons, and was thus fulfilling the government contract, escaped damage. In addition, much new machinery that was due to be installed was saved. Charcoal wood, so important to the production processes, accounted for $18,000 of the total loss.

A large funeral was held for the victims, attended by most of Santa Cruz's residents. The powder company paid all costs, including erection of a monument over the fresh graves. Several weeks later the powder works was back in business, with its manufacturing capacity suffering hardly a hiccup, and still much-needed to prosecute the war against Spain.

Ends and Beginnings

Minus the aspect of tragedy, disasters offer a rough yardstick for progress and change in society. This is certainly true of California during the nineteenth century. While some constants endure, others recede into the past as relics of a sort.

Fires, the great bane of towns and cities during the flimsily-built Gold Rush era—destroying some localities several times over—had greatly lessened in their impact by the turn of the century. With the use of canvas and wood on the decline, and with more construction consisting of brick and concrete, it became harder for whole settlements to go up in smoke. Whereas every major city in California suffered through a major blaze during the 1850s, the proliferation of better construction and well-equipped fire companies held losses much lower by the 1890s. During that latter decade, the worst of the blazes were restricted to smaller towns, such as Guerneville, Woodland and Georgetown. No corresponding fires were hitting major urban areas by that time, and their incidence in the twentieth century—San Francisco in 1906, Berkeley in 1923 and 1992, and Bel-Air in 1961—has been relatively infrequent.

The petering-out of California's great steam-related tragedies roughly parallels the end of its great fire era. With the increased use of coal and petroleum-based fluids for motive power, and better attention paid to safety factors, boarding a ship became less of a calculated risk and more of a routine act. The *Julia*'s demise, in 1888, marked the end of these horrible and generally unanticipated incidents in California. It was the passing of an era which, surely, no one mourned.

Another momentous change worth noting: from self-reliance in the wake of tragedy, to today's declarations of federal disaster areas and millions in insurance payouts, should the companies neglect to invoke the "act of God" clauses in their policies. In those faraway times, people did not rely on government for help in times of disaster. They relied on their family, friends and neighbors, their own courage and frequently the unsought aid of a great many strangers. Whenever there was a great catastrophe of any kind, the victims were immediately welcomed into homes and supplied with clothes, food and anything else they needed. While shopkeepers frequently donated supplies of every kind, government was usually the last to be asked for aid. These days, it tends to be the first resource.

Terrible as the disaster roster was, there were—and are—reasons to be thankful upon reviewing it. California has been and continues to be a worldwide center of mining operations, all of which are rife with danger and potential mishaps. Yet relatively few mining-related disasters hit anywhere in the Golden State during the nineteenth century, with the most notable examples (Bodie, 1879 and the Utica Mine, 1889 and 1891) documented in this book. Few others are found in the records. Considering the thousands of personnel and locations which have been involved in this industry, the fact it compiled such a relatively light record of casualties is astounding.

Another surprise is the relative paucity of railroad disasters in nineteenth-century California, considering how dominant a means of transportation it was after the 1860s, and that this dominance continued until the automobile's advent, well after the century's turn. Even in the worst of the train-related mishaps (Santa Cruz, 1880 and Tehachapi, 1883) the fatality rates were low. Considering the risks inherent on the rails in those days—no computerized safety systems, susceptibility to avalanches and floods, and a huge reliance on human judgment and its accuracy—it again seems remarkable that the derailments and collisions were as rare as they were.

Then—sadly—there are the threats that never end and never will. Californians of today remain equally vulnerable to earthquakes as they were during its earliest days of habitation. And here there is reason to view the future with ample trepidation. With the exception of 1906, no shakes equal to those felt in 1812, 1857 and 1872 have reoccurred. The state was fortunate in that the population was scantier in those years, and the construction less extensive. If any of those shocks are re-created in the near future, property losses will be in the billions, and the human toll is almost too much to contemplate.

Flooding and landslides likewise remain a threat to California and Californians. In fact, the continued advance of residential areas into scenic mountain and cliff locales has, to some extent, exacerbated this risk factor. Thanks to ubiquitous news coverage, almost everyone has seen an image of a canyon filled with mud, or a home perched precariously on dissolving ground—usually somewhere in the greater Los Angeles area.

It seems a bit odd to ascribe certain trends to disasters, since their very nature is rooted in the unexpected. Yet their evolution is inextricably tied to the activities of humans and these, inevitably, dictate their terms and types. So they did in the California of long ago, and so they do today, giving us relief that some of the old fears need no longer be heeded—and, at the same time, giving us some new reasons for worry. As the sage once said: "The more things change, the more they remain the same."

The Authors

MAJOR CALIFORNIA DISASTER LOG, 1812-1899

The list which follows attempts to summarize California disasters for the period which can fairly be described as "major," although that determination is, by necessity, subjective. All events mentioned at length in the main text are included, along with a number which possess obvious significance, but which could not be covered at length due to space limitations. Here, we have attempted to assemble a record of all fires in which either the dollar loss was great, or all or nearly all of a town or city was consumed by flames; all rail and maritime disasters in which there was large-scale economic loss, and/or deaths; all earthquakes in which there was widespread and significant property destruction; and all explosions in which there was widespread property damage. We have tried to account for the number of dead and injured, and for total dollar losses (non-adjusted for inflation), but these data are not always available from the records, and are sometimes not reported in the most reliable fashion. Despite the gaps and question marks this is, to the best of our knowledge, the first log of its kind to ever appear in print.

Date	Disaster	Location	Casualties	Losses	Remarks
1812-1813	Earthquakes	Southern California	Unknown	Unknown	See text for details.
1833	Epidemic	California	Thousands of deaths	N/A	Widespread malaria epidemic. See text for details.
January 7, 1836	Shipwreck	Golden Gate	Unknown	Unknown	Schooner *Peor es Nada* stranded, all aboard lost.
1847	Donner Party	Northern California	43 deaths	N/A	Stranded party of emigrants in the Sierra which resorted to cannibalism for survival. See text for details.
December 24, 1849	Fire	San Francisco	Unknown	$1,000.000+	First major fire to hit San Francisco. See text for details.
April 4, 1850	Fire	Sacramento	Unknown		First major fire to hit Sacramento. See text for details.

Date	Disaster	Location	Casualties	Losses	Remarks
May 4, 1850	Fire	San Francisco	Unknown	$4,000,000+	Second major fire to hit San Francisco. See text for details.
June 14, 1850	Fire	San Francisco	Unknown	$5,000.000+	Third major fire to hit San Francisco. See text for details.
August 1850	Explosion	San Francisco Bay			Steamer *Fawn*'s boiler exploded, first such tragedy in California waters. See text for details.
October 29, 1850	Explosion	San Francisco Bay	50 or so deaths	Unknown	Steamer *Sagamore*'s boiler exploded despite no warning of trouble. See text for details.
November 9, 1850	Fire	Sacramento	Unknown		Second major fire to hit Sacramento. See text for details.
Late 1850	Epidemic	Northern California	250-300+ Deaths, many ill	N/A	See text for details.
March 11, 1851	Fire	Nevada [City]	Unknown	$500,000	First major fire to hit Nevada City. See text for details.
May 3, 1851	Fire	San Francisco	6 deaths	$12,000,000+	Fourth major fire to hit San Francisco; most costly of all nineteenth-century fires in California, unmatched until the 1906 earthquake and fire. See text for details.
May 6, 1851	Shipwreck	Humboldt Bay	None	Unknown	*Commodore Preble* run aground. Said to be first major shipping disaster on the Pacific coast.
May 7, 1851	Fire	Stockton	Unknown	$1,000,000+	Most severe fire to hit city during Gold Rush era; heavy losses to business district.
August 31, 1851	Fire	Marysville	Unknown	$500,000+	First of a succession of major fires to hit Marysville. See text for details.
September 10, 1851	Fire	Marysville	Unknown	$80,000+	Second major fire to hit Marysville. See text for details.

Date	Disaster	Location	Casualties	Losses	Remarks
February 19, 1852	Fire	Downieville	Unknown	$150,000+	First major fire to hit town. See text for details.
June 19, 1852	Fire	Sonora	1 death	$2,000,000	First major fire to hit Sonora, also resulting in highest losses. See text for details.
July 14, 1852	Fire	Georgetown	Unknown	Unknown	First major fire to hit Georgetown; approximately two-thirds of town destroyed. See text for details.
August 16, 1852	Shipwreck	San Simeon Bay	20 deaths	Unknown	Steamship *Pioneer* run aground after experiencing mechanical failure and sustaining damage in bad weather.
November 2-3, 1852	Fire	Sacramento	4 deaths, many injured	$10,000,000	Third major fire to hit Sacramento, and the most extensive of all; second greatest fire in nineteenth-century California. See text for details.
November 7, 1852	Fire	Marysville	Unknown	$75,000+	Third major fire to hit Marysville. See text for details.
1852-1853	Storms/ Floods	California	Unknown	Unknown	Harsh winter season resulted in much property loss. See text for details.
January 6, 1853	Ship collision	Carquinez Straits	At least 10	Unknown	Steamships *Comanche* and *J. Bragdon* collided, with the former sinking.
March 6 , 1853	Shipwreck	near Point Bonita (Tennessee Cove)	None	$300,000+	Steamer *Tennessee* ran aground; see text for details.
March 7, 1853	Fire	Weaverville	Unknown	$100,000+	First major fire; two-thirds of town destroyed.
March 21, 1853	Explosion	near Nicolaus	24 deaths	Unknown	Steamship *R.K. Page* exploded during race with *Governor Dana*.
April 9, 1853	Shipwreck	3 miles north of Bolinas Bay	None	$150,000+	Steamship *S.S. Lewis* run aground and dashed to pieces in rough seas.

Date	Disaster	Location	Casualties	Losses	Remarks
April 11, 1853	Explosion	San Francisco Bay	31 deaths, 19 injured	Unknown	Steamer *Jenny Lind*'s boiler unexpectedly exploded. See text for details.
June 14, 1853	Fire	Shasta	Unknown	$250,000	Most of town destroyed; heavy losses to business district.
June 28, 1853	Fire	Rough and Ready	Unknown	$60,000	Most of town destroyed.
July 8, 1853	Fire	French Corral	Unknown	$42,000+	Most of town destroyed.
July 12, 1853	Fire	Ophir	Unknown	$100,000+	Most of town destroyed in only one hour.
August 25, 1853	Fire	Kelsey's Diggings	Unknown	$30,000+	Most of town destroyed.
October 4, 1853	Fire	Sonora	1 death	$300,000	Second major fire to hit Sonora. Large portion of town and business district reduced to ashes in only one hour.
October 18, 1853	Explosion	Three Sloughs	4 deaths, 6 injured	Unknown	Steamer *American Eagle*'s boiler exploded.
October 18, 1853	Explosion	New York Landing	2 deaths, some injuries	Unknown	Steamer *Stockton*'s boiler exploded.
December 1853	Shipwreck	Anacapa Island	Some injuries	Unknown	Steamer *Winfield Scott* ran aground, placing crew and passengers at great peril. See text for details.
January 8, 1854	Explosion	San Francisco Bay	2 deaths	Unknown	Steamer *Ranger*'s boiler exploded.
January 19, 1854	Explosion	San Francisco Bay	2 deaths, 10 injured	Unknown	Steamer *Helen Hensley*'s boiler exploded.
April 15, 1854	Explosion	San Pablo Bay	40+ deaths, some injuries	Unknown	Steamer *Secretary*'s boiler exploded during race with another vessel. See text for details.
April 21, 1854	Shipwreck	10 miles south of Mendocino	11 deaths	Unknown	Bark *William Claxton* capsized while sailing to San Francisco.
May 12, 1854	Fire	Yreka	Unknown	$147,000+	Upper business district destroyed.

Date	Disaster	Location	Casualties	Losses	Remarks
May 25, 1854	Fire	Marysville	Unknown	$200,000+	Fourth major fire to hit Marysville. See text for details.
July 7, 1854	Fire	Minnesota	Unknown	$52,000+	Town destroyed except for three buildings.
July 10, 1854	Fire	Columbia	Unknown	$500,000+	First major fire to hit town; most of business district destroyed.
July 13, 1854	Fire	Sacramento	Several injuries	$300,000+	Twelve blocks of city destroyed.
July 27, 1854	Fire	Marysville	Unknown	$250,000+	Fifth major fire to hit Marysville. See text for details.
August 2, 1854	Fire	Bidwell	Unknown	Unknown	All but six buildings in town destroyed within one hour.
August 17, 1854	Fire	Campo Seco	Unknown	$100,000+	Entire town destroyed within an hour.
August 19, 1854	Fire	St. Louis	Unknown	$150,000+	Town destroyed.
August 20, 1854	Fire	Mokelumne Hill	Unknown	$500,000+	All but two buildings in town destroyed.
October 1854	Shipwreck	Point Arguello	30+ deaths,	$500,000+	Steamer *Yankee Blade* ran aground, with general confusion and looting ensuing. See text for details.
January 27, 1855	Explosion	near Sacramento	20+ deaths, many injured	Unknown	Steamer *Pearl*'s boiler exploded during race with another vessel. See text for details.
June 4, 1855	Fire	Auburn	Unknown	$250,000+	Most of town destroyed.
June 24, 1855	Fire	Angels Camp	Unknown	$40,000+	Town destroyed.
June 24, 1855	Ship Fire	Crescent City	None	$140,000+	Steamer *America* burned; passengers rescued despite extreme hazards.

Date	Disaster	Location	Casualties	Losses	Remarks
June 24, 1855	Fire	Crescent City	Unknown	$140,000+	Steamer *America* burned while in harbor.
September 7, 1855	Fire	Weaverville	Unknown	$200,000+	Second major fire to hit town; most of it destroyed.
September 13, 1855	Fire	Grass Valley	Unknown	$400,000+	Almost entire town destroyed in two hours, with blaze covering 25 to 30 acres.
October 6, 1855	Fire	Scott's Bar	Unknown	$100,000	All but one building in town destroyed.
November 23, 1855	Explosion	Petaluma	5 deaths	Unknown	Steamship *Georgia* explodes; captain later held responsible.
January 8, 1856	Shipwreck	Half Moon Bay	At least 2 deaths	$120,000	Clipper *Isabelita Hyne* found washed ashore, with possible evidence of mutiny on board.
February 6, 1856	Explosion	11 miles north of Sacramento	10+ deaths, 18 injured	Unknown	Steamer *Belle*'s boiler failed unexpectedly during normal run. See text for details.
July 7, 1856	Fire	Georgetown	Unknown	Unknown	Second major fire to hit Georgetown; town destroyed. See text for details.
July 7, 1856	Fire	Placerville	Unknown	$1,000,000+	All but two buildings in business district destroyed, along with most of the town.
July 19, 1856	Fire	Nevada [City]	At least 10 deaths	$1,500,000+	Second major fire to hit town, most of which was destroyed in a half-hour. See text for details.
August 1856	Fire	Marysville	Unknown	$145,000	Sixth major fire to hit Marysville. See text for details.
August 5, 1856	Fire	Diamond Springs	Unknown	$500,000+	Most of town destroyed.
January 9, 1857	Earthquake	California	1 death	Unknown	Shock centered near Fort Tejon, but severe and felt widely; see text for details.

Date	Disaster	Location	Casualties	Losses	Remarks
February 2, 1857	Fire	Iowa Hill	Unknown	Unknown	Business district of town destroyed.
June 15, 1857	Fire	Drytown	Unknown	$100,000+	Most of town destroyed.
August 1, 1857	Fire	Calaveritas	Unknown	$30,000+	Town destroyed.
August 25, 1857	Fire	Columbia	6 deaths	$650,000+	Second major fire to hit town; all but a few buildings destroyed.
January 1, 1858	Fire	Downieville	Several injuries	$500,000+	Second major fire to hit town, and the most destructive of all. See text for details.
April 10, 1858	Fire	Forest City	Unknown	$180.000+	Most of town destroyed.
May 22, 1858	Fire	Nevada [City]	Unknown	$207,000+	Third major fire to hit town. Large portion of business district destroyed. See text for details.
June 2, 1858	Fire	San Andreas	Unknown	$200,000+	Most of town destroyed.
June 4, 1858	Fire	Mariposa	Unknown	Unknown	Most of business district destroyed.
August 17, 1858	Fire	Georgetown	Unknown	$50,000	Third major fire to hit town. All but four structures in business district destroyed; see text for details.
November 8, 1858	Shipwreck	Farallon Islands	10-20 deaths	Unknown	Ship *Lucas* ran aground; reportedly first wreck in the island chain. See text for details.
November 26, 1858	Earthquake	Northern California	Unknown	Unknown	Felt most strongly at San Francisco and San Jose, both of which experienced notable property damage.
April 19, 1859	Fire	Georgetown	Unknown	Unknown	Fourth major fire to hit town; east side of Main Street consumed by flames. See text for details.

Date	Disaster	Location	Casualties	Losses	Remarks
June 17, 1859	Windstorm	Santa Barbara	Unknown	Unknown	Hot gale-force wind destroyed large numbers of trees, plants and wild/ domesticated animals.
June 25, 1859	Fire	Tehama	Unknown	$100,000+	Business district of town destroyed.
July 8, 1859	Fire	Chips' Flat	Unknown	$15,000+	Most of town destroyed.
July 8, 1859	Fire	Rough and Ready	Unknown	$75,000+	All but two buildings in town destroyed.
July 23, 1859	Fire	Grizzly Flat	1 death	Unknown	All but two buildings in business district destroyed.
August 12, 1859	Fire	Vallecito	1 death 2 injuries	$60,000+	Business district of town largely destroyed.
August 21, 1859	Fire	Murphys	Unknown	$100,000	Business district of town largely destroyed.
January 5, 1860	Shipwreck	Humboldt Bay	38 deaths	Unknown	Steamer *Northerner* ran aground, with great loss of life. See text for details.
January 28, 1860	Fire	Forbestown	Unknown	$20,000+	All but four buildings in town destroyed.
November 15, 1860	Shipwreck	Big River	10 deaths	Unknown	Brig *J.S. Cabot* capsized.
July 27, 1861	Fire	La Porte	Unknown	Unknown	Most of town destroyed.
August 1, 1861	Fire	Forbestown	Unknown	$35,000+	Most of town destroyed.
August 7, 1861	Fire	Sonora	Unknown	$100,000+	Third major fire to hit Sonora. Large portion of town destroyed.
August 25, 1861	Explosion	near Knight's Landing	15 deaths	Unknown	Steamer *J.A. McClelland*'s defective boiler exploded while on a run to Red Bluff. See text for details.
1861-1862	Storms/ Floods	California	Unknown	Unknown	Harsh winter season resulted in much property loss. See text for details.

Date	Disaster	Location	Casualties	Losses	Remarks
1862-1863	Epidemic	Southern California	"Hundreds"	N/A	Smallpox outbreak killed many living on Indian reservations, especially in San Diego County.
August 23, 1862	Fire	Jackson	Unknown	$300,000	Most of town destroyed, 2,000 made homeless.
September 12, 1862	Fire	Snelling	Unknown	$22,000+	Large portion of town destroyed.
February 22, 1863	Shipwreck	Humboldt Bar	13-15 deaths	Unknown	Tugboat *Merrimac* broken up in rough seas.
April 27, 1863	Explosion	San Pedro Harbor	50 or so deaths	Unknown	Steamer *Ada Hancock*'s boiler water shifted suddenly, causing high pressure and explosion. See text for details.
November 8, 1863	Fire	Nevada [City]	Unknown	$550,000+	Fourth major fire to hit town; most of it destroyed. See text for details.
December 30, 1863	Shipwreck	22 miles south of Cape Mendocino	14 deaths	Unknown	Schooner *Dashaway* wrecked.
February 27, 1864	Fire	Downieville	Unknown	$200,000+	Business district of town destroyed.
May 30, 1864	Fire	Michigan Bluff	Unknown	$50,000	All but two buildings in business district destroyed.
September 4, 1864	Fire	Goodyear's Bar	Unknown	Unknown	Most of town destroyed.
September 5, 1864	Explosion	near Rio Vista	80+ deaths unknown injuries	Unknown	Steamer *Washoe*'s boiler exploded during race with other vessels. See text for details.
October 26, 1864	Explosion	Suisun	At least 7 deaths, 7 injuries	Unknown	Steamer *Sophie McLane* succumbed, apparently to defective boiler.
October 30, 1864	Fire	Horsetown	Unknown	Unknown	Most of town destroyed.
January 17, 1865	Shipwreck	Pigeon Point	13 deaths	Unknown	*Sir John Franklin* ran aground, cargo saved but ship lost.

Date	Disaster	Location	Casualties	Losses	Remarks
January 17, 1865	Shipwreck	Pigeon Point	13 deaths	Unknown	*Sir John Franklin* ran aground, cargo saved but ship lost.
June 27, 1865	Fire	Forest City	1 death, 1 injured	$50,000	Most of town destroyed.
July 30, 1865	Shipwreck	Point St. George	166 deaths	Unknown	Steamer *Brother Jonathan* ran aground, with only nineteen escaping. The most significant maritime disaster in nineteenth-century California. See text for details.
October 8, 1865	Earthquake	Northern Caifornia	Unknown	Unknown	Extensive damage to buildings in San Francisco, Santa Clara and San Jose.
April 16, 1866	Explosion	San Francisco	12 deaths, some injuries	Unknown	Mishandling of crate with nitroglycerin lead to detonation. See text for details.
June 29, 1866	Fire	Montezuma	Unknown	Unknown	Town destroyed.
August 25, 1866	Fire	Mariposa	Unknown	Unknown	All but five or six buildings in town destroyed.
August 27, 1866	Explosion	Petaluma	5 deaths 7 injured	Unknown	Railroad locomotive explosion, cause undetermined.
November 28, 1866	Shipwreck	Pigeon Point	26 deaths	Unknown	Bark *Coya*, carrying coal and passengers, ran aground.
April 12, 1867	Shipwreck	San Francisco Heads	7 deaths	$10,000	Pilot boat *Caleb Curtis* capsized, with a number of crew members drowning.
August 16, 1867	Fire	Washington	Unknown	$40,000+	Business district of town destroyed.
December 23, 1867	Cloudburst/ Flood	Auburn	Unknown	Unknown	Many buildings washed away or significantly damaged.
March 4, 1868	Avalanche	Keystone	5 deaths	Unknown	Significant property damage to mining camp.

Date	Disaster	Location	Casualties	Losses	Remarks
July 4, 1868	Mechanical	Oakland	10 deaths, some injuries	Unknown	Ramp leading to ferryboat failed, plunging many into water. See text for details.
August 27, 1868	Fire	Hornitos	Unknown	$60,000+	Most of town destroyed.
October 21, 1868	Earthquake	Northern California	Unknown	$700,000+	Severe series of shocks, greatest felt in San Francisco until 1906. See text for details.
November 19, 1868	Shipwreck	Pigeon Point	11 deaths	Unknown	*Hellespont*, carrying cargo of coal, went aground.
January 8, 1869	Shipwreck	10 miles north of Santa Cruz, on coast	5 lost	Unknown	Schooner *A. Crosby* sank unexpectedly overnight.
May 28, 1869	Fire	Georgetown	5 deaths	$32,000+	Fifth major fire to hit Georgetown; half of town destroyed. See text for details.
July 31, 1869	Fire	Moore's Flat	Unknown	$80,000+	All but two buildings in town destroyed.
November 1, 1869	Fire	Cisco	Unknown	Unknown	Town destroyed.
November 14, 1869	Train	Simpson's Station	15 deaths, many injured	Unknown	Switchman's inability to read timetable resulted in collision. See text for details.
November 26, 1869	Explosion	San Francisco	2 deaths, 7 injured	Unknown	Accident at Giant Powder Works, cause indeterminate.
August 15, 1870	Fire	New Almaden	Unknown	Unknown	Most of town destroyed.
September 23, 1870	Train derailment	near Vallejo	1 death, 2 injured	Unknown	Train failed to brake properly when cow obstructed tracks; thrown off course and six cars demolished.
October 17, 1870	Fire	Mendocino	Unknown	Unknown	Business district of town destroyed.
March 29, 1871	Fire	Truckee	1 death	Unknown	Widespread destruction, with all of Chinatown destroyed.
July 4, 1871	Fire	Yreka	Unknown	$300,000+	One-third of town destroyed.

Date	Disaster	Location	Casualties	Losses	Remarks
July 17, 1871	Fire	Marysville	Several injuries	$100,000+	Heavy losses to business district.
June 18, 1872	Fire	Mineral Hill	Unknown	$80,000+	Most of business district destroyed.
April 26, 1872	Earthquake	Owens Valley	16+ deaths, 60+ injuries	Unknown	Most severe earthquake ever recorded in California, felt throughout all the central section. See text for details.
October 13, 1872	Train derailment	near Truckee	4 or more deaths, several injured	Unknown	Three cars jumped tracks and went over embankment due to brake chain failure
October 23, 1872	Fire	Howland Flat	Unknown	Unknown	Business district of town destroyed.
November 25, 1872	Fire	Oroville	Unknown	$50,000+	Chinatown destroyed.
April 20, 1873	Fire	Chico	Unspecified deaths	$100,000+	Half of town destroyed.
November 5, 1873	Fire	Dutch Flat	Unknown	Unknown	Most of town destroyed and all of Chinatown.
December 16, 1873	Tornado	Milton	None	$7,000	Scattered property damage; first tornado of note to strike in California.
April 22, 1874	Fire	Colfax	Unknown	Unknown	Business district destroyed, along with numerous houses.
April 7, 1875	Explosion	San Francisco	5 or more deaths, several injured	$650,000	Accidental fire detonated powder box, leading to explosiv e chain reaction. See text for details.
May 20, 1875	Fire	Milton	Unknown	$10,000+	Most of town destroyed.
May 29, 1875	Fire	Truckee	Unknown	$50,000+	Chinatown destroyed.
April 18, 1876	Shipwreck	Humboldt Bar	5 deaths	Unknown	Schooner *Albert and Edward* capsized.
October 30, 1876	Stampede	San Francisco	19 deaths, many injured	N/A	Hasty theater evacuation in Chinatown leads to great tragedy. See text for details.

Date	Disaster	Location	Casualties	Losses	Remarks
April 4, 1877	Train collision	Cascade	3 deaths, several injured	Unknown	Collision between two locomotives owing to engineer's error.
October 10, 1877	Fire	Vacaville	Unknown	$250,000+	Most of business district destroyed.
November 22, 1878	Shipwreck	Humboldt Bar	7 deaths	Unknown	Ship *Laura Pike* wrecked.
January 14, 1879	Explosion	San Francisco	7 deaths	$50,000	Accident at Giant Powder Works, apparently caused by misuse of hammer and nails.
February 12, 1879	Explosion	Santa Cruz Mountains	Many injured	Unknown	Coal oil gas ignited by accident, leading to tragedy. See text for details.
February 22, 1879	Explosion	Stockton	15 deaths, many injured	Unknown	Public demonstration of inadequate boiler leads to explosion. See text for details.
July 9, 1879	Fire	Coulterville	Unknown	Unknown	Half of town destroyed.
July 10,1879	Explosion	Bodie	7 deaths, 18+ injured	Unknown	Accidental detonation of powder magazine located next to Standard mine. See text for details.
September 7, 1879	Fire	Marysville	Unknown	$50,000	Seventh major fire to hit Marysville. See text for details.
October 5, 1879	Balloon crash	San Francisco	2 deaths	N/A	Possible improper ballast leads to irregular flight and crash. See text for details.
November 18, 1879	Explosion	Wright's	27+ deaths, 17+ injured	Unknown	Coal oil gas ignited by accident, leading to tragedy. See text for details.
April 17, 1880	Explosion	Berkeley	24 deaths	Unknown	Accident at Giant Powder Works, apparently caused by using metal hammers to seal powder packing crate.

243

Date	Disaster	Location	Casualties	Losses	Remarks
May 23, 1880	Train derailment	Santa Cruz Mountains	10+ deaths, 30+ injured	Unknown	Train ran away after being backed up to summit, going out of control. See text for details.
November 19, 1880	Fire	Jamison	Unknown	Unknown	Town destroyed.
November 26, 1880	Train	Oakland	1 death, injuries	Unknown	Main locomotive jumped track and three cars derailed due to fast braking.
August 31, 1881	Fire	Sierraville	Unknown	$50,000	Business district of town destroyed.
September 26, 1881	Shipwreck	Half Moon Bay	11 deaths	Unknown	Sailship *Alice Buck* ran aground with a cargo of coal.
November 10, 1881	Fire	Modesto	1 death	$100,000	Much of business district destroyed.
March 11, 1882	Windstorm	Kern County	Unknown	Unknown	Large sand clouds obscured visibility. Numerous buildings blown down by gale-force winds.
May 30, 1882	Fire	Willows	Unknown	$175,000+	Most of town destroyed.
June 19, 1882	Shipwreck	Golden Gate	25 deaths	Unknown	Iron steamship *Escambia* unexpectedly sank, losing most of its crew.
August 11, 1882	Explosion	near Vallejo	Unknown	Unknown	Hardy Powder Works destroyed; fifteen tons of powder detonated by accident.
August 17, 1882	Fire	Red Bluff	Unknown	$500,000+	Heart of business district destroyed.
October 4, 1882	Shipwreck	7 miles south of Navarro	7 deaths	Unknown	Ship *Emily Stevens* capsized.
January 1883	Train	Tehachapi	21+ deaths, many injured	Unknown	Improperly-set or defective brakes caused train to roll backward, derail, and smash up cars. See text for details.

Date	Disaster	Location	Casualties	Losses	Remarks
January 21, 1883	Explosion	Fleming's Point, 2 miles north of Berkeley	40+ deaths, 6+ injured	$150,000	Destruction of the Giant Powder Works and San Francisco Chemical Works by accidental detonation.
March 16, 1883	Fire	Forest City	Unknown	$100,000	All but a few buildings in town destroyed.
May 23, 1883	Fire	Guerneville	Unknown	$75,000	Business district and much of residential area destroyed.
May 25, 1883	Explosion	Petaluma Creek	11-13 deaths	Unknown	Steamer *Pilot* exploded.
June 15, 1883	Fire	San Mateo	Unknown	$40,000	Business district of town destroyed.
September 30, 1883	Explosion	Pinole	30+ deaths	$7,000+	Accidental explosion at California Powder Works.
August 5, 1884	Fire	La Porte	Unknown	Unknown	Most of town destroyed.
June 21, 1885	Fire	Merced	Unknown	$60,000+	Much of business district destroyed.
August 20, 1885	Shipwreck	near Point Reyes	17 deaths	$187,000+	Bark *Haddingtonshire*, due to broken navigational equipment, ran aground in fog and rough seas.
December 24, 1885	Explosion	San Francisco	2 deaths, 3 injured	Unknown	Accidental boiler explosion at Spring Valley Water Works.\
December 25, 1885	Shipwreck	near Humboldt Bay	7 deaths	Unknown	Bark *Lili of Elseffeith* ran aground.
June 30, 1886	Fire	Independence	Unknown	$285,000	Business district destroyed, along with much of residential areas.
July 5, 1886	Fire	Wrights	Unknown	Unknown	Excepting railroad company buildings, town destroyed.
August 13, 1886	Fire	Folsom	Unknown	$150,000	Business district mostly destroyed.
December 7, 1886	Shipwreck	San Francisco, near Cliff House	30 deaths	Unknown	Whaling bark *Atlantic* run aground in heavy fog.

Date	Disaster	Location	Casualties	Losses	Remarks
January 16, 1887	Explosion	San Francisco	2 injured	Unknown	Schooner *Parallel*'s cargo of powder, caps and coal oil detonated by accident after ship drifted out of control. See text for details.
April 1, 1887	Fire	Monterey	None	Unknown	Hotel Del Monte, one of California's great luxury resorts, burns to ground. See text for details.
May 30, 1887	Fire	Santa Cruz	Unknown	$50,000+	Large portion of central city destroyed.
July 24, 1887	Fire	Los Angeles	Unknown	$50,000	Most of Chinatown destroyed.
July 26, 1887	Fire	Camptonville	Unknown	$100,000	All but a few buildings in town destroyed.
September 4, 1887	Fire	Calico	Unknown	$100,000	All but seven or eight buildings in town destroyed.
September 19, 1887	Fire	Marysville	Unknown	$155,000+	Eighth major fire to hit Marysville. See text for details.
December 14, 1887	Windstorm	Southern California	2 deaths, 14 injured	$100,000+	Hotels at Crescenta Canyon, San Gabriel and Lordsburg destroyed, along with Cucamonga depot.
December 20, 1887	Fire at sea	Pigeon Point	12 deaths	Unknown	Steamship *San Vicente* burned at sea; total loss.
February 27, 1888	Explosion	Vallejo	16 deaths, 18 injured	$250,000	Commuter steamer *Julia* explodes, cause indeterminate. See text for details.
July 9, 1888	Fire	Suisun	1 death	$500,000+	All but two buildings in business district destroyed, along with much of residential area.
November 7, 1888	Fire	Vacaville	Unknown	$200,000+	Most of business district destroyed.

Date	Disaster	Location	Casualties	Losses	Remarks
July 7, 1889	Fire	Bakersfield	Unknown		Total of fifteen square blocks and most of business district destroyed. See text for details.
July 24, 1889	Cloudburst/ Flood	Siskiyou County	Unknown	Unknown	Heavy damage to agricultural and mining properties located along the Klamath River and its tributaries.
August 1889	Fires	Mariposa County	Unknown	Unknown	Succession of forest fires which threatened the Mariposa Grove of Big Trees.
August 26, 1889	Fire	Port Costa	Unknown	$650,000+	Fire at wharves destroyed three ships, forty-two railroad cars of wheat, wheat warehouse, docks and other property.
November 16, 1889	Shipwreck	Humboldt Bar	8 deaths	Unknown	Schooner *Fidelity* capsized.
December 1889	Storms/ Floods	Southern California	Unknown	$450,000+	Heavy property damage to railroads and transportation facilities throughout the region.
December 22, 1889	Mine accident	near Angels Camp	16 deaths	$10,000	Cave-in at Lane (Utica) Mine. See text for details.
January-February 1890	Storms/ Floods	Northern California	Unknown	Unknown	Harsh winter season resulted in much property loss. See text for details.
April 17, 1890	Train derailment	Tehachapi	3 injured	Unknown	Air brake failure resulted in derailment of ten cars.
May 30, 1890	Train derailment	Oakland	13 deaths, many injured	Unknown	Train leaped from tracks when drawbridge was improperly engaged. See text for details.
June 4, 1890	Fire	Daggett	Unknown	$23,000+	Most of business district destroyed.
June 15, 1890	Fire	Chinese Camp	Unknown	$12,000+	Most of business district and some residences destroyed.

Date	Disaster	Location	Casualties	Losses	Remarks
July 12, 1890	Fire	Redding	Unknown	Unknown	Much of business district destroyed.
July 13, 1890	Collision	near Baden	15 deaths, 4+ injured	Unknown	Wagon full of German picknickers collided with locomotive.
August 22, 1890	Train derailment	Cascade	4 deaths, some injured	Unknown	Brake failure caused train to roll backward from summit, causing cars to derail and crush against each other. See text for details.
November 13, 1890	Fire	Tiburon	Unknown	$25,000	All but railroad property destroyed.
January 5, 1891	Mine accident	near Angels Camp	12 deaths	Unknown	Cable skip at Utica Mine broke, plunging miners to their deaths. See text for details.
February 21, 1891	Shipwreck	Tennessee Cove	20+ deaths	$100,000+	Ship *Elizabeth* wrecked in rough weather. See text for details.
June 15, 1891	Train collision	near Port Costa	2 deaths, 6 injured	Unknown	Los Angeles Express and gravel-carrying trains collided due to conductor and engineer negligence.
July 16, 1891	Fire	Boulder Creek	Unknown	$30,000+	Large portion of central town destroyed.
August 23, 1891	Fire	Sheridan	Unknown	$15,000+	Most of business district destroyed.
December 21, 1891	Shipwreck	Point Arena	10 deaths	Unknown	Screw steamship *West Coast* wrecked.
March 27, 1892	Shipwreck	Rockport	5 deaths	Unknown	Steam schooner *Ventura* broke in two after striking rocks.
April 19, 1892	Earthquake	Northern California	Several injuries	$200,000+	Heaviest damage suffered in Vacaville, Winters and Dixon.
June 13, 1892	Explosion	Mare Island Naval Shipyard	15 deaths, many injured	Unknown	Shell manufacturing accident detonated powder and adjacent magazine. See text for details.

Date	Disaster	Location	Casualties	Losses	Remarks
July 2, 1892	Fire	San Jose	Unknown	$200,000	Large portion of business distric t affected.
*July 1892	Fire	Woodland	1 death		
July 20, 1892	Fire	Rio Vista	Unknown	$100,000+	Business district of town and some residences destroyed.
October 21, 1892	Explosion	Los Angeles	7 deaths, may injured	Unknown	Powder added to fireworks led to major explosion. See text for details.
November 1892	Windstorms	Northern California	Unknown	Unknown	Gales cause ships to leave moorings in San Francisco, many buildings damages and roads washed out.
February 17, 1893	Fire	Los Alamos	Unknown	$30,000+	Much of town destroyed.
July 18, 1893	Fire	Susanville	Unknown	$300,000+	Business district destroyed, along with many residences.
September 7, 1893	Fire	Copperopolis	Unknown	$30,000+	Business district destroyed.
February 2, 1894	Shipwreck	Point Sur	6 deaths	Unknown	Propeller ship *Los Angeles* ran aground on rocks near lighthouse.
February 14, 1894	Train derailment	Austin Creek, near Fort Ross	5 deaths	Unknown	Train fell off flood-weakened bridge. See text for details.
April 15,1894	Fire	Santa Cruz	Unknown	$100,000+	Heavy losses in central city, including county courthouse.
August 25, 1894	Fire	Guerneville	2 deaths, several injured	$150,000+	Most of town destroyed.
April 9, 1896	Shipwreck	Mission Bay (San Francisco Bay)	6 deaths	Unknown	Square-rigger *Blairmore* capsizes under freak conditions. See text for details.
November 24, 1896	Shipwreck	Point Arena	6 deaths	Unknown	Ship *San Benito* hit rocks and broke in two.

Date	Disaster	Location	Casualties	Losses	Remarks
June 14, 1897	Fire	Georgetown	2 deaths, 1 injured	$150,000+	Sixth major fire to hit Georgetown; most of town destroyed. See text for details.
June 20, 1897	Earthquake	Northern California	Unknown	Unknown	Damage heaviest at Hollister, Salinas and Gilroy. Said to be severest earthquake in California since 1868.
March 10, 1898	Storm	Northern California	Unknown	Unknown	Steamer *Patterson* collided with bark *Martha Davis*, nearly severing the latter; many vessels damaged.
March 30, 1898	Earthquake	Northern California	Unknown	$300,000+	Heavy damage inflicted at Mare Island Naval Shipyard, and scattered throughout San Francisco Bay Area.
April 14, 1898	Earthquake	Northern California	Unknown	Unknown	Much damage at Mendocino, Greenwood and Point Arena.
April 26, 1898	Explosion	Santa Cruz	5 deaths, many injuries	$75,000	Apparent accidental detonation at California Powder Works. See text for details.
April 2, 1899	Shipwreck	Humboldt Bar	10 deaths	Unknown	Steamship *Chilkat* wrecked.
September 26, 1899	Fire	Forbestown	Unknown	$9,000+	Business district of town destroyed, along with some residences.
December, 1899	Earthquake	Southern California	6 deaths, 8 injured	$60,000+	Heavy damage in San Jacinto, Hemet and Highland.
December 24, 1899	Train derailment	Pomona	3 deaths, 20+ injured	Unknown	Broken drive wheel caused three cars to jump tracks.

Chapter Sources

1812 EARTHQUAKE

Bancroft, Hubert Howe. *History of California, Vol. II, 1801-1824.* San Francisco: The History Company, 1886.

Engelhardt, Rev. Zephyrin, O.F.M. *The Missions and Missionaries of California.* San Francisco: James H. Barry, 1916.

_____. *Santa Barbara Mission.* San Francisco: James H. Barry, 1923.

Geiger, Maynard.O.F.M., and Clement W. Meighan. *As the Padres Saw Them: California Indian Life and Customs as Reported by The Franciscan Missionaries, 1813-1815.* Santa Barbara, Califormia: Santa Barbara Mission Archive Library, 1976.

Johnson, Paul C., ed. *The California Missions: A Pictorial History.* Menlo Park, California: Lane Book Company, 1964.

Pararas-Carayannis. *The Santa Barbara, California, Earthquakes and Tsunamis of December, 1812: A Study of Historical Tsunamis in California.* Marina Advisors, U.S. Regulatory Agency and the U.S. Army Coastal Engineering Research Center.

Phillips, George Harwood. *Indians and Intruders in Central California, 1769-1849.* Norman and London: University of Oklahoma Press, 1993.

Senan, Padre Jose, O.F.M. *The Biennial Report from Mission San Buenaventura, 1811-1812.* Translated by Maynard Geiger, O.F.M. Santa Barbara, California: Old Mission, 1974.

Trask, John B. "A Register of Earthquakes in California from 1800 to 1863." San Francisco *Daily Alta California*, August 8, 1864.

1833 EPIDEMIC

Briggs, Carl, and Duff Chapman. "For Profit and Empire."*The Californians*, May/June 1984.

Cook, Sherburne F. *The Conflict Between the California Indian and White Civilization.* Berkeley and Los Angeles: University of California Press, 1976.

_____. *The Epidemic of 1830-1833 in California and Oregon.* Berkeley and Los Angeles: University of California Press, 1954.

Latta, Frank F. "San Joaquin Primeval." Tulare *Daily Times*, July 29 and 30, 1931.

Maloney, Alice B., ed. *Fur Brigade to the Bonaventura: The Journal of John Work.* San Francisco: California Historical Society, 1945.

Mann, Charles C. "The Pristine Myth." *Atlantic Monthly*, March 7, 2002.

Phillips, George Harwood. *Indians and Intruders in Central California, 1769-1849.* Norman and London: University of Oklahoma Press, 1993.

Warner, Jonathan J. Letter, Los Angeles *Star*, August 22 and 23, 1874.

■ 1847 THE DONNER PARTY

The California Star, January 16; February 13 and 27; April 3; and May 22, 1847.

Californian (newspaper), March 27, 1847.

Houghton, Eliza P. Donner. *The Expedition of the Donner Party and its Tragic Fate.* Chicago: A.C. McClurg & Co., 1911.

King, Joseph A. "The Real Breens versus Persistent Donner Party Mythology, Critiquing the Chroniclers." *The Californians*, July/August 1992.

_____. *Winter of Entrapment, A New Look at the Donner Party.* Lafayette, California: K & K Publishers, 1992.

McGlashan, C. F. *History of the Donner Party, A Tragedy of the Sierra.* Stanford, California: Stanford University Press, 1940.

Steed, Jack and Richard. *The Donner Party Rescue Site, Johnson's Ranch on Bear River.* Fresno: Pioneer Publishing, 1988.

■ 1850 CHOLERA EPIDEMIC

Carter, John Denton. "George Kenyon Fitch, Journalist." *California History Society Quarterly,* December 1941.

Morse, John Frederick, M.D. *First History of Sacramento City* (as published in *The Sacramento Directory for the Year 1853-54*). Sacramento, California: Samuel Colville, 1850.

Nagel, Charles E. "Sacramento's Cholera Epidemic of 1850." Term paper, Department of Social Science, Sacramento State College, 1956.

Sacramento *Daily Transcript*, November 12 and 13, 1850.

San Francisco *Daily Alta California*, October 8, 13, 23, 24, 25, 26, and 27; and November 6, 7, 9, and 12, 1850.

San Francisco *Daily Morning Call*, June 8, 1890.

■ 1850 EXPLOSION OF THE SAGAMORE

De Massey, Ernest. "A Frenchman in the Gold Rush." *California Historical Society Quarterly*, March 1927.

MacMullen, Jerry. *Paddle-Wheel Days in California.* Stanford, California: Stanford University Press, 1944.

McGaw, William Cochran. *Savage Scene: The Life and Times of James Kirker, Frontier King.* New York: Hastings House, 1972.

San Francisco *Daily Alta California*, August 19 and 23; October 31; and November 1, 1850.

San Francisco *Daily Evening Picayune*, October 30, 1850.

■ 1849-51 SAN FRANCISCO FIRES

Barker, Malcom E., comp. *San Francisco Memoirs, 1835-1851: Eyewitness Accounts of the Birth of a City*. San Francisco: Londonborn Publications, 1994.

Barry, T.A. and B.A. Patten. *San Francisco, California, 1850*. Oakland, California: Biobooks, 1947.

Brown, John Henry. *Early Days in San Francisco*. Oakland, California: Biobooks, 1949.

Johnson, Kenneth M. *San Francisco as It Is: Being Gleanings from the Picayune, 1850-1852*. Georgetown, California: Talisman Press, 1964.

Marryat, Frank. *Mountains and Molehills*. London: Longman, Brown, Green and Longmans, 1855.

Mullen, Kevin. *Let Justice Be Done: Crime and Politics in Early San Francisco*. Reno and Las Vegas: University of Nevada Press, 1989.

_____. "Torching Old San Francisco." *The Californians*, January/February 1991.

San Francisco *Daily Alta California*, December 16, 1850.

Sacramento *Daily Union*, May 6, 7, and 12, 1851.

San Joaquin Republican (Stockton), June 25, 1851.

Soule, Frank, John H. Gihon, M.D., and James Nisbet. *The Annals of San Francisco*. New York: Appleton, 1854.

■ 1851 FIRE IN MARYSVILLE

Chamberlain, William, and Harry Wells. *History of Yuba County, California*. Oakland, California: Thompson & West, 1879.

Sacramento Daily Union, September 2, 1851.

San Francisco *Daily Alta California*, September 2, 1851.

San Joaquin Republican (Stockton), September 3, 1851.

■ 1852 GREAT FIRE IN SONORA

Borthwick, J. D. *Three Years in California*. Oakland, California: Biobooks, 1948.

Buckbee, Edna Bryan. *The Saga of Old Tuolumne*. New York: Press of the Pioneers, 1935.

Marryat, Frank. *Mountains and Molehills*. London: Longman, Brown, Green and Longmans, 1855.

Stoddart, Thomas Robertson, ed. by Carlo M. De Ferrari. *Annals of Tuolumne County*. Fresno: Valley Publishers, 1977.

San Francisco *Daily Alta California*, October 6, 1853.

San Joaquin Republican (Stockton), June 19, 21, 23, and 25, 1852.

■ 1852 SACRAMENTO'S GREAT FIRE

History of Sacramento County, California. Oakland: Thompson & West, 1880.

Reed, G. Walter, ed. *History of Sacramento County, California*. Los Angeles: Historic Record Company, 1923.

Sacramento *Daily Union*, November 4, 5, 6, 7, and 8, 1852.

San Francisco *Daily Herald*, November 4 and 5, 1852.

■ 1853 EXPLOSION OF THE JENNIE LIND

Kemble, John Haskell. *San Francisco Bay: A Pictorial History*. New York: Bonanza Books, 1957.

MacMullen, Jerry. *Paddle-Wheel Days in California*. Stanford, California: Stanford University Press, 1944.

Marysville *Herald*, October 29, 1850.

San Francisco *Daily Alta California*, April 10, 12, 13, 1853

San Francisco *Herald*, August 13 and October 3, 1852; April 12, 13, and 14, 1853.

Wiltsee, Ernest A. *Gold Rush Steamers of the Pacific*. San Francisco: Grabhorn Press, 1938.

■ 1853 FLOODS IN THE VALLEYS

Buck, Franklin A., ed. by Katharine A. White. *A Yankee Trader in the Gold Rush*. Boston and New York: Houghton Mifflin, 1930.

Doble, John, ed. by Charles L. Camp. *John Doble's Journals and Letters from the Mines*. Denver: Old West Publishing Company, 1962.

Morse, John Frederick, M.D. *First History of Sacramento City* (as published in *The Sacramento Directory for the Year 1853-54*). Sacramento, California: Samuel Colville, 1850.

Sacramento *Daily Union*, January 1, 3, 4, 5, 10, 11, and 14, 1853.

San Francisco *Daily Alta California*, January 8, 9, 17, 1853.

San Francisco *Herald*, January 3, 1853.

San Joaquin Republican (Stockton), January 12 and 19, 1853.

Williamson, Lieutenant R. S. *Reports of Explorations and Surveys to Ascertain the Most Practicable and Economical Route for a Railroad from the Mississippi River to the Pacific Ocean made under the Direction of the Secretary of War, in 1853-4...* Volume V. Washington: A.O.P. Nicholson, 1856

■ 1853 SINKING OF THE WINFIELD SCOTT

Bosqui, Edward, *Memoirs of Edward Bosqui*. Oakland, California: Holmes Book Company, 1952.

Cardone, Bonnie J., and Patrick Smith. *Shipwrecks of Southern California*. Birmingham, Alabama: Menasha Ridge Press, 1989.

Sacramento *Daily Union*, December 7 and 9, 1853.

San Francisco *Daily Alta California*, December 7, 1853.

San Francisco *Daily Herald*, December 7, 1853.

Wiltsee, Ernest A. *Gold Rush Steamers of the Pacific*. San Francisco: Grabhorn Press, 1938.

1854 EXPLOSION OF THE SECRETARY

Gibbs, James. *Shipwrecks of the Pacific Coast*. Portland: Binfords & Mort, 1957.

MacMullen, Jerry. *Paddle-Wheel Days in California*. Stanford, California: Stanford University Press, 1944.

San Francisco *Daily Alta California*, April 16 and 17, 1854.

San Francisco *Daily Herald*, April 16 and 17, 1854.

1854 WRECK OF THE YANKEE BLADE

Bell, Horace. *Reminiscences of a Ranger*. Santa Barbara: Wallace Hebberd, 1927.

Knight, Donald G., and Eugene D. Wheeler. *Agony and Death on a Gold Rush Steamer*. Ventura, California: Pathfinder Publishing, 1990.

San Francisco *Daily Alta California*, September 27, 28, 29, 30; October 10, 11, 1854

San Francisco *Daily Herald*, October 10, 1854

Spearman, C. F. "The Wreck of the Yankee Blade." *San Diego Historical Society Quarterly*, April 1959.

Wiltsee, Ernest A. *Gold Rush Steamers of the Pacific*. San Francisco: Grabhorn Press, 1938.

1855 EXPLOSION OF THE PEARL

San Francisco *Daily Alta California*, January 29, 1855.

San Francisco *Daily Herald*, January 28 and 29, 1855.

San Joaquin Republican (Stockton), January 31, 1855.

1856 EXPLOSION OF THE BELLE

Sacramento *Daily Union*, February 5 and 6, 1856.

San Francisco *Daily Alta California*, February 6, 1856.

San Francisco *Daily Herald*, February 6 and 7, 1856.

1856 GREAT NEVADA CITY FIRE

Bean, Edwin F., comp. *Bean's History and Directory of Nevada County, etc.* Nevada City: Daily Gazette, 1867.

Davis, H. P. *Gold Rush Days in Nevada City*. Nevada City: Berliner & McGinnis, 1948.

San Francisco *Daily Evening Bulletin*, July 21, 1856.

1857 EARTHQUAKE AT FORT TEJON

Barker, John. *San Joaquin Vignettes, The Reminiscences of Captain John Barker*. Bakersfield, California: Kern County Historical Society, 1955.

Cullimore, Clarence. *Old Adobes of Forgotten Fort Tejon*. Bakersfield, California: Kern County Historical Society, 1949

Mitchell, Annie R. *The Way it Was: The Colorful History of Tulare County*. Fresno: Valley Publishers, 1976.

Richter, Charles F. *Elementary Seismology*. San Francisco: W.H. Freeman, 1955.

Sacramento *Daily Union*, January 10, 1857.

San Francisco *Daily Herald*, January 10, 13, 1857.

San Jose *Tribune*, January 14, 1857.

Santa Barbara *Gazette*, January 15, 1857.

Stockton *Daily Argus*, January 12 and 16, 1857.

Stockton *San Joaquin Replican*, January 14, 1857.

■ 1858 DOWNIEVILLE FIRES

Fariss and Smith. *History of Plumas, Lassen & Sierra Counties, California* [1883]. Reprint. Berkeley, California: Howell-North Books, 1971.

Sinnott, James J. *History of Sierra County, Vol. 1: Downieville*. Fresno: Mid-Cal Publishers, 1977.

San Francisco *Daily Alta California*, January 4 and February 24, 1858.

Stockton *Argus*, January 5, 1858.

Stockton *San Joaquin Republican*, January 5, 1858.

■ 1858 SHIPWRECK OF THE LUCAS

Sacramento *Daily Union*, November 13, 1858.

San Francisco *Daily Alta California*, November 12, 1858.

Stockton *Daily Argus*, November 13, 1858.

■ 1860 THE NORTHERNER DISASTER

Carranco, Lynwood. "Two Tragic Shipwrecks of the 1860s." *The Californians*, May-June 1987.

Genzoli, Andrew M. and Wallace E. Martin. *Redwood Cavalcade... Pioneer Life, Times*. Eureka, California: Schooner Features, 1968.

Humboldt Times (Union), January 4, 6, 14 and 15, 1860.

Marshall, Don B. *California Shipwrecks, Footsteps in the Sea*. Seattle: Superior Publishing, 1978.

San Francisco *Daily Alta California*, January 15, 1860

■ 1861 WHEN THE McCLELLAND BLEW

MacMullen, Jerry. *Paddle-Wheel Days in California*. Stanford, California: Stanford University Press, 1944.

Sacramento *Daily Union*, August 26, 27 and 28, 186.

San Francisco *Daily Alta California*, August 25, 1861.

■ 1861-62 THE GREAT FLOOD

Coggins, Paschal H. "A Reminiscence of the Flood of '61."*Out West*, July 1902.

Elliott, Wallace W., pub. *History of Fresno County, California...* San Francisco, 1882.

Sacramento *Daily Union*, December 9 and 10, 1861.

San Francisco *Daily Alta California*, December 15 and 17, 1861; January 9, 10, 12, 17, 20, and 21, 1862.

San Francisco *Herald*, December 5 and 10, 1861.

Santa Cruz *Pacific Sentinel*, December 12, 1861; January 30, 1862.

Severson, Thor. *Sacramento, An Illustrated History: 1839 to 1874...* San Francisco: California Historical Society, 1973.

Wheat, Carl I., ed. "California's Bantam Cock." *Quarterly of the California Historical Society*, December 1931.

■ 1862-64 THE GREAT DROUGHT

Bancroft, Hubert Howe. *History of California, Volume VII, 1860-1890*. San Francisco: History Company, 1890.

Brewer, William H., ed. by Francis P. Farquhar. *Up and Down California, 1860-1864*. Third edition. Berkeley, Los Angeles and London: University of California Press, 1966.

Cleland, Robert Glass. *The Cattle on a Thousand Hills, Southern California 1850-1880*. Revised edition. San Marino: The Huntington Library, 1951.

Cleland, Robert Glass and Osgood Hardy. *March of Industry*. San Francisco, Los Angeles and Chicago: Powell Publishing, 1929.

Guinn, J.M. "Exceptional Years: A History of California Floods and Drought." *Historical Society of Southern California Annual Publication*. Los Angeles: The Society, 1890.

Mason, Jesse D. *History of Santa Barbara County, California*. Oakland: Thompson and West, 1883.

Newmark, Harris. *Sixty Years in Southern California, 1853-1913*. Third edition. Boston: Houghton Mifflin, 1930.

■ 1863 ADA HANCOCK TRAGEDY

Gleason, Duncan. *The Islands and Ports of California*. New York: Devin-Adair, 1958.

Krythe, Maymie. *Port Admiral: Phineas Banning, 1830-1885.* San Francisco: California Historical Society, 1957.

MacMullen, Jerry. *Paddle-Wheel Days in California*. Stanford, California: Stanford University Press, 1944.

Marshall, Don B. *California Shipwrecks, Footsteps in the Sea*. Seattle: Superior Publishing, 1978.

Newmark, Harris. *Sixty Years in Southern California, 1853-1913*. Third edition. Boston: Houghton Mifflin, 1930.

San Francisco *Daily Alta California*, May 1 and 2, 1863.

■ 1864 EXPLOSION OF THE WASHOE

Hull, David (Editor). *Up the River, Steam Navigation above Carquinez Strait*. San Francisco: The Book Club of California, 2003

Kemble, John Haskell. *San Francisco Bay: A Pictorial History*. New York: Bonanza Books, 1957.

MacMullen, Jerry. *Paddle-Wheel Days in California*. Stanford, California: Stanford University Press, 1944.

Marshall, Don B. *California Shipwrecks, Footsteps in the Sea*. Seattle: Superior Publishing, 1978.

Sacramento *Daily Union*, September 6, 7, 8, 9, 10, and 11, 1864.

San Francisco *Daily Alta California*, September 7, 8, 9, 10, and 11, 1864.

San Francisco *Daily Morning Call*, September 7 and 8, 1864.

San Jose *Daily Mercury*, September 8, 1864.

Smith, Jesse M., ed. *Sketches of Old Sacramento*. Sacramento, California: Sacramento Historical Society, 1976.

■ 1865 THE WRECK OF THE BROTHER JONATHAN

Carranco, Lynwood. "Two Tragic Shipwrecks of the 1860s." *The Californians*, May-June 1987.

DeWolf, Marie. Undated holograph manuscript. Del Norte County Historical Society, Crescent City, California.

Gibbs, James. *Shipwrecks of the Pacific Coast*. Portland: Binfords & Mort, 1957.

San Francisco *Daily Alta California*, July 26, August 2, 3, 4, 5, 6, 7, 8, 1865.

Schlicke, Carl P. *General George Wright, Guardian of the Pacific Coast*. Norman, and London: University of Oklahoma Press, 1988.

Stockton *Daily Evening Herald*, August 3, 4, 7, 8, 10, 12, 15 and 21, 1865.

■ 1866 DEADLY EXPLOSION IN SAN FRANCISCO

San Francisco *Daily Alta California*, April 16 and 17, 1866.

San Francisco *Daily Examiner*, April 16 and 17, 1866.

San Francisco *Daily Evening Bulletin*, April 16, 1866.

Placer Herald (Auburn), April 21, 1866.

Stockton *Daily Evening Herald*, April 17, 18, 19, 21, 27, 1866.

Van Gelder, Arthur Pine, and Hugo Schlatter. *History of the Explosives Industry in America*. New York: Columbia University Press, 1927.

■ 1868 OAKLAND FERRY DISASTER

Halley, William. *The Centennial Yearbook of Alameda County*. Oakland: The Author, 1876.

Harlan, George H. *San Francisco Bay Ferryboats*. Berkeley: Howell-North Books, 1967.

Merlin, Imelda. *Alameda, A Geographical History*. Alameda, California: Friends of the Alameda Free Library, 1977.

Oakland *Daily News*, July 11, 1868.

San Francisco *Daily Alta California*, July 3, 6, 7, 8, 9, 11, and 12, 1868.

■ 1868 THE GREAT HAYWARD EARTHQUAKE

Halley, William. *The Centennial Yearbook of Alameda County*. Oakland: The Author, 1876.

Neville, Amelia Ransome. *The Fantastic City*. Boston and New York: Houghton Mifflin, 1932

San Francisco *Daily Alta California*, October 22, 1868.

San Francisco *Morning Call*, October 22, 1868.

Stillman, M.D., J.D.B. "Concerning the Late Earthquake." *Overland Monthly*, November 1868.

Stockton *Daily Evening Herald*, October 21, 22 and 24, 1868.

Townley, Sidney D., and Maxwell W. Allen. *Bulletin of the Seismological Society of America. Descriptive Catalog of Earthquakes of the Pacific Coast of the United States, 1769 to 1928*. Berkeley: University of California Press, 1939.

■ 1869 ALAMEDA LOCOMOTIVE COLLISION

Alameda County *Gazette*, November 15, 16 and 18, 1869.

Beebe, Lucius. *The Central Pacific & the Southern Pacific Railroads*. Berkeley, California: Howell-North Books, 1963.

Deverell, William. *Railroad Crossing, Californians and the Railroad, 1850-1910*. Berkeley, Los Angeles and London: University of California Press, 1994.

Halley, William. *The Centennial Yearbook of Alameda County*. Oakland: The Author, 1876.

Oakland *Daily Transcript*, November 15, 16, 17, and 18, 1869.

San Francisco *Chronicle*, November 15, 16, 17, and 18, 1869.

San Francisco *Daily Alta California*, November 15, 16, 17, and 18, 1869.

Stockton *Daily Evening Herald*, November 15, 16, 1869.

■ 1871-72 DISASTROUS STORMS

San Francisco *Chronicle*, February 4, 21 and 22, 1872.

San Francisco *Daily Alta California*, December 19, 20, 21, 22, 23, 24, 26, 27, 28, 29, 30, and 31, 1871; January 2, 3, 4, 5, 6, 7, 8, 9, 10, 11, 13, 14, 18, 25, and 26, 1872.

■ 1872 THE GREAT INYO EARTHQUAKE

Chalfant, W. A. *The Story of Inyo*. Revised edition. Independence, California: The Author, 1933.

Cragen, Dorothy Clora. *The Boys in the Sky-Blue Pants*. Fresno, California: Pioneer Publishing, 1975.

Johnston, Philip. "Inyo's Roaring Cataclysm." *Westways*, February 1941.

Los Angeles *Daily News*, March 27, 30 and 31, 1872.

Mulholland, C. "The Owens Valley Earthquake of 1872." *Historical Society of Southern California Annual Publication*. Los Angeles: The Society, 1894.

San Francisco Chronicle, April 21, 1872.Stockton *Daily Evening Herald*, March 27, 1872.

Whitney, Josiah D. "The Owens Valley Earthquake." *Overland Monthly*, August 1872.

Visalia *Weekly Delta*, March 28, 1872.

■ 1875 BLACK POWDER TRAGEDY

San Francisco *Chronicle*, April 8, 9 and 10, 1875.

San Francisco *Daily Alta California*, April 8 and 9, 1875.

■ 1876 CHINESE THEATER TRAGEDY

Farkas, Lani Ah Tye. *Bury My Bones in America*. Nevada City, California: Carl Mautz, 1998.

Lloyd, Benjamin E. *Lights and Shades in San Francisco*. San Francisco: A.L. Bancroft, 1876.

San Francisco *Chronicle*, November 1 and 2, 1876.

San Francisco *Daily Alta California*, October 31, November 1 and 2, 1876.

Wilson, Thomas B., L.L.,D. "Old Chinatown." *Overland Monthly*, September 1911.

■ 1879 STOCKTON STEAM EXPLOSION

Gilbert, Col. F. T. *History of San Joaquin County, California*. Oakland California: Thompson & West, 1879.

San Francisco *Chronicle*, February 23, 1879.

San Francisco *Daily Morning Call*, February 23, 1879.

Stockton *Daily Independent*, February 23, 24 and 25, 1879.

Tinkham, George Henry. *History of San Joaquin County, California*. Los Angeles: Historic Record Company, 1923.

Wood, R. Coke, and Leonard Covello. *Stockton Memories*. Fresno: Valley Publishers, 1977.

■ 1879 RAILROAD TUNNEL EXPLOSION

Arbuckle, Clyde, ed. by Leonard McKay. *Clyde Arbuckle's History of San Jose*. San Jose: Smith & McKay Printing Co., 1985.

Bruntz, George G. *The History of Los Gatos, Gem of the Foothills*. Fresno: Valley Publishers, 1971.

Harrison, E. H. *History of Santa Cruz County, California*. San Francisco: Pacific Press Publishing Company, 1892.

Koch, Margaret. *Santa Cruz County, Parade of the Past*. Fresno: Valley Publishers, 1973.

San Francisco *Chronicle*, November 19 and 20, 1879.

San Francisco *Daily Alta California*, February 14, 16 and 19, 1879.

San Jose *Daily Mercury*, November 10, 19, 20, 21, and 22; December 7, 1879.

■ 1879 THE GREAT BODIE EXPLOSION

Cain, Ella M. *The Story of Bodie*. San Francisco: Fearon Publishers, 1956.

Daily Bodie Standard, July 14, 1879.

San Francisco *Chronicle*, July 11 and 12, 1879.

Watson, James and Doug Brodie. *Big Bad Bodie: High Sierra Ghost Town*. San Francisco: Robert D. Reed, 2002.

Wedertz, Frank S. *Bodie 1859 - 1900*. Bishop, California: Sierra Media, 1969.

■ 1879 BALLOON ASCENSION TRAGEDY

Kurutz, Gary F. "An Informal History of Ballooning in California." *The Californians*, July-August 1988.

Lloyd, Benjamin E. *Lights and Shades in San Francisco*. San Francisco: A.L. Bancroft, 1876.

San Francisco *Chronicle*, October 4, 5, 6, 7, 12, and 15, 1879.

San Francisco *Daily Alta California*, October 6, 1879.

San Francisco *Daily Evening Bulletin*, October 6, 1879.

■ 1880 SANTA CRUZ EXCURSION TRAIN DISASTER

Harrison, E. H. *History of Santa Cruz County, California*. San Francisco: Pacific Press Publishing Company, 1892.

Koch, Margaret. *Santa Cruz County, Parade of the Past*. Fresno: Valley Publishers, 1973.

Santa Cruz *Sentinel*, May 15, 22 and 29; and June 5 and 12, 1880.

Stern, Daniel K. "Last Stop Before Eternity." *Westways*, November 1952.

Young, John V. *Ghost Towns of the Santa Cruz Mountains*. Santa Cruz: Western Tanager, 1984.

■ 1883 TEHACHAPI RUNAWAY TRAIN

Kern County Californian, January 27, February 3, and March 31, 1883.

Kern Weekly Record, January 26 and February 3, 1883.

Morgan, Wallace M. *History of Kern County, California*. Los Angeles: Historic Record Company, 1914.

Reed, Robert C. *Train Wrecks, A Pictorial History of Accidents on the Main Line*. New York: Bonanza Books, 1968.

San Francisco Chronicle, January 21, 22 and 28, 1883.

Visalia Weekly Delta, January 26 and February 2, 1883.

■ 1887 THE PARALLEL DISASTER

O'Brien, Robert. *This is San Francisco*. New York and Toronto: McGraw-Hill, 1948.

San Francisco *Daily Alta California*, January 16 and 17, 1887.

San Francisco *Chronicle*, January, 16, 17 and 19, 1887.

San Francisco *Daily Morning Call*, January 16 and 17, 1887.

■ 1887 DEL MONTE HOTEL FIRE

Fink, Augusta. *Monterey County: The Dramatic Story of its Past.* Fresno: Valley Publishers, 1978.

San Francisco *Daily Alta California*, April 2, 1887.

San Francisco *Chronicle*, April 3, 24 and 28, 1887.

San Francisco *Daily Examiner*, April 3, 4 and 24, 1887.

■ 1888 THE JULIA EXPLODES

MacMullen, Jerry. *Paddle-Wheel Days in California.* Stanford, California: Stanford University Press, 1944.

San Francisco *Chronicle*, February 28 and 29, 1888.

San Francisco *Daily Alta California*, February 28 and 29, 1888.

■ 1889 BAKERSFIELD'S TRIAL BY FIRE

Kern County Californian (Bakersfield), June 29, 13 and 20, 1889.

Morgan, Wallace M. *History of Kern County, California.* Los Angeles: Historic Record Company, 1914

Scanlan, Nicholas Patrick, ed. *Kern County Pioneer Recollections.* Bakersfield, California: Kern County Library, 1985.

San Francisco *Daily Alta California*, July 8, 1889.

San Francisco Chronicle, July 8, 1889.

■ 1889 THE UTICA MINE DISASTER

Buckbee, Edna Bryan. *Pioneer Days of Angel's Camp.* Angel's Camp, California: Calaveras Californian, 1932.

Clark, W. B. *Gold Districts of California.* Bulletin 193, California Department of Conservation, Division of Mines and Geology. Sacramento: The Department, 1970.

Wood, Richard Coke. *Calaveras, The Land of Skulls.* Sonora, California: Mother Lode Press, 1955.

Mokelumne Hill *California Chronicle*, December 28, 1889 and January 4, 1890.

San Francisco *Chronicle*, December 24, 25 and 27, 1889; and January 6 and 7, 1891.

San Francisco *Daily Alta California*, January 7, 1891.

■ 1890 DISASTROUS CALIFORNIA STORMS

Downieville *Mountain Messenger*, January 11, 1890.

Huestis, W.A. "Story of the China Slide." *Trinity County Historical Society Yearbook*, 1956.

Jones, William A. "Yreka's Chinese and The Great Flood of '90." *The Californians*, September/October 1986

Sacramento *Sunday Union*, January 5, 1890.

San Francisco *Chronicle*, February 14, 1890.

San Francisco *Daily Alta California*, February 14 and 20, 1890.

Yreka *Weekly Journal*, February 12, 19 and 26, 1890.

■ 1890 OAKLAND TRAIN TRAGEDY

Merritt, Frank C. *History of Alameda County. California.* Chicago: Clark, 1928.

Fresno *Daily Morning Expositor*, May 31 and June 4, 1890.

San Francisco *Chronicle*, May 31 and June 2, 3 and 4, 1890.

San Francisco *Examiner*, May 31 and June 1 and 2, 1890.

■ 1890 RUNAWAY TRAIN OVER THE SIERRA

San Francisco *Chronicle*, August 23, 1890.

San Francisco *Daily Alta California*, August 23, 1890.

San Francisco *Daily Morning Call*, August 23, 1890.

San Francisco *Examiner*, August 23, 1890.

■ 1891 TRAGIC WRECK OF THE ELIZABETH

Marshall, Don B. *California Shipwrecks, Footsteps in the Sea.* Seattle: Superior Publishing, 1978.

San Francisco *Daily Morning Call*, February 22 and 23, 1891.

San Francisco *Examiner*, February 22, 23 and 24, 1891.

■ 1892 MARE ISLAND NAVAL EXPLOSION

San Francisco *Chronicle*, June 14 and 15, 1892.

San Francisco *Daily Alta Calaifornia*, June 13, 1892.

San Francisco *Examiner*, June 14 and 15, 1892.

San Francisco *Daily Morning Call*, June 14, 1892.

■ 1892 LOS ANGELES COLUMBUS DAY EXPLOSION

Los Angeles *Herald*, October 22, 1892.

Los Angeles *Times*, October 22, 23, 24, 25, 26, 27, and 28, 1892.

■ 1894 AUSTIN CREEK TRAIN DISASTER

"Going the Rounds." *The War Cry*, Salvation Army publication, *circa* 1895-1897, courtesy Gary Rodgers.

Rodgers, Gary, Cazadero historian. Personal knowledge regarding Austin Creek train disaster.

San Francisco *Daily Morning Call*, January 16, 1894.

San Francisco *Examiner*, January 16 and 17, 1894.

Sonoma *Democrat*, January 20 and 27, 1894.

Stindt, Fred A. *Trains to the Russian River*. Redwood City, California: Pacific Coast Chapter, Railway & Locomotive Historical Society, 1974.

▮ 1896 TRAGEDY STRIKES THE *BLAIRMORE*

Gibbs, James. *Shipwrecks of the Pacific Coast*. Portland: Binfords & Mort, 1957.

Los Angeles *Times*, April 10 and 19, 1896.

San Francisco *Daily Morning Call*, April 10, 1896.

San Francisco *Examiner*, April 10, 1896.

Washington *Post*, November 22, 1896.

▮ 1897 GEORGETOWN FIRES

Baird, Newton. "Thousand-tongued Destroyer: Fire!" *Los Angeles Westerners Brand Book*, Vol. 12, 1965.

Coloma *Empire County Argus*, July 12, 1856.

Georgetown *News*, March 20, 1856.

Georgetown *Gazette*, June 17, 1897.

Gudde, Erwin G. *California Gold Camps*. Berkeley, Los Angeles and London: University of California Press, 1975.

Sacramento *Daily Union*, July 17, 1852 and August 17 and 18, 1858.

San Francisco *Chronicle*, June 15, 1897.

San Francisco *Daily Alta California*, July 17, 1852; August 19, 1858; and May 29, 1869.

San Francisco *Daily Herald*, July 17, 1852.

San Joaquin Republican (Stockton), July 9, 11, 1856.

Yohalem, Betty. *"I remember."* Placerville: El Dorado County Chamber of Commerce, 1977.

▮ 1898 SANTA CRUZ POWDER PLANT EXPLOSION

Harrison, E. H. *History of Santa Cruz County, California*. San Francisco: Pacific Press Publishing Company, 1892.

Koch, Margaret. *Santa Cruz County, Parade of the Past*. Fresno: Valley Publishers, 1973.

San Francisco *Chronicle*, April 27, 28, 1898.

Santa Cruz *Sentinel*, April 16, 27 and 28, 1898.

INDEX

About the Authors

William B. Secrest, Sr. (standing) and
William B. Secrest, Jr. (seated)

Chronicler of the American west for almost 50 years, William B. Secrest, Sr., is the author of five books about early California crime, including *Lawmen and Desperadoes; California Desperadoes;* and *Perilous Trails, Dangerous Men*. He has also written a history of California's Indian wars, *When the Great Spirit Died*; a biography of San Francisco's legendary chief of detectives, Isaiah Lees (*Dark and Tangled Threads of Crime*); and, most recently, a biography of Harry Love, captain of the California Rangers who hunted down Joaquin Murrieta (*The Man from the Rio Grande*). Now semiretired, he divides his time between the Fresno County Library's California History and Genealogy Room and various history-minded pursuits.

His son, William B. Secrest, Jr., also works in the Room, where he serves as librarian and archivist. He has coauthored two local history books, including *Fresno County—The Pioneer Years*, and has edited five other published works about central California's past. His efforts in helping document Fresno's architectural and design heritage led to the Room's winning a Governor's Award in Historic Preservation for the year 2005.

This book marks the first extended collaboration between father and son in their favorite field of endeavor, and the first general history of California disasters to ever appear in print. As such, it fills a notable gap in the story of the Golden State.

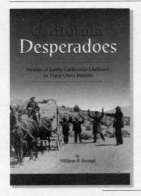